# A Complete Guide to Making

# A Public Stock Offering

*Every man who knows how to read has it in his power to magnify himself, to multiply the ways in which he exists, to make his life full, significant and interesting.*

—ALDOUS HUXLEY

# A
# COMPLETE GUIDE
# TO
# MAKING A PUBLIC
# STOCK OFFERING

by Elmer L. Winter

PRENTICE-HALL, INC., Englewood Cliffs, N. J.

Seventh printing . . . . . . . . November, 1968

PRINTED IN THE UNITED STATES OF AMERICA
16017—B&P

## DEDICATION

To AARON SCHEINFELD, my very good friend and close business associate over the past 25 years

## About the Author

ELMER L. WINTER is President and co-founder of Manpower, Inc. After graduating from the University of Wisconsin Law School in 1935, Mr. Winter practiced tax and corporate law in Milwaukee, Wisconsin and Chicago, Illinois. In 1948 he was instrumental, with Aaron Scheinfeld, his law partner, in organizing Manpower, Inc. In 1954 Mr. Winter gave up the practice of law to devote his full time, attention and energies to the further development of the Manpower program. He has maintained a very close relationship with the field operations of the company and travels extensively visiting and working with the offices in this country and abroad.

Manpower, Inc. is the world's largest temporary help service and has 240 offices in the United States and Canada. In addition, the company maintains offices in 15 cities in Europe and the Near East, from Stockholm to Tel Aviv. The company also has an office in Tokyo, Japan.

Mr. Winter recently wrote a book entitled *A Woman's Guide to Earning a Good Living*. He is a director of a number of corporations and has written many articles for trade magazines. Mr. Winter is a member of the Taxation Committee of the United States Chamber of Commerce, and serves as first vice president of the International Franchise Association. He is an award-winning painter and a mosaicist.

# Preface

As we move forward into the highly dynamic 60's and 70's, many financial changes will take place in the life of a large number of corporations. New industries, unknown five or ten years ago, will be springing up daily and developing new products in the fields of science, medicine, electronics, foods, etc. As a result, our manufacturing, distribution and merchandising plans will need to be revised constantly to keep pace with these new developments. But what about our financial planning and needs? What will the future hold in store in this important area of corporate life and existence?

The times call for a realistic appraisal of corporate financing. We must determine whether family-owned corporations can continue to operate successfully on a closely held basis or whether they will prosper by "going public." If the past can be used as a guide, it would appear that in the next 10 years, thousands of corporations for the first time will go to the public for expansion funds, hoping to become a part of the cult of growth stocks. Public offerings may well be the order of the day—provided, of course, that the public maintains its present appetite for new issues, which they hope will be the blue chips of tomorrow.

Is the "public offering" path strewn with roses—or would it be well to pause and pay close attention to the hidden thorns that can make the going difficult? A timely good road sign might point out: "Those interested in going public, proceed with caution." Some companies have ignored this warning and have gone to the public before they were matured and seasoned. Perhaps it looked too easy for them as they saw others in their field acquire the label of a "hot issue." They missed the sense of timing as they failed to realize that there is a right and a wrong time for a public offering. If the public and the company are ready, a success story can be written. If the timing is off, the results can be disastrous.

More and more executives are considering a public stock offering for their company for the first time. They are searching for answers and looking for the pitfalls to be avoided. I have heard many executives say "It all sounds good to me, but I am not sure this is the right time for my company to go public." In talking to these executives, I find, that while they have a strong desire to have a public stock offering, they hesitate to take the necessary steps because of many fears which concern them. They have said to me "I like the idea of a public stock offering for my Company but I don't want to get mixed up with lawyers, accountants, underwriters or the SEC." They also have said "I'm not sure that our company has sufficient appeal to the investing public and am afraid that we would be unsuccessful with our public offering." Are their fears real—or are they imagined? Are they alone in hesitating to take the steps leading to a public stock offering? Definitely "no"—everyone has the fear of the unknown, and these doubts loom particularly large as one considers a public stock offering for his company.

I, too, had such fears when we first talked about selling a part of the stock of our company, Manpower, Inc., in the summer of 1959. We had been a family-held corporation for twelve (12) years, operating profitably with increased earnings each year. We had no particular need for outside capital. However, my business associate, Aaron Scheinfeld, and I realized as our company grew and expanded, that there were many advantages that could accrue by "going public." We, too, had many questions in our minds as we considered a public stock offering. Fortunately, having a background in the practice of law, it was not too difficult for us to resolve some of the doubts as we analyzed the records of other companies, SEC regulations, underwriter proposals, contracts, etc.

When we embarked upon our public stock offering, I searched the libraries and research departments of investment banking firms to find information—legal as well as non-legal, to answer the many problems confronting us as we entered this new phase of our business and financial life. To my surprise, I could not find any books or reports that would answer fully my many questions. The answers, therefore, had to come from discussions with our investment bankers, our attorneys, our accountants and business associates.

When we had concluded our initial public stock offering, it seemed clear to me that there was need for a book that would analyze the problems facing those executives who wish to have their corporation "go public" for the first time. Hence this book.

I have limited my discussions to the problems of a public stock offering. Space does not permit a complete analysis of other methods of financing—important as they may be to the corporate executive.

Although my background has been in the field of law, I have written this book in non-legal terms, with the idea of giving down-to-earth advice, and practical suggestions to the business executive who is thinking of a public stock offering for his company. My main target is the uninitiated in this field. I have tried to write as informally as though I was sitting on the 8:15 commuter train with you, Mr. Corporate Executive, discussing your contemplated move of "going public."

Before saying "All Aboard" let me express my appreciation for the assistance given to me by many corporate executives, too many to list completely, who have in the past several years steered their corporations through the uncharted seas of a public stock offering. It could well be said that this book is a result of the suggestions and ideas of over 200 corporate executives, whose experiences I have analyzed and summarized in an effort to present objectively the many problems facing the corporate executive as he considers "going public" for the first time. I have had the benefit of the advice and assistance of many specialists who have great experience in the field. I am indebted to them for their valuable assistance.

I owe a special debt of gratitude to my wife and three daughters for their understanding and patience during the many months I worked on this book.

ELMER L. WINTER

# Contents

# A Complete Guide to Making

# A Public Stock Offering

# 1

## Seven Deadly Fears Facing the Corporate Executive Wishing to Go Public

I have talked to many presidents, executive vice-presidents, and corporate treasurers of companies who have a genuine interest in a public stock offering for their companies. What holds them back? What keeps them from discussing their problems with an investment banker? As I analyze the problems and fears facing them, it appears to me that their problems fall into seven separate categories:

1. *Does my company have sufficient appeal to insure success of a stock offering?*

All of us know about the stock issues that have done extremely well from the date of the first offering. Sometimes we overlook the companies where the public was not excited about the issue and the stock was not well received. As a matter of fact, in some of these issues the price declined after the initial offering date. How does the unsure executive gain confidence that his own company will fall into the first category of successful companies rather than the unsuccessful group? The answer to this question requires a great deal of corporate soul-searching—examinations of records of past performance and goals for the future.

We struggled with this weighty question in our own company for quite some time. As we considered a public stock offering, we analyzed and compared our company with others also operating in the service field which had gone public. We found that there were relatively few companies in the service field that were publicly owned. We knew full well that we did not have what is customarily found in public stock offerings—plant equipment and inventory. We asked ourselves how would the public react to the fact that we did not have brick and mortar, commonly thought to be an important part of any company seeking public financing. Our brick and mortar is our management, our person-

1

nel, and the quality of the service that we have to offer. Would the public accept this in place of physical plants, warehouses, factory equipment, etc.? Would the public be excited by the fact that we, at Manpower, Inc., for example, employed over 135,000 people in 1961 and that we serviced over 90,000 different firms? How would the public react to the fact that within 13 years we had grown from a start of two offices to 240 offices in the United States and Canada, plus 15 offices abroad? Would this give our company the necessary appeal to insure the success of our issue? Would the buying public readily understand our type of operation, which is a new business tool; namely, leasing staff to stores, offices, industrial concerns, service organizations, etc. Would the buyers place the label "A good growth potential" on our company since we had increased our net earnings 550 per cent in the four years from fiscal 1955 to fiscal 1959?

These and many other questions needed answers. Fortunately our investment bankers, through their many years of experience, were able to give us the necessary confidence to enable us to move forward with a public stock offering in September 1959. This is one of the important roles that investment bankers play as they guide you along the way. Their evaluation of the market for your company's stock, their estimates of the growth potential of your company as well as proper timing is of great value to the corporate executive considering a public stock offering for his company.

I have outlined in Chapter 8 areas for an executive to analyze in determining whether his corporation has the proper appeal to bring about a successful stock offering. It is important that you be honest with yourself and your underwriter in reviewing the guideposts set forth in this chapter. If you rationalize or give your company's activities a "once over lightly" treatment, you might end up with an unhappy stock offering. If your company is not ready for a public stock offering, you would be well advised to wait for a better time.

On the other hand, "Don't sell your company short"—your company may have an appeal far greater than you anticipate. You may be too close to the picture to be able to appraise the public's appetite for your stock. It isn't necessary that your company fall into the glamor category if it has a sound record of earnings and management strength. Select a top grade investment banker and let him evaluate your chances for a successful offering. You will generally get an impartial decision. He will be cautious and judicious since he does not want to have his name attached to a failure. Be sure, however, that you pick the very best investment banker available. There are good and bad ones. Your lawyer can help you decide on the proper choice.

2. *Is our company large enough for a public stock offering?*

You will ask your advisors, "Are we big enough for an offering? Will it pay for us to go through all the steps and costs involved in a public stock offering?

There are no pat answers to these questions. A great deal depends on the goals that you wish to accomplish. If equity capital is urgently needed for your company or if you are very anxious to sell a part of your stock to diversify your holdings or ease the way out of estate tax problems, you might be willing to go into a public offering even in a borderline case.

Generally speaking, your company, if interested in a public stock offering, should have earnings of at least $100,000 a year and a net worth in excess of $1,000,000. The issue should be for $500,000 or more. Obviously, there are many public offerings that do not meet these standards but the underwriting fraternity usually applies these three tests in determining whether your company is large enough for a public stock offering.

Judgments in this area are influenced by the future prospects of earnings and dividends. In some companies the possibilities of growth and expansion are so dynamic that the general rules of the game are discarded. Keep in mind that the costs of a public offering run high in small issues and a great deal of time is involved in the preparation of the offering. Be sure that the net results to your company—and to you if you are selling your stock—are sufficiently rewarding.

In Chapter 8 I discuss this question. Size alone is not the criterion. There are many issues of $300,000–$400,000 being offered to the public today. If your company measures up to the tests set forth in Chapter 8, you might well be ready for a public stock offering even though by normal tests your company might be considered "too small."

Don't try to determine for yourself whether your company is the right size for an underwriting. Discuss this with an investment banker and determine whether your company has the sales, earnings, and potential which will make for an attractive stock offering. This is the best way to get an answer to this question.

3. *Will I lose control of my corporation to outside stockholders?*

In most public stock offerings today, the company or the stockholders sell 25 to 33⅓% of the common voting stock. A sale of this type means many new stockholders. However, there is no reason to expect that you will lose control of your corporation. While you must recognize that selling a portion of your stock to the public requires the company to make periodic accounting to the stockholders; nevertheless, the day-to-day running of your business will not be affected if you are providing good management to your company. Normally your stock will be widely held as a result of your public offering and no one group will attempt to influence your management decisions. You must, of course, keep in mind that management will have a fiduciary duty to act for the benefit of all stockholders.

You might think that a *private* placement of a portion of your stock with several institutions will place you under less pressure since you would have to conform only to the wishes of the few holders of your stock. This does not necessarily follow. A private placement may create greater pressure than a public offering since in the latter case the stockholders are spread throughout the country and are generally content to let you manage the company without any dictation of policy.

You must recognize that if your company has a public stock offering, you and your associates in effect will be living in a goldfish bowl where whatever you say or do will have an impact upon your stockholders and will be noticed by them. You will have in effect 500 to 1,000 or possibly 2,000 "partners" who will be inactive partners as long as you offer sound management to your company.

What protection exists to prevent raiders from taking over? The best protection lies in limiting the public offerings to 25 to 33⅓% of the outstanding capital stock. This will always leave you with control.

If you are planning to sell only 25 or 33⅓% of your stock, you will control the remaining 75 or 66⅔% at all times. Even though the stockholders may be unhappy at some point with your management, as long as you control the majority of the stock outstanding, there is very little that they can do other than bring court proceedings on the grounds of mismanagement. Suits of this type can be disruptive to management. If your company has cumulative voting, minority stockholders may be able to place a representative on your board of directors. However, in the normal operations of your business, you will not be faced with any problem of loss of control.

What about a situation where the stock is owned by two men who went into business together and each owns one-half of the common stock of the company? Obviously they are each in a deadlock position. Neither one can have control of the corporation. Now each would like to sell a portion of his stock to the public but he fears that then as an individual he would be in a minority position. If each sold 25% of his stock to the public, each would own after the sale 37½% of the outstanding stock and the public would own 25%. In case of a dispute, one stockholder owning 37½% of the stock could be forced out by the stockholders siding with the other 37½% stockholder. This situation usually can be controlled through a voting trust agreement between the two principal stockholders or other form of voting agreement.

*4. Will I be able to live with outside Directors?*

Most family-owned corporations do not have outside directors. Possibly the attorney or the banker will serve on the Board. The President or principal stockholders dominate the Board. Now as you consider a public stock offering, will you need to bring in outside directors and subject yourself to limitations and direction? At the outset, keep in mind that many companies do not add outside directors to their Board of Directors after a public stock offering. On the other hand, some underwriters require that outside persons, in some cases, a representative of the underwriter, be placed on the Board of Directors.

In Chapter 33 I discuss the pros and cons of bringing in outside directors. Let me assure you that if you are required to have non-company directors on your board, you might well find many advantages will accrue to your company. Outside directors who have good business background in fields other than yours can bring to your company many benefits since they are not too close to the forest to see the trees. If you select well qualified men and women to serve on your Board, you will get the advantage of their sound judgment and experience in fields other than yours. Don't fear the addition of new persons from outside your company to your Board. Turn this into an advantage. You are getting extra and valuable assistance in the running of your corporate affairs.

5. *Won't the State and Federal regulations make it impossible to have a successful stock offering?*

Many of us have been conditioned to think of the Securities and Exchange Commission as a regulatory body firmly situated behind impregnable walls with complicated rules and regulations which will prevent registration of a small issue. This attitude, in my opinion, is harmful to the corporation and is not based upon facts. The SEC regulations, while firm, still permit a corporation without undue difficulty to proceed with a public stock offering.

It is true that a great deal of time, effort and cost accompanies a registration with the SEC. You also must keep in mind that there is a continuing responsibility to file reports annually with the Commission. But it can well be worth the effort—the high cost of executive time involved as well as the expenses of underwriters, attorneys and accountants. Actually your advisors, including your attorney, accountants and investment banker will lead you carefully through the Federal and State securities laws. In Chapters 22 and 23 you will find the road map which will help you understand the SEC requirements. Don't turn down a public stock offering for your company because you are concerned about the SEC regulations. The SEC rules and regulations work fairly and the information it requires from your company is good for you to have in the management of your business.

6. *Aren't the costs of financing prohibitive?*

A public stock offering is an expensive venture. There is no question about that. On the other hand, the costs must be measured in terms of future values. In Chapter 16, I review the many costs that you and your company will incur in a public stock offering.

Is it worth it? I would certainly say "yes" if you can gain for yourself or your company many of the advantages which I describe later.

Financing costs are relative. The initial costs are high. You will pay substantial fees now to sell a portion of your stock but look to the many advantages that will accrue to you as a result of your public stock offering. Actually, in terms of results, it could be considered that the costs are low. If all other conditions are favorable for a public offering now, it would be well to pay the initial costs and reap the advantages in the years ahead.

7. *Will I get the right price for the stock I sell?*

You won't get the right price if you proceed on the basis of getting the last dollar at the time of the initial offering. I have seen many underwritings die a-borning because at the last moment the underwriter and the company could not agree on price. The company or selling stockholder wants $20 a share and the underwriter wants to pay $18. Neither side will move from this position and as a result months of work are lost and the stock issue never becomes a reality.

Who was right and who was wrong in refusing to concede? No one will ever know. Possibly, however, the company will some day regret that it held out for the last dollar because it missed its opportunity to get into a favorable and bullish market. Possibly the company will have lost a real opportunity by holding out for the last dollar.

Let me again relate this to our own situation. Our underwriting group suggested a price of $15. The general market was strong at the end of September 1959 when our registration statement was filed and we felt that the public might well pay $17 or $18 for our stock rather than $15. Our underwriters were strong in their desire to have the issue sold at $15 a share on the basis that this was a proper price for the stock. They pointed out that the aftermarket was important and that the price could decline if the stock was overpriced. Having practiced law for many years prior to entering the Manpower program, it was always my opinion that clients should not second-guess their counselors. I had to follow the same rules in accepting the advice of our investment bankers. And how right our underwriting group was! Within 6 months our stock rose from $15 a share to $50. Would the stock have had this dramatic increase if the initial price had been $17 or $18? Possibly so, but on the other hand it might not have. There may have been some who felt that it was overpriced initially and would not have been in the market for our stock. Suffice it to say that the over-all result was extremely good. It points out the importance of working with competent investment bankers who guide you in these matters.

It's advisable before taking any steps toward a public offering to be familiar with the advantages and disadvantages of an underwriting for your company's stock. Let's examine the pros and cons.

# 2

## Advantages of a Public Stock Offering

As you sit back in your easy chair at home some evening, your mind might start wandering back towards the office—the problems that are confronting you daily as your company is expanding and reaching new highs in sales and profits. There are new pressures on you for more working capital to increase the current asset ratio, provide for a new plant or the replacement of obsolete equipment, or the need to automate. Bank loans aren't providing the answer to your problems.

You have considered and discarded a private placement of a portion of your companys' stock and customary debt financing arangements will not serve your purpose. You start to think in terms of a public stock offering for your company to help answer your problems. You begin to ask yourself, "What are the advantages and disadvantages of a public stock offering to my company? You also think of the possibility of selling a portion of your stock to the public to get diversification, create a market for your families stock holdings, etc." Will "Going Public" offer the best answer to all of these problems?

It will be helpful to you in analyzing your company's financial problems to learn what other companies have done in similar situations. Why have others gone public? In many underwritings, the major purpose of the sale of stock to the public is to satisfy the company's need for additional working capital, or repay outstanding loans. The company may need to improve its debt-equity ratios. Cash may also be needed for increased inventories, accounts receivable, plant and equipment. In other cases, the company may wish to establish a market for its stock.

It would be well to examine carefully the basic reasons why a company sells a portion of its stock to the public. The following categories cover most of the public offerings in today's market and point up the advantages that can be gained through a public stock offering.

7

*Provide Additional Capital*

Many corporations find themselves in a position where retained earnings and short term loans do not meet their capital requirements. Short term loans of this type must be repaid periodically and quite often the due date falls at a disadvantageous time. A company may have plans to expand into new areas—bring out new products for diversification—open new markets, establish plants abroad, etc. Permanent capital is the only practical answer for long term expansion. A private placement of long term debt or capital stock has been explored and is not deemed to be advisable. A public stock offering may well be the answer to help provide the additional working capital for that expansion program.

John R. Janssen, secretary and treasurer of Wolverine Shoe and Tanning Corporation, in analyzing the over-all advantages of their public stock offering stated,

> Our Board decided that we were not generating enough earnings to finance our anticipated expansion. While we did have satisfactory tentative arrangements with our banks, the effect of debt capital would not really give us a very strong balance sheet, and that is why we pursued the equity route.

*New Plants and Equipment*

Many companies today are faced with a desperate need for new plant facilities and new automated equipment, both in the office and in the plant. Obsolescence produces limited and decreasing production capacity. Replacement of plants and equipment is needed by many companies to meet the challenge of competition, not only from this country but from foreign sources as well.

The need for automation in plants and offices requires substantial amounts of capital. The costs cannot always be met out of funds or from borrowings of surplus. Surplus itself provides nothing. "Going Public" has enabled many companies with limited capital to construct a new plant and equip it with fully productive machinery and stay ahead of competition.

*Acquisitions*

Many companies today are seeking to acquire other corporations as part of their expansion and diversification program. Very often these companies cannot be purchased because the buying corporation either does not have sufficient cash or the selling corporation is not willing to take stock in a closely held corporation.

However, if the buyer is a publicly owned company the sellers might well be willing to take a portion or all of the purchase price in marketable stock. In determining the purchase price, there will be substantial advantages to the buying company that is publicly owned. Generally the selling corporation, if a family owned corporation will be priced on the basis of book value or a price earnings formula, which is considerably less than the P/E ratio of the buying company.

William R. McLain, president of Kusan, Incorporated, in pointing out the advantages of a public stock offering for his company stated:

> A sound example of the value of our stock offering was our acquisition of a small machine and die shop during the past year. We purchased the assets of this company with stock of our corporation. This was done at a time when the market value of our shares was close to double the book value. The purchase was thus for a much reduced book cost to our corporation and it actually increased the value of the individual shares slightly. On the other hand the owners of the company acquired received a better price than expected, and could hold the stock as investment, or sell on the market as desired (subject to security regulations). They thus converted their frozen assets into live marketable securities, and became a part of our organization. This condition of a firm market of securities selling at an appreciated value makes possible many of the mergers and acquisitions being made today. Under these conditions both parties can often benefit greatly by a sale of assets for securities or by exchange of stock. Such a sound market also provides our employees with a place of investment in their own company and its future.

## Repayment of Loans

Many companies have large interest and maturity commitments to meet on their outstanding loans, either short or long term. They would like to get relief from the fixed interest charges and are often troubled with the need of meeting maturity dates which may be coming due. A public stock offering will permit the company to retire the loans and eliminate the interest charges.

## Establishing a Market for the Company's Stock

As a by-product of a public stock offering, the company establishes a market for its stock. This can prove to be an advantage for the corporation as it seeks credit, negotiates for acquisitions or establishes deferred compensation plans. The principal stockholders also benefit by having a readily accessible market for their stock. Many valuation problems can be eliminated by having a market value for the company's stock.

## Increased Bank Loans

If after the public stock offering, the company is still in need of additional short term financing, the opportunities for borrowing from banks is enhanced by the fact that the company has had a public stock offering. In these cases, larger loans can normally be obtained. Equity financing creates a more favorable atmosphere for future borrowing.

Your commercial banker, in looking at your company's financial statement after a public stock offering, will not be guided only by the book value as shown on the balance sheet. Since the stock is quoted daily either on an "over the counter" basis or on an exchange, your banker in valuing your company may well project the value of your stock by multiplying the number of shares outstanding by the current market price at the time of the loan. Normally, this produces a value considerably higher than book value, and loans can be made on a much more desirable basis.

## Competitive Advantages to be Gained by Going Public

There is an old adage which says "success breeds success." By bringing the public into your corporation, you are stepping into a new area of business activity. Your company becomes well known in the market places. Your company also attains a certain "success status" as a result of a successful public stock offering. People generally like to deal with successful firms.

All things being equal, we tend in our purchases, to buy from the successful firm because we feel that the product will be well made and the company will stand behind the product or the service it offers. While it will not always be true, generally, it can be said that a public stock offering will give you a status that indicates success for your company. The public will consider that your company "has arrived." You will gain a greater respect from your vendors, suppliers, customers and the public generally.

## Improved Employee Relations

Will you have improved employee relations as a result of a public stock offering? Many corporate executives are of the opinion that this question should be answered "yes"; some say "no." I queried some executives who had recently steered their company through an underwriting. They evaluated their stock offering and its effect on employee relations in different ways.

Raymond D. Stevens, Jr., executive vice president of Pierce and Stevens Chemical Corporation, stated,

> In our judgment "Going Public" has had a favorable effect on employee relations. The influence of public ownership has taken two directions as far as employees are concerned. First, many of our people were stockholders prior to the offering(s). In the absence of a market and definitive information on

company progress, their shares lacked liquidity and were accordingly difficult to valuate. To the extent that the offering remedied this situation, it promoted employee relations.

The second effect is less definable but, we feel, has exerted quite a direct impact. We have detected that employees in all ranks seem more responsible and sympathetic to the problems which underscore corporate progress. The "new boss" concept appears to have created a pride in being identified with a publicly-held company. This is particularly true when the success or failure of their efforts is reflected in daily market quotations for all to see.

Mr. Theodore Rossman, president of Pentron Electronics Corporation, in describing the reaction of his employees to the company's public stock offering stated,

> Our employees seem to have developed a sense of pride in the company now that the stock is publicly traded.

Mr. L. Every Landon, president of Nalley's Inc., considers employee stock ownership to be of great value. Mr. Landon reports,

> Approximately half of our outstanding stock is held by employees bought from previous private owners and we have found that our employee relationship is excellent because of their stock ownership. A limited number bought bonds under the recent public offering. We have hired only one new executive recently and he was brought in primarily because of our public offering. I doubt that we could have attracted him had we not been going into the public market.

While many companies are of the opinion that a public stock offering strengthens employee relations, Eric William Passmore, executive vice president of Simplicity Manufacturing Company, was of a contrary opinion and pointed out:

> The change from private ownership by persons in immediate charge and control of operations to public ownership tends to make junior executives uneasy as to the duration of their employment. They know and rely on the attitude of the private owners but fear that the top management may be changed and that other personnel changes may follow.

Consideration must be given to the importance of a public stock offering in attracting new employees. In a family held corporation, generally, stock ownership by employees is not provided, or at best, is quite limited. A public offering gives management the opportunity to attract employees by offering stock options not generally available in a family corporation.

Mr. G. H. Bruns, Jr., president of Syston-Donner Corporation, pointed out the advantages of the company's public stock offering on employee relations, as follows:

> I believe that our recent stock offering had a beneficial effect on our employee relationships in two ways. First, it enabled some 50% of our people to participate directly in the growth of the organization through their direct purchase of shares in their company. Secondly, I believe it pointed up to all of our people the fact that Systron-Donner Corporation is now a publicly owned organization of national stature.

### Customer Relations

Many customers of your company, having confidence in the future of your plans, might well want to own stock in your company if the opportunity was offered to them. This, of course, can be accomplished through a public stock offering. Your customers, identifying themselves as stockholders, could have a greater interest in your company and the products it sells. A more permanent relationship can be created through a dual relationship. On the other hand, customer-stockholders may question your prices by referring to a healthy after tax profit shown in your operating statement.

One word of caution might be added at this point. If your company decides to "Go Public," you will in all likelihood receive calls from many of your customers throughout the country suggesting in no uncertain terms that they will expect you to use your influence to obtain 100 to 500 or 1,000 shares at the initial offering price on them. This type of request imposes a difficult burden on you because of the possibility of disturbing good customer relationships. Nevertheless, your prospectus will have to disclose whether the underwriters are reserving shares for your customers. Consequently, I recommend that these requests be turned over, as tactfully as possible, to your underwriters without any firm commitment from you that the customers' demands will be met.

### Stockholder's Interest in Your Company's Products

As a publicly held company, you may well find many of your stockholders will take a personal interest in the welfare of your company. They will become purchasers and be boosters of your company's products or services, particularly if your company is in the consumer field. From time to time, through the mail, you will receive many good suggestions from your stockholders. You will find that your stockholders identify themselves with your company and its products and take a personal interest in its welfare. This is a program that you will want to encourage.

Before turning to the consideration of the disadvantages of a public stock offering for your company, it is important to bear in mind the many advantages that accrue to the family stockholders by going public. Many public stock offerings today are made to accomplish individual goals. The advantages of a public stock offering by you and your family will be discussed in Chapters 4 and 5 following.

# 3

## Disadvantages of a Public Stock Offering

It would be well to review the disadvantages of a public stock offering. It is always easy to look at the advantages—the increased capital for your company— the new equipment that the stock offering will provide for you. However, your corporate life will change as you bring in new stockholders. Make up your mind to that. The advantages had better outweigh the disadvantages before you put your signature on the registration statement.

Not all will agree that a public stock offering is the best method of raising capital. Mr. G. M. Jones, president of Row, Peterson & Company, offers this bit of advice:

> It would be my advice that nobody contemplate a public stock offering unless they were compelled to that move by the financial necessities of their capital requirements or by the tax penalties on their stockholders. A privately owned company is undoubtedly the best form of operation that business can have if it meets the necessities of the business.

Let's examine carefully the disadvantages of a public offering. Don't sweep them under the carpet. They are real, but they should not deter you from going ahead with your plans—as long as you are aware of them at the outset.

### Management of Your Company

There is no denying you will find a serious change in your corporate activities as a result of a public stock offering. Family owned corporations are run on a somewhat informal basis. Decisions can be reached quickly through a telephone call or two with the other directors—or possibly the president runs the show pretty much as he sees fit. There has been no need for many formal meetings. The president just goes ahead and does the necessary.

As a publicly owned corporation, you have to follow the rules of the game— carefully and with exactness. Your stockholders must be considered every inch

14

of the way, and there is no short cut in this area. Action must be taken in accordance with the by-laws. You will have to obey the letter as well as the spirit of the rules regulating your company. This may sound ominous and foreboding; but it is not difficult. The rules are clear; they can and must be followed. You won't be asked in running your business to do the impossible, but on the other hand, you won't be as free and easy with making decisions as you were before. Your Board of Directors in all likelihood will play a greater role in the operation of your business. This may well work to your advantage as you share the "thinking through" of problems with your Board.

It would be well for you to review with your attorney the rights that stockholders will have in your company. You will want to review the state statutes which cover the rights of stockholders to hold and transfer securities, participate in new stock offerings, receive reports, inspect records, etc. Stockholders have the right to vote for directors and attend stockholders' meetings. You must keep in mind that stockholders have the right to vote on major questions affecting the company. Stockholders have the right to receive dividends, although the declaration of dividends is in the discretion of the directors.

The Securities and Exchange Commission will continue to maintain an interest in your company as long as it is publicly owned. For example, annual reports must be filed with the Commission—but again this does not pose any serious problem. Your advisors can handle well the reporting requirements.

Suffice it to say, as a publicly owned corporation, there will fall upon your executives an increased responsibility in dealing with the public, the company stockholders, Board of Directors and regulating agencies. Most companies have successfully met this responsibility. There is no reason to expect that you will fail.

*Relations with Employees*

Your employees will know a great deal about your company's financial condition after a public stock offering. Privately held corporations do not publicize their earnings. This, of course, has certain advantages which are lost when a company goes public.

When you have outside stockholders, you will issue reports that are available to all stockholders. The employees or your organization will have access to this information. They may not be happy with the amount paid to the executives and their pension plan. They may feel that they should receive a greater part of the earnings of the company. On the other hand, a proper explanation of the profits can be an advantage in that your employees may have assumed that the company had considerably greater earnings. Many companies through their Annual Report point out in a constructive way to their employees the small share of employees have a misconception about corporate earnings and are surprised to see the small amount left for stockholders.

### Pressure to Keep Up Growth Pattern

Many corporations are able to sell a portion of the stock to the public because they fall into the category of "Growth Company." It is important that you give consideration to the continuous pressures that will be placed upon you, as an executive of a public corporation, to continue and expand your company's growth pattern.

The public will expect that your company sales and profits will move forward substantially each year on a steady basis. As a family-owned corporation you and your immediate family were the only ones affected if the corporation had some lean years. The situation changes, however, when your company "goes public" since the investing public is very actively interested in your company's successes and failures.

If the public is "hot" on your company's stock you will be under pressure to justify the maintenance of this attitude. You must realize fully that a bad quarterly report or two may cause some of your stockholders to become apprehensive and jittery and sell their stock in your company. They may feel that the "bloom is off the rose" and look to other companies for growth potential. There are many who will take the "long look" at your company and will not be disturbed unduly by several poor reports. But even these stockholders will always be weighing the advantages of an investment in your company as compared to another growth situation.

Don't underestimate the pressures that will be placed upon you as an executive of a public corporation to continue its success pattern. You have assumed obligations to the public and you will consciously as well as subconsciously be aware of this at all times as you manage the affairs of your company. As you consider expansion of plant facilities, addition of new research departments, or new lines, you will be aware of the impact of the expenditures on your company's operating statement. However, you have to make decisions that are best for the company in the long pull and not be swayed by the short term effects of expansion on your company's current Profit and Loss Statement.

### Pressure to Pay Dividends

Once you establish a dividend pattern as a publicly owned corporation, it will be difficult to change—unless, of course, your Board of Directors decides to increase the amount of the dividend. You will find that the investing public and the security dealers will react unfavorably to a reduction in the dividend regardless of the reason. You may be justified in passing a dividend because the company needs all of its funds for expansion purposes but the investing public won't easily accept an action of this type. The pressure will be on your company to maintain and increase the dividends.

### Information Available to Competitors

As a publicly owned corporation, your financial statements will be available to your competitors. If you have not given out financial reports to credit agencies in the past, you must recognize that your company's operating statements will be available to your competitors who may find pricing patterns, operating ratios, markups, and other information that may be helpful to them in pricing their products or services.

As you carefully weigh the advantages and disadvantages of a public offering to your corporation, it would be well to withhold reaching any conclusion until you carefully consider the effects of an offering upon you and the other stockholders of your company. What will an underwriting mean to you personally?

# 4

## Should Stockholders Have All Their Eggs in One Corporate Basket?

While in many public stock offerings, the corporation is the sole seller of stock, there is an increasing number of underwritings where the principal stockholders join the corporation in selling stock to the public. In many offerings, the stockholders alone are the sellers of stock and none of the proceeds of the sale go to the corporation. Why do stockholders sell their stock as part of a public offering?

### DIVERSIFICATION OF INVESTMENTS

The order of the day among corporations is "diversify." This recommendation has applicability to the corporate executive as he thinks about his own investments and his personal portfolio. During the past 20 years, thousands of family corporations have developed and grown into substantial business organizations. As you pull back the curtains and look behind the corporate scene of many of these companies, you will find stock held by either one individual, a family, or two. The company normally was started with a small amount of capital and earnings were left in the company to help finance the business. Whenever needed, short term loans were made by the stockholders, and possibly some preferred stock or debentures were issued for long term financing. In many of these situations, the banks have been the major source of financing, either through short term or long term loans.

By and large, in the average family corporation, the major investment in the president's portfolio consists of his stock in his family owned corporation. With personal income taxes at their high level, he has not had much opportunity to diversify his holdings by purchasing stock in other companies.

18

### To Provide a Market for Stock

Many individuals, as well as corporations, are desirous of establishing an over-the-counter market for their stock. There may be many times when an individual would like to dispose of a portion of his stock not only for diversification purposes, but to make investments in other enterprises, etc. Sales of stock are very difficult to accomplish in a family owned corporation. Buyers do not want to purchase stock in a closed corporation that will place them in a minority position. Having "gone public," with an over-the-counter market, or listing on an exchange, the selling stockholders generally have a market to sell portions of their stock in the future, subject to SEC regulations.

### To Insure Protection for Your Family

The owner of a family corporation, often in the quiet of his study, asks himself such questions as "What would happen to my investment in my corporation if I became permanently disabled or if I died?" "How would my family operate the company upon my death?" "Would the company be sold to pay inheritance taxes?"

These are real and serious questions confronting the corporate owner of a family corporation. Some of these problems can be answered through the purchase of insurance or buy and sell agreements. But today's executives often prefer to have a substantial part of their holdings outside of their business, so that whatever the fates may decide for their family corporations, they and their families will be more secure through outside investments.

### To Provide for Your Own Income

The president of the family corporation, since he normally controls the Board of Directors, can vote himself salary increases; but after taxes, will there be enough left to purchase securities of other companies? Dividends can be declared and paid—but after taxes—what will be left? In most cases, diversification of investments can only be accomplished by an executive of a family corporation through the sale of a portion of his stock, either on a private placement basis or through a public offering. Here's where a good sound tax lawyer can be of great assistance. Be sure to discuss the capital gains taxes that must be paid if you sell a part of your company's stock during your lifetime.

#### PREPARING FOR THE PROBLEMS OF YOUR ESTATE'S EXECUTOR

I suggest that you check over your investment portfolio with your tax lawyer to determine the effect of federal estate and state inheritance taxes upon your estate. He will advise you as to basis of valuing your family held stock upon your death and the taxes that must be paid.

Your tax lawyer will point out to you the many difficulties that will confront your executor, upon your death, in the valuation of the stock in your family held corporation. The Internal Revenue Service under Section 2031 of the Code, through a series of interpretative bulletins, has established the factors which it will use upon your death in determining the value of your stock in your closely held corporation. There is no exact formula that can be used. A sound valuation will be based upon all relevant facts.

## Tax Evaluation of Stock in a Closed Corporation

Under Revenue Ruling 59–60 the following indicia will be considered in valuing stock in a closed corporation:

1. The nature of the business and the history of the enterprise from its inception;
2. The economic outlook in general and the condition and outlook of the specific industry in particular;
3. The book value of the stock and the financial condition of the business;
4. The earning capacity of the company;
5. The dividend paying capacity;
6. Whether or not the enterprise has good will or other intangible value;
7. Sales of the stock and the size of the block of stock to be valued;
8. The market price of stocks of corporations engaged in the same or a similar line of business having their stocks actively traded in a free and open market, either on an exchange or over-the-counter.

Your executor may wish to value your stock in your family-owned company on the basis of book value, but the government will not accept this valuation if through the use of capitalized earnings, dividend and other tests, a higher valuation will be reached.

Even though your executor can obtain a favorable valuation of your closely held stock under the provisions of the Federal estate tax laws, there are still state inheritance taxes to be considered. Quite often the valuations which the State taxing authorities impose on stock in a family held corporation are higher than those established by the Internal Revenue Service. Your tax lawyer will also advise you as to the potential State inheritance tax liability that will be imposed against your heirs as a result of the valuations that might be placed upon your corporate stock.

It is true that estate tax payments due to the Federal Government can be made over a period of years. Your family-owned corporation, under certain rules, also can redeem a portion of your stock to pay estate taxes but this presupposes that your company will have the financial ability to buy some of your stock. Key-man insurance will help bridge this gap if your corporation cannot afford to buy a part of your stock. In all events your estate must have the necessary funds to meet the tax liability even though time is allowed for the payment on an extended basis.

### Using Insurance to Pay Taxes

You can well argue, "I carry a large amount of insurance and my estate can use the insurance to pay the taxes." Keep in mind that if you own the insurance, the proceeds from your insurance policies are also subject to Federal Estate and State Inheritance Taxes. Again, your tax attorney will advise you how much of the insurance that you carry will be needed by your wife and family when your salary from your corporation ceases as a result of your death. You don't want your family to use the principal of the insurance. In all likelihood your family will need all of the income from your insurance policies to take care of their family needs. With inflation, the needs become even greater for additional amounts of insurance.

I suggest that you check with your tax attorney to determine whether your estate actually could use any major part of your insurance for the payment of estate and inheritance taxes. If the answer is "no," then your executor, faced with a stiff Federal Estate Tax and State Inheritance Tax, might be forced upon your death to sell some or all of your corporate stock to outsiders to pay taxes. A part or all of your stock may be sold at prices far below the true value, thereby causing serious financial loss to your family. As a result of this sale, control of the business you have built up during your lifetime may pass to others and your family may be left in a minority position.

To remedy what may be a disastrous situation, many executives find it personally advantageous to sell a portion of their stock to the public. All of their eggs will not then be in one corporate basket.

At the time of death, the taxing authorities will have no difficulty in valuing your corporate stock if your company has had a public stock offering since a fixed market price exists. This can work to your disadvantage as well as your advantage. It will be an advantage to your estate if upon your death the market value of your stock will be lower than the price which the government would have determined by using the various valuation formulae set forth above. On the other hand, your estate may be at a disadvantage if the stock, at the time of your death, may be selling on the market at prices which may be considerably beyond the price that the government might have determined for closed corporations by using capitalized earnings, book value, etc. This is a calculated risk which you take upon selling stock in your corporation.

Through the sale of a stock to the public you have established a price which will vary from day to day. The government will normally use the quoted market value of your stock upon your death. However, an alternate value may be allowed if your executor wishes to use a value based upon the price of the stock one year after death. Without a market for your stock, your estate would be in a position to present arguments to oppose the government's high valuations. This opportunity to argue for a lower valuation does not exist where you have a public market and the stock is sold on a day to day basis.

### Using Blockage Rules for Tax Benefits

There are tax benefits that your estate can receive under blockage rules. Recently a man died owning 1,440 shares of Common Stock of an insurance company which was listed on the American Stock Exchange. The Internal Revenue Service, for estate tax purposes, applied its usual rule for listed securities which meant setting the valuation between the high and low price on the date-of-death.

Since the stock was quoted at a low of $86.50 and a high of $87.50, the stock was valued at $87.00 per share. The Executor, however, prevailed in establishing a price of $84.00 per share at the date-of-death under the blockage rule since he could show that the block of stock to be valued was so large in relation to the actual sales on the existing market that the stock could not be liquidated in a reasonable time without depressing the market. The price at which the block could be sold outside of the market was a more accurate indication of value than market quotations.

Basically you must keep in mind that through the sale of your stock to the public you have created a public market and a price which can either benefit or hurt your estate on future tax valuations.

# 5

## The Personal Income Tax Costs and the Effects of Bailing Out

Where the corporation is the sole seller of stock, there are no income tax problems for the individual stockholder until he sells a part of his stock. However, if and when, you consider the sale of a portion of your company stock to the public, then you will be confronted by a set of tax considerations. Again a good long visit with your tax attorney will give you the answers to the tax questions facing you. Since you are selling a portion of your stock in your company, you will be required to pay the capital gains taxes provided under the Federal Income Tax laws.

In talking to your tax attorney, check with him on the state income taxes that also might be due on the sale of a portion of your stock. Many state tax laws will tax the gain in a manner similar to the federal government, but at lower tax rates.

You might well argue: "I don't want to pay out a large sum of money for capital gain taxes." Since the tax dollars on the sale of your own stock must be paid by you and not by your corporation, you should consider that the taxes in effect are being paid out of the proceeds of the sale of your stock to the public. In effect, the gross amount that you receive from the sale of your stock will be reduced by the Underwriter's commissions, your share of the expenses and by the amount of the capital gain taxes.

On the other hand, it is important to remember that you will have a substantial amount of money remaining after the sale which can be invested by you, as you determine, outside of your business. Be sure that you are completely familiar with the capital gains laws that affect the sale of your stock.

### Gifts of Stock

As part of your tax planning you might want to make gifts of your common stock to your children or grandchildren. Your tax attorney will point out to you the problems of valuation of common stocks. Again, as in the case of estate taxes, you will have established a valuation on your stock for gift tax purposes through the sale of a portion of your stock to the public. At any time that you wish to make a gift of your stock to your children, relatives, or friends, you have an easily determined value by making reference to sales of the stock on the day of your gift. This might be a disadvantage since you no longer have the opportunity to present the usual arguments against the valuation imposed by the taxing authorities as they use various formulas for establishing market value of closely held corporate stock. The market price, as established by sales of your company stock, is the valuation that will be placed upon the gifts that you make.

### Are You Bailing Out?

Your underwriters will be most interested in knowing whether as the result of your selling a portion of your stock, you intend to gradually step out of the active management of your company. If they sense a plan on your part that you are selling or bailing out, they are not going to be anxious to underwrite your stock issue, particularly if top management in your company is very thin.

The underwriters and the public in effect will ask you, "Why are you selling a portion of your stock?" If there is an impression that you are planning to retire from active business after you sell a part of your holdings, the underwriter and investing public might not look favorably upon the intended public issue. This is a natural conclusion because the future growth of your company would normally depend to a large degree upon your continued management. Even though you may have a strong management group, the underwriters and the public are normally looking to you to continue the record of the past and bring about the same high earnings for the future. If you are selling a portion of your stock, the SEC in its deficiency letter generally will ask for a letter from you, explaining your reasons for selling.

By all means, be candid with the underwriters as you discuss your future plans with them. Review carefully with them your own personal work timetable for the future. If you do have in mind retirement in the not too distant future, let them know your thinking, so that they can more closely evaluate the management group in your organization.

# 6

## Advantages of Private Placement vs. Public Stock Offering

Before considering a public stock offering, you should give serious consideration to a private placement of a portion of your company's stock. A program of this type is normally used where the issue is too small for a public stock offering. Under a private placement plan, a portion of your company's stock is sold directly to one or two purchasers without need to register with the SEC. Normally, purchasers sign a letter indicating that they are purchasing the stock for investment and they do not intend to resell it. While some private sales are negotiated directly between the company and the buyers, many private placements are handled by investment bankers who will normally place the issue with financial institutions, pension funds, insurance companies, investment funds, endowment funds, etc.

How many buyers may purchase a single issue without having the transaction considered a public offering? The answer to this question is not simple; offers to sell as well as actual sales to different people must be considered. There is no simple definition of whether a proposed offering will or will not be a private placement. As far as the SEC is concerned, each situation must be judged on the basis of its particular facts and circumstances. Important factors taken into consideration are the type of security offered, the size of the offering, the number of persons to whom the offering is made, and the type of purchaser. Your attorney is in the best position to advise you after a thorough study of the SEC Act of 1933 and the ruling thereunder. See Chapter 23 for a discussion of this subject.

### Why Consider a Private Placement?

If you consider a private placement of your company's stock, it would be well to weigh the following advantages:

1. Under the Securities Act of 1933, securities which are to be sold to the

public in interstate commerce must be registered. This is a costly procedure. On private sale, registration is not required. This means savings in attorney and accountant fees, and the elimination of printing costs, filing fees, etc. Since SEC registration is not required on a private placement, the company does not have to put in a prospectus, information it prefers not to make public. It is important that your attorney advise you whether the contemplated sale is exempt under the SEC regulations.

2. Securities can be sold immediately where there is a private sale. This can be a great advantage if funds are needed quickly. If the offering must be registered under the Securities Act of 1933, as a public rather than a private sale, considerable time is involved. Delays may have a serious effect on the company's financial position.

3. In some cases securities are sold on a private placement basis without the services of an investment banker and, of course, there are no fees paid. If the sale, on the other hand, is negotiated by an underwriter, the commissions are paid—but they are considerably less than in a public offering.

4. If the company subsequently has financial problems, it is sometimes easier to negotiate an extension or an adjustment if the stock is held by one or two institutions instead of a large number of investors.

5. Sometimes a company that is in a stage of transition or change, can explain this satisfactorily to a few sophisticated investors but would find it difficult to spell it out in a prospectus.

### Disadvantages of a Private Placement

On the negative side there is the possibility that the private investors may impose tight covenants which would be more restrictive than those required in a public offering. Also, in a private placement, the investors may rush to exercise some degree of control if they are not satisfied with the progress of the business. It is not always possible to sell stock on a private placement basis. The answer may be, "We would prefer to wait until your company is seasoned."

### Making the Private Placement

It is usually desirable to employ an investment banker or underwriter to undertake the private placement. Large companies with active financial departments or smaller companies that are actively solicited by insurance companies do in some instances place debt securities privately with institutions without the aid of an underwriter. There have also been some, but very few, private placements of common stock without the assistance of an investment banker. In most instances the fee paid for the banker's services is more than made up in the terms secured by the seller. Also the private placement of common stock is usually difficult to accomplish without the services of an investment banker since unless the seller is a large nationally known company many institutional purchasers have no interest.

In a private placement the investment banker acts as an agent for the seller, he does not make any kind of commitment to sell the securities and is paid a fee for his services. The fees paid are impossible to define as they are the subject of negotiation between seller and banker and depend upon the difficulty, time and amount of work required to make the placement. Obviously a private placement that is arranged in a day as a result of two or three telephone conversations, calls for an entirely different fee from one where a detailed study of the company has to be made and numerous prospective purchasers approached requiring sometimes three or four months. The fee in no case is likely to be less than the equivalent of two stock exchange commissions were the stock listed on the N.Y.S.E. and for a fairly difficult placement might run two or three times this amount.

Another factor in considering the cost of a private placement of common stock is that invariably the purchaser when he signs an investment letter requires a concession from the market price to compensate him for his lack of liquidity. This again varies depending upon whether the particular stock is in good demand. If the stock to be privately placed has no existing market, the purchaser will only pay a price that represents a substantial concession from the price at which he believes the stock would sell if it had a public market.

As you weigh the merits of a private sale, it would be well for you to discuss your problems frankly with a very competent investment banker and your lawyer. They are in the best position to help you steer your course and prevent making an unwise decision for your corporation. Remember that a private placement will not create a public market for your company's stock if there has been no prior public offering.

# 7

## Will an Underwriter Consider Your Company Ready?

You may think that your company is ready, willing and able to "go public" but, before you get your hopes up too high, you will want to sound out an underwriter and get his opinion. Timing is of utmost importance, as well as past earnings, potential, etc.

Mr. Robert E. Linton, partner in Burnham & Company, in a paper that he presented before the American Management Association in New York stated his views on the types of companies that his firm is looking for to underwrite a stock issue as follows:

> Here we are looking for good small companies with a solid record of earnings, good management, and better than average growth prospects. We are not so much looking for electronic or missile component manufacturers to bring out at fancy multiples of earnings, but rather solid small manufacturing and service companies whose securities can be sold to the public at a reasonable price relative to current earnings.

Have frank and honest discussions with your underwriter to determine if they think that your company is ready to go to the public for financing.

Richard Jenrette, of the firm Donaldson, Lufkin & Jenrette, in analyzing his company's methods of examining a company for a potential underwriting, advises:

> When we originate an underwriting, we want it to be a company of exceptional potential, above all, and secondly of large enough size so that it might be bought by some of the more enterprising institutional investors, such as Putnam Growth Fund, Chase Fund, Fidelity, or some of the large pension funds and college endowments. This stems from our view that the best way to success on Wall Street long-term, is to acquire a reputation for making

good investment recommendations. Turning out a number of underwritings in companies that may or may not work out well long-term may be good for immediate profits, but in time may come back to haunt the banker if subsequent results prove disappointing.

Your investment bankers must be satisfied that your company's stock issue will be successful. Their name is attached to the offering and they don't want to come in with a failure. If the underwriters do not consider your company ready for an offering, they will ask you to wait and you would be well advised to hold off until they give you the green light.

How will your underwriters reach a conclusion as to whether or not to proceed? They will ask many questions, study facts and figures and analyze the potential appetite of the public for your company's stock.

It is not necessary that your company fall into the "Growth Company" category. Many stock offerings are underwritten for companies that have a long and continuous record of good sales and earnings. They may not be on the spectacular side but are offered to the public as a good investment and priced at a reasonable price-earnings ratio. The investing public has an interest in these companies for the long pull.

On the other hand, many investors today are interested solely in "Growth" situations. They look for new issues in this category hoping that there will be a rapid rise in the market price of the stock. How will the investing public look at your company? Will they place the stamp of "Growth Company" on your stock offering?

## Determining Whether or Not Yours Is a Growth Company

The world is moving so quickly, investors find it difficult to stay abreast of the changes in our dynamic world economy. They find that stocks that were attractive in the fifties are becoming less important as new products and services come into the market. Investors, in examining available stock for purchase, are influenced by the changes in population, increased leisure time, the political situation, etc. They gravitate in their investments toward companies that will be important in the next decade.

Your company will have to measure up favorably against those companies that are engaged in many of the new dramatic fields. Investors will try to determine whether yours is truly a "growth company." How do investors and analysts make this determination?

Carl M. Loeb, Rhoades and Company, defines a "growth company" as one which is showing a 12 to 15% growth in per share earnings compounded yearly. Growth stocks are the fashion and every corporate executive would like to have the investing public consider the stock of his company in that category.

Potential growth and earnings alone do not constitute the sole test. Consideration also must be given to the company's competitive position, dividend policies, management, maturity of the company and the industry. A growth company generally has a high return on invested capital, a sizable percentage of sales spent each year on research and a large flow back of earnings into additional plant and equipment.

Philip Fisher, an investment counselor on the West Coast, and author of a book entitled *Common Stocks and Uncommon Profits* points out in his book that in analyzing a corporation, to determine if it meets the test of a growth company, one should review carefully the inner workings of a corporation and measure management at various levels. He should study carefully the relationships between the executives, depth, and personnel policies. Mr. Fisher also points out the need to analyze the effectiveness of the sales organization, sales program, cost and accounting controls, research and development, etc.

It would appear that a company, in order to qualify as a "growth company," must not only have an increasing record of sales and per share earnings, as well as sound management, but also a good record of new products. The company should be in a field where there is dynamic growth potential through the use of new products and services as well as an increasing market. The size of the company alone is not a test. A company may be small, but if it dominates the market, it can measure up as a "growth company."

## Determine Whether or Not the Public Is Ready

As you consider a public offering, you might find your company in the position where it has a fine record of earnings, is a well managed company, and has a good growth potential. You are ready to proceed but the underwriter tells you to hold off until a subsequent date.

You might rightfully ask yourself, "Why should we wait when everything is in our favor at this time?" The answer, of course, lies in the fact that the public has to be in a proper buying mood at the time your stock will come out in the market. If the market is "bearish" and the public is selling rather than buying, your investment banker might well tell you that the time is not right for selling your stock to the public. In most cases, however, your underwriter will tell you, despite the bearish trend, to proceed with your company's underwriting if they feel that it is an attractive offering. Many issues are brought to the market even though the market generally is not bullish.

Your underwriters may adjust their thinking on the price that can be obtained during a bearish period. If they feel that the public will look favorably upon your company's stock, the underwriters will normally recommend that you move forward with the sale. Basically it is the underwriter's function to sell new issues, whether the market is bearish or bullish.

You might find in a bearish market that the investing public will be looking for the stock offered by your company so that they can come in on the ground floor. In a depressed market, certain investors might sell securities that have reached a price-earnings ratio which is beyond reason, and purchase your company's stock as a replacement. Your underwriter is the best judge as to whether the public is ready to buy stock in your company.

Your investment banker is in a position to sense the pulse of the market and you would be well advised to take his opinion as to the timing on the sale of your stock. You might find that there are certain times of the year which are not appropriate for the sale of stock. If you wish to come out with an issue in December, your investment banker may tell you to wait until January or February. He may be of the opinion that the summer months are not as good as the fall for introducing your stock to the public. Experience shows that timing is very important. Your investment banker is in the best position to advise you.

# 8

## Your Company Under Public Examination

You might think you have the finest company in America, but will the public agree with you as it examines every phase of your corporation operation? You may say to yourself, "We have been doing very well for many years, sales have been increasing, profits are up; what more can the public want?" Actually the public wants to know many things about your company, and it is important that you do a great amount of corporate soul searching before you put your name on the bottom line of the registration statement.

*By all means be honest with yourself.* The investing public has a way of evaluating your company's stock based upon many tests. The security analysts all over America will be going over your company's prospectus, with a fine-tooth comb. They will be looking for your corporate weaknesses as well as your strength.

If you cannot bring a sound corporate picture to the investing public, you would be well advised to hold off until such time as your company's house is in order and it has the necessary appeal.

Let's review the various phases of your corporation activity that will come under close scrutiny.

1. *Industry, Position and Economic Function.* Before the public specifically evaluates your company, it will want to form an impression of the industry of which you are a part. Questions will be asked of you such as:

"Has your industry grown rapidly in the past 5 to 10 years?"

"Is the group of which you are a part a 'growth industry'?"

"How permanent is your industry?"

"Is your industry subject to technological changes?"

"Is your industry recession-proof?"

"Has your industry reached its peak or does it have the potential of many new industries?"

The public must be satisfied that your industry is not only "here to stay," but that there is a good possibility of dynamic growth in the years ahead. If the public is satisfied that your industry has a growth potential, it can attach to this growth increased protfis in the years ahead. The trend of your industry is very important.

Most industries have made studies of the potential market for the future. These studies are of importance in presenting the potential of the industry of which you are a part.

The public will also want to know that your company serves a definite and important economic function. If your company is in the service field, you will be asked for evidence that your company renders an essential service and that it renders it well.

2. *Your Company's Position.* Your company's position among your competitors will be reviewed carefully to determine your position of leadership. The public will want to know whether your company is one of the leaders in a competitive field. Is your company ahead of the parade? You will be asked to define the share of the market that your company has in relationship to your competitors. It will be well for you to point out the strength that your company has gained in the previous years in relationship to your competitors.

The reputation of your company in the business community also will be checked carefully. There is no substitute for an established reputation. Wishful thinking should not be allowed to color your judgment. The prestige of your company cannot be built up overnight in preparation for the stock offering. There is no magical formula. This is something that must be established over a period of years. If your company is not highly regarded in its own community, the public might not readily accept its stock in the market place.

3. *Book Value.* Investors and analysts, in reviewing your company's financial statements, will quickly look to the book value as a guide for investment. They will take the assets, subtract the liabilities to creditors and preferred stock, and divide the remainder by the number of shares of common stock outstanding and arrive at the book value of your company. In some businesses the book value test is important. Book value is often compared to market price and the price of your stock will be compared to other companies which may have a higher book value.

The book value of your company alone is not an important indication of value. However, it will be seriously considered along with earnings, dividends, management, etc.

4. *Capital.* The capital structure of your company will be reviewed carefully to determine whether there is an excessive amount of debt, bonds, or preferred stock. The existence of these obligations will be of concern to the public. Naturally the capital structure of firms varies, but it will be important to investors and

analysts particularly, that your company has a sound capital structure in which the debt and preferred stock are limited.

The public will want to be certain that you can meet your obligations to your creditors and preferred stockholders when the obligations are due. If you are in the manufacturing field, the analysts particularly will want to be certain that you have sufficient capital to finance your accounts receivable and your inventories. If your company is not in a strong capital position, the public will be concerned that dividends may be passed when the company's profits decline. The public will want to know whether the commitments on your company's debt structure and preferred stock can be met even under adverse conditions.

5. *Cash Flow.* In recent years cash flow has become increasingly more important as a test of a company's financial strength. With a proper cash flow, the public will be assured that the company has the wherewithal to expand without borrowing or withholding dividends. The cash flow of companies varies but security analysts particularly will want to review the cash flow of your company.

6. *Earnings.* The earnings of your company will be subject to x-ray examination by the investing public and the security analysts. Its current and past earnings will be reviewed carefully to determine whether earnings have moved forward each year. The company profits will be examined to determine if they have been affected by adverse business conditions. The effect of the business cycle on earnings will also be carefully scrutinized to determine whether there has been an erosion of earnings.

You will be asked to demonstrate how your company's earnings compare to the earnings of its competitors. You will be asked to furnish operating statements for the past 10 years at least, if available. The security analysts particularly will want to know what proportion of the annual income has been retained by the company. If your company can show a strong earning record through all phases of the business cycle, through war and peace, your company will form a strong and favorable impression upon the buying public.

Increased earnings each year place an "excellent" on management's ability. The public will place considerable emphasis on the price-earnings ratio of your company's stock. The ratio is determined by dividing the current selling price of the stock by the annual earnings. For example, if a stock sells at $20 a share and the earnings of the company are $2 a share for the year, the price-earning ratio will be ten to one.

The public naturally will try to purchase stocks, all things being equal, in companies with a low price-earning ratio. Your corporation will be measured against others to determine whether your stock is offered at a low price-earnings ratio. Many corporations have a price-earnings ratio of ten to fifteen times earnings. On the other hand, many corporations have price-earnings ratios in excess of 25 times. Those stocks that are priced at 25 or more times current earnings generally are considered by the investing public as having excellent growth possibilities.

7. *Statistics and Ratios.* The investment banking industry will want statistical information about your company so that comparisons can be made with your competitors and related industries. The ratios which you will be asked to present are as follows:

(a) *Current ratios.* This is the most popular of all ratios and represents the total current assets in relationship to the current liabilities. Normally the investing public will expect you to have at least a two-to-one ratio, particularly if your company is in the manufacturing field. Your stock will be held in higher regard if the ratio improves from 2 to 1 to, for example, 3 or 4 to 1.

(b) *Operating ratios.* The operating expenses of your company will be related to sales to determine the amount that is paid out for material, wages, and other operating expenses. The public will hope to find a low operating expense ratio to insure high earnings. This ratio is particularly important if your company is in the service field.

(c) *Ratio of net receivables to sales.* Your accounts receivable will be compared with sales to determine whether the collection program of the company is sound. The lower the ratio of receivables, the more attractive your company will be.

(d) *Ratio of inventory to sales.* If your company is required to carry inventories, the analysts will review the ratio of your inventory to sales to determine whether your inventories are in line with others in your field. Again, the lower the percentage of inventory to sales, the more attractive your company stock will be.

(e) *Ratio of net profit to net worth.* This ratio provides a sound analysis of the stockholders' equity. In determining this ratio, the net income is divided by the net worth. This ratio gives the answer as to how much the company is earning on its net worth. It is important to calculate this ratio to determine if there is sufficient return to the stockholders on the net worth to the company.

(f) *Pretax profit margin.* The analysts will determine the ratio of profit before taxes to sales. This ratio is found by dividing the operating profit by sales. The analysts will review prior years operations to determine whether there is an improvement in profit margins with increased sales.

(g) *Liquidity ratio.* This ratio shows the relationship of cash and marketable securities to current liabilities. This ratio supplements the current ratio as it indicates the company's ability to meet its current obligations and pay increased dividends.

(h) *Capitalization ratio.* These are the percentages of each type of investment in the company to the total investment. The analysts will want to find a high percentage of common stock and surplus.

(i) *Sales to fixed assets.* The analysts will compute this percentage by dividing the annual sales by the value, before depreciation and amortization, of plant, equipment and land at the end of the year.

(j) *Dividend return.* The analysts will determine the return on the common stock by dividing the annual dividend per share by the current price of the stock. This will give the current dividend yield.

8. *Management.* One of the most important factors considered today in evaluating a company is "management." If your company is about to embark on a public stock offering, the management will be scrutinized carefully by the investing public and by the security analysts in particular. The public will want to know about your management group to determine whether its executives work together as a team, inspire confidence in the employees of the organization, have long-range potential, etc. Does your management have the experience and has it demonstrated its ability to operate at a profit under all business conditions? If your company cannot receive an "E" for executive evaluation, you had better defer thinking about a public stock offering until a later date.

You will receive many visitors from investment banking firms, trust companies, stock dealers, investment trusts, etc., all wanting to closely scrutinize the executive group in your organization. It is important to the analysts that your management group has depth and works together closely towards the same goals. Through meeting your executives, the analysts will formulate an opinion of the ability, skill, intelligence, leadership and soundness of your executive staff. They will hope to find a squad of bright and aggressive experts. Comparisons will be made to other executive groups. Your company's past record will be reviewed carefully to determine executive turnover.

Benefit plans, insurance programs, and incentives also will be considered to determine whether you are providing properly for your executives. Are your top men content to stay in your organization? Do they think they have a future in your company? Do your executives delegate well? Are they engaged in communal work? These and other similar searching questions will be asked of you many times.

If the investing public reaches the conclusion that yours is a "one-man" organization, your company's stock will not be as attractive as a company with a well-rounded top executive team. The public will be concerned with the future of the business in case anything were to happen to you.

A challenge will be placed at your doorstep to prove that you have an astute executive staff not only at the first level, but the second, third, and fourth as well. You will want to be able to prove that your management methods are paying off for stockholders as reflected by an excellent rate of return on the stockholders' equity.

In analyzing management, the investing public will want to know whether the top management of your company is strong on long-range planning. A careful look will also be given to the depth of your management and the organizational structure of your company.

Your company will be checked carefully to see whether there is a clear delegation of authority and responsibility. Is your management flexible and is it able to quickly shift its product lines to meet new demands? Do you have a centralized policy control and decentralized operational control?

Of great importance, of course, is your program to develop your future management—the men who will handle the future affairs of your company and meet the challenge of the years ahead.

The public and the analysts will want to know whether the officers of the company are large stockholders. The market will consider large holdings by your officers to be desirable. Salaries of executives will be checked carefully and compared with others in similar fields.

Stanley A. Winter, vice president of A. G. Becker and Company, in commenting on the importance of management stated:

> An appraisal of the company's management is of overriding importance to any investment recommendation. Yet, it often defies analysis—publicity to the contrary notwithstanding. The personality and the salesmanship of top executives sometimes becloud the significant issues. Specific standards are therefore virtually useless in appraising management. Past performance is, of course, an indicator of management ability. The age of top officials, the continuity and experience of management talent, methods of compensation and of recruiting and training executives, the depth of the organization, etc., are significant considerations. Reliance is placed upon the opinions of suppliers, customers, bankers, competitors and others who have worked with the company over many years. However, in the final analysis one has to rely on intuitive judgments concerning management philosophy. Is the management still "hungry" or are they getting "fat" on past success? Where does management propose to take the company and how does it propose to get there?

William R. Johnson, vice president of Northwestern National Insurance Company, set forth his tests as to how his company analyzes the management of a company by stating:

The first question which must be answered by any potential investor is the following: "Are the individuals responsible for the success of this venture people with whom I wish to entrust my funds?" Purchasing stock for investment purposes is much the same as buying a part interest in a business venture and should be analyzed in much the same manner.

Perhaps the most important attributes of any management team in today's competitive market are desire and enthusiasm. These qualities must emanate from strong leadership and can only be fostered by excellent communication and effective delegation. In a personal visit with management, attitudes such as these reveal themselves and one can sense a harmony or lack of it within a management team, and can note whether or not a profit consciousness is communicated throughout the organization. Especially important in a research-oriented firm is the existence of a permissive atmosphere, for a creative mind cannot operate effectively in a highly restrictive surrounding. It is important, therefore, to have a management check with operating heads, in addition to the chief executive officer.

The general attitude of management in employee, consumer, and stockholder relations can also be detected through a plant tour, a review of advertising material, a history of labor relations and incentive programs, public statements by officials, management's role in community affairs, industry opinion of the company as a competitor, and consumer attitudes towards the firm.

The moral and ethical standards of top management are also important in that they often reflect the structure of the entire organization and portend future results. Here, management or employee turnover can give a clue as to the type of organization under review. Past training and experience of key people are valuable guides to potential effectiveness, but almost more important is the management beneath this first tier, and how such talent is being utilized and trained. At this point, it is important to determine if potential problems exist relating to nepotism or to absentee management or control.

It is equally important that management has set goals for itself, and has a constructive and realistic plan for attaining these goals. Past statements by management and consequent results are guideposts in this area, and can give indications as to the accuracy of current pronouncements or estimates.

Finally, does management itself show confidence in the venture for which it is responsible through stock ownership, stock options, or other equitable profit oriented incentives. A potential stockholder must always assure himself that management's objectives are consistent with the investor's best interests.

9. *Board of Directors*. In addition to evaluating your management team, the public will carefully scrutinize your board of directors. The public will look

to see whether you have outside directors. Customarily, in smaller companies, the board does not have outside representatives; however, the investing public prefers to find outside directors on your board as they can bring to your company, knowledge, experience, objectivity and prestige.

The public will want to know the names of the directors of the company, their background, their outside business interests, compensation and stock ownership in the company. The degree of activity of the directors on the board will be of interest to the public. In other words, the public will want to be satisfied that the board is composed of capable men and women chosen from within the company and outside of the company.

10. *Fiscal Programs.* The fiscal policies of your company will be examined carefully to determine whether they are sound. Your budgeting programs will be reviewed as well as your inventory methods and your depreciation policies.

The public will want to know whether your company has had any financial re-organizations in the past years. Reserves will be examined carefully. Inventory control systems will be scrutinized. Your company's fiscal policies will be compared with others in your industry.

11. *Dividends.* As the investing public and the analysts evaluate the stock in your corporation, they will want to have full information about the dividends that have been paid in the past as well as an indication of future dividend policy. You will be asked such questions as:

"What has been the dividend policy of your company for the past 5 to 10 years?"

"How much has been paid in dividends and has there been any interruption in the payment?"

"Are there any restrictions on the payment of dividends in your company?"

"Have there been any stock dividends or splits?"

The yield on your stock is very important to many investors. The yield is the ratio of the dividend paid annually per share to the current price of the stock. For example, if your company pays dividends at the rate of $1.00 per year and its stock sells at $25.00 a share, the yield is 4 per cent.

Investors interested in buying the stock in your company will compare the yield on your company's stock to other companies.

Potential stockholders will want to know what percentage of your company's earnings will be paid out in dividends. Some companies pay 50 to 75 per cent of their earnings. Others pay a very small dividend and some few corporations pay none.

If your corporation will be considered as a growth company, it is possible that your dividend can be small. The public then will be buying your stock not on the basis of yield, but because of its growth potential.

If a dividend is to be paid, it is important that your Board of Directors establish a dividend rate at a level which will permit your company to pay out at least the same dollar amount of dividends each year. If your company dividends are stable, this is generally an indication that the earnings are sound and that the company has adequate working capital. Your Board also shows a confidence in the future by having a dividend policy that is consistent over the years.

The cash flow as well as the cash required in the business will certainly have a direct effect on the dividend policy of your company. Be certain, as you establish your first dividend policy with your underwriter, that you do not declare a dividend which might become unrealistic and difficult to pay in the years ahead.

12. *Research and Development.* "Describe to us the research and development program of your company." This request will be made of you time and time again in the early stages of your company's public offering as well as the years following.

Security analysts particularly want to know the answers to such questions as:

"Does your company have a centralized research department?"

"What are the current projects under research?"

"How much has the company spent for research during the past five years?"

"What is the ratio of the research budget to gross sales?"

"What market research activities are carried on?"

"What basic important discoveries have been made by the company?"

These questions must be answered clearly and fairly as the security analysts try to determine whether your company is keeping ahead of its competitors.

It is important to show that management is fully behind the research program and that your company is leading the field, if this is the case. Research laboratories in and of themselves are only a part of the answer. More important is the intelligence and ability of the men assigned to the research program.

The security analysts will want to be certain that your company is attracting qualified men and women for your research department. They will examine closely your program to determine whether the research is done in an atmosphere conducive to the development of new products and the improvement of old ones. They will analyze the team work that exists in your organization, as this is an important factor in determining the strength of a research program. If your men work together well in this area, good results will be forthcoming. The dollars that your company spends on research are not the measure of your success. It is the "people" in research, the attitude of management and the results accomplished that will be of interest to the public.

The public will compare your company's research program with that of other firms in the same field. The investing public knows that in the years ahead, more and more dollars will be spent for research and development regardless of sales and protfis. Competition and pressures on prices will require increased expenditures for research and development.

Your company's research program will be examined closely to determine not only whether you are keeping up with the Joneses in your industry but whether you are setting the pace. You will come out well if you can show that you have developed the latest techniques to develop your company's long range potential.

13. *Labor.* As the investing public analyzes your company, it will want to know about your company's labor relations. You will be asked such questions as, "What have been the relations with the union?" "What is the record of strikes during the past 5 years?" "What are your employee benefits?" "What is your annual labor turnover?"

Labor plays an important part in most every organization and the public will want to know that your labor relations have been better than satisfactory. If you have had a considerable amount of turnover, work stoppages, shutdowns and labor strife, the public might well draw certain unfavorable conclusions about your labor relations.

Your employment philosophy will come under close scrutiny. If you have high turnover in your organization, the security analysts in particular will want to know the reasons for this. They will want to check your recruiting procedures, indoctrination programs, advanced training programs, plans for promotions from within, job evaluation programs, etc. The investing public is interested in companies that have well rounded labor relations and are particularly partial to companies that have a low ratio of labor cost to total sales.

14. *Plant Facilities.* The geographical location of your company plant facilities will be carefully analyzed by your underwriter, analysts, and the public. You will be asked whether the areas in which your plants are located are today the best from a transportation standpoint, attracting employees, and closeness to employees. Your company's buildings and equipment will be reviewed to determine whether you are operating with efficiency and on a competitive basis.

The analysts will want to see your plant so they can form an opinion as to the adequacy of your equipment and machinery. They will attempt to determine how much obsolescence has crept into your plant and whether you can operate on a competitive basis. They will want to know whether your facilities are out-dated and whether they are sufficiently automated. Your depreciation policies will be reviewed to determine whether you are plowing back sufficient earnings to replace your equipment when it becomes obsolete.

15. *Production.* "Is your company operating on an efficient basis?" "How do you compare to your competitors in production efficiency?" These and many other questions will be asked of you, particularly if you are in the manufacturing and distribution field, to determine whether you are manufacturing quality

products at the right price. The degree of automation in your plant will be analyzed. "How much mechanization has taken place?" "Are you getting the maximum output from your plants?" These are questions which you will be asked as the analysts evaluate your production strength and vitality for the future.

16. *Patents and Trademarks.* Your balance sheet won't show the value of your company's patents and trademarks. These are intangibles which may have a great value to you, particularly if you are a leader in your field. The public will have a greater interest in your company if it recognizes your trademark and your brand names. Security analysts will want to know whether you have protected your patents and trademarks through proper registration and whether you have any litigation pending, contesting your rights to the use of such patents and trademarks.

The public will have a greater interest in your company if you own important patents and trademarks. Many of America's large corporations today own trademarks and brand names which have become a household word. These intangible assets are important to the investing public.

17. *Sales and Service.* The sales program and policies of your company will be appraised carefully. Obviously the sales strength and vigor of your organization has a direct bearing upon the profits to be made by your company. The public will want to know about the products or services that your company sells. It will try to determine if you have diversified markets for your products. Your sales policies will be analyzed as well as your distribution system. The analysts will want to know how many customers you have and the turnover among customers, dealers, or distributors. They will want to know whether your company has many customers or few. There are certain dangers inherent in having few customers since the loss of one or two would materially affect the sales of the company. Companies that manufacture products that are consumed daily by the public are sometimes more attractive than the stocks of companies that manufacture products that are not replaced for long periods of time. The public will want to know whether the products that are being sold by your company will be bought in recession periods as well as during prosperous times.

Your service policies and programs will be reviewed and the sales staff, its selection, training, compensation, etc., will come under close scrutiny. Basically, the investing public will want to know if your company has the ability to sell more efficiently than your competitors. If you do not have a strong sales organization, the public will doubt your ability to grow. Investors tend to buy securities in companies that have a strong sales organization.

Many firms have marketing divisions which provide special selling aids. Will your company be able to show that it has developed these programs and that it has a strong concept of service?

Your customer relations will be carefully analyzed to determine whether you have built up goodwill among your customers. Investors will want to know that your customers will stay with you and not drift off to your competitors in the years ahead. The public will try to estimate your future sales both on a short term and long term basis. If the public is optimistic and feels that your company's sales will grow in the years ahead they will find your company's stock to be attractive.

The advertising policy of your company will play an important role also in determining whether your company is sales oriented and has a maximum of sales vitality and strength.

18. *Government Business.* "What percentage of your company's business is done with the United States Government and subcontractors for the government?" This question will be asked of you since normally the public prefers to make its investment in companies where there is a higher percentage of civilian orders than military business. While the government can provide large volume orders, quite often the profits are lower. Government contracts are subject to renegotiation and can be canceled. Non-government business generally has greater stability.

19. *Government Regulations.* You will be asked, "Is your company subject to government regulations and control?" The public takes a second look in making investments in companies that are under government control and are likely to be subject to constant investigation.

20. *Expansion.* "What are your company's expansion plans?" The public will want to know the answer to this question as it evaluates the stock in your company. Are you planning to open new plants or introduce new lines? The public has a greater interest in companies that are moving forward rather than those that are interested in the status quo.

21. *Mergers and Acquisitions.* If your Board of Directors has an interest in acquiring other companies through mergers and acquisitions, this may add an additional flavoring to your company's stock.

The investing public today is aware of the acquisition programs of many companies. Your corporation will be compared to others who have had acquisitions. Does your company subscribe to the theory that it will go backwards if it does not grow through acquisitions? The analysts also will want to know if your company has any unassimilated acquisitions.

22. *Foreign Facilities.* With the growing importance of the European common market, it is necessary for American manufacturers to give consideration to opening up plants abroad. The investing public will want to know, particularly if you are a manufacturer, whether you have developed overseas operations.

23. *Is Your Company Recession-proof?* The public, in analyzing your company, will want to know whether your company is "recession-proof." There are

many companies, such as, for example, the electric utilities which are considered a defensive industry as well as having growth possibilities. Electric utilities are usually able to show gains in a short recession period as well as in good times.

Your company's earnings will be closely examined for the years 1949, 1954, 1958 and 1960 which were the recession years. The public will want to know how your company was affected by the recession and its record will be compared with other companies in its industry group.

If your company's earnings dropped in those recession years, it will be necessary for you to be able to show what changes have been made in its operations if you claim your company is now recession-proof.

24. *Public Relations Program.* The success or failure of a corporation's first public stock issue may well hinge on the extent to which it has built up a public awareness of the firm's name, its sphere of activity, and its achievements in this sphere. To do this, it must not only have turned in a good performance, it must have managed to convey to the public a knowledge of this performance.

The simplest definition of public relations is: "Good performance publicly appreciated, because adequately communicated." It is this job that must have preceded any effective attempt to sell stock. The company must have reached that stage in its relations with both the financial and the general community that will insure a demand for a share in its ownership. Before any corporate management makes the decision to go public, it should ask itself whether the firm has been sufficiently publicized. It is important that you consult with your attorney who will guide you as to the limits which must be imposed in public relations prior to an offering.

25. *Future Outlook and Growth Potential.* The average investor who purchases your company's stock must have confidence in the future of your company. The investor will expect you to have a sound philosophy for growth in the years ahead and a more than reasonable opportunity to move forward saleswise and profitswise.

The analysts who will visit with you will be quick to determine whether your company can qualify as a "growth company." They will want evidence of foresight, vision and planning. If there is evidence of a general status quo attitude or, "We've done it this way before, there is no reason to change," the analyst will not look with favor upon your company's future outlook and growth.

The possibilities of a successful public stock offering depends, to a great extent, upon your ability to convince the public and the invesment industry that your company has a strong growth potential in the years ahead.

# 9

## Function of an Investment Banker

As you and your associates give serious thought to the sale of a portion of your company's stock to the public, you will want to meet and discuss this program with an investment banker, also known as an "underwriter."

You might well ask, "What is an investment banker and what is his function?" Actually an investment banker is a middleman who brings together sellers and purchasers of securities. While he serves many functions, as will be described later, one of his major functions consists of purchasing securities from companies wishing to go public—or which have already gone public and selling them directly or through other security dealers to dealers or to the investing public.

An investment banker normally purchases the securities to be offered to the public on a fixed commitment basis and assumes the risk of being able to sell all the stock purchased. For example, the investment banker will purchase stock from a company or a selling stockholder at a determined price, for example, $10 and sells the stock to the public at $11 on the initial offering. The difference of one dollar, known as the "spread" or underwriter's commission, is the compensation that is paid to the investment banker to cover his expenses and his services and compensate him for his risk and permit him to make a profit.

The underwriter assumes the risk of outright purchase in most issues. The risk can be for a short duration if he markets the issue within a few hours or days after the initial offering. It is possible, however, that the issue may not sell as anticipated and the underwriter can take some losses.

At the outset do not confuse investment bankers with commercial bankers. The latter are institutions that handle savings accounts, make loans and provide checking facilities for both individual and business organizations. They do not underwrite stock issues.

### Are Underwriting Firms Necessary?

It is possible to conduct your own public stock offering without an investment banker. However, this practice is not generally recommended. The final cost of a direct sale may be much higher than the underwriter's "spread." Distribution of the stock may be poor and the job of selling the stock may be difficult without an underwriter's sponsorship. Your corporation, in effect, receives such an approval when a reputable underwriter sells your company's issue.

There are many reasons for you to sell your securities through an investment banker rather than selling directly to the public on your own. In most cases the investment banker will agree to purchase all of the stock that you wish to sell thereby assuring you that you will sell all of the stock that you wish to place on the market. If, on the other hand, you attempt to sell your stock on your own you will have no assurance that you will be successful in selling all of the stock. You might end up selling less than you had anticipated or needed.

If you have legal problems you consult a lawyer. If you have medical problems you consult a physician. By the same token, if you intend to sell a substantial amount of stock in your corporation, you will be well advised to consult an investment banker and the best you can obtain. He has a familiarity with the market conditions. He knows the public's mood and frame of mind on the acquisition of new issues. An investment banker is familiar with the prices of stock of companies in businesses similar to yours and is in the best position to advise you as to the best offering price for your stock as well as the proper time for the sale.

An investment banking firm, through its syndication channels and sales organization, will obtain for you the type of distribution that is best for your company. If your investment banker has an outstanding reputation in the minds of the investing public, your stock issue will generate more interest and you will have a better chance for a successful sale.

### Investment Bankers' Activities

Investment bankers perform many functions beyond the placing of new issues. These services are quite uniformly offered by the large firms operating on a national basis.

The principal activities of an investment banker are described as follows:
1. Origination, registration, underwriting and syndicating of corporate stock and bond issues.
2. Public distribution of issues through wholesale and retail channels.
3. Trading as principal and broker in many issues, including securities of banks, insurance companies, public utilities and industrial corporations.

4. Purchase of large blocks of listed or unlisted stock for secondary distribution through security marketing channels.
5. Acts as agent in arranging private financing with insurance companies, banks, investment trusts and other institutional accounts.
6. Arranges contracts for sale and lease-back of properties.
7. Acts as agent in negotiating purchase and sale of controlling or major stock interests in going business concerns.
8. Consults and assists in effecting corporate mergers, consolidations, liquidations, recapitalizations, etc.
9. Purchase for temporary investment of entire or substantial equity interests in going concerns for subsequent public or private sale.
10. A major factor in buying and marketing bonds of states, municipalities, and other governmental bodies.

### *Services Offered by an Investment Banking Firm*

If you contemplate a public stock offering, it is important that you be very conversant with the various departments of an investment banking firm. Your discussions with your underwriter will bring you into close contact with most of these divisions. While investment banking firms operate differently, most of the large firms have the following departments:

1. *Buying or Corporate Finance Department.* The work of this group consists of originating underwriting business, investigating, preparing issues for a public offering and the purchase of securities from companies. If you intend to have a public stock offering, you will work primarily with the representatives of this department.
2. *Syndicate Department.* This department organizes groups of underwriters to participate in the sale of issues which the firm will manage and forms a selling group composed of other security dealers to participate in the distribution.
3. *Sales Department.* This department distributes the securities to investors. Most investment banking firms have salesmen who contact individual and institutional buyers for the purpose of selling stock.
4. *Research Department.* It is customary for investment banking firms to have a Research Department that studies the securities of corporations who not only seek financing but who have securities in the public market. The employees of the Research Department study statistical reports, make comparisons of companies in similar fields, and issue reports which are very often widely circulated.
5. *Investment Counseling Department.* Many investment banking firms offer a counseling service to investors.

# 10

## How to Select an Underwriter

As you give serious consideration to a public stock offering you will ask the question, "How can I select the investment banking firm that will do the best underwriting job for our corporation?" This is not an easy assignment because there are many fine firms from which to choose. Your task in selecting an underwriter may be made easier for you if you can find a corporation executive who recently has had a public stock offering. He will give you the benefit of his thinking and experience. You might find that a particular underwriting firm specializes in selling issues in your particular field, and in all likelihood could do an excellent underwriting job for you.

### Seek the Best

Clearly it is to your company's interest to try to find the very best investment banking firm to sell your issue. In offering the stock of your company to the public for the first time, the reputation of the underwriter is of great importance. You will find that if the public, in reviewing your prospectus, finds the name of one of the large high-grade investment banking organizations as managing underwriter for your issue, it will have greater confidence in your stock.

The most important consideration in selecting your investment banker is his reputation. Before contacting an investment banker, discuss with your attorneys, accountants, bankers and your management consultant, if you have one, the type of investment banker best suited for your needs. Try to select the one that is most highly regarded and one that has underwritten issues similar to yours.

It is important to keep in mind that after the sale of your stock, you will want to work closely with your underwriter. Never consider your initial stock offering as being the one and only time that you will work with your investment banking firm. In all likelihood there will be a continuing relationship, and it is important that you have complete confidence in the integrity and ability of the investment banking firm that you have selected.

It is imperative that you have a highly qualified underwriting firm because many of the negotiations which you conduct with the underwriter are not reduced to writing. A handshake very often is all that is required. You must be in a position where you can rely upon the word of your underwriter, whether it be verbal or in writing.

Robert Dickerman, president of Microdot, Inc., warns:

> My initial advice to a corporate executive considering a public stock offering for the first time would be to avoid, if at all possible, the small so-called "boiler-plate" investment banking houses which impose all sorts of management and stock restrictions and excessive commissions. I would suggest that the executive seek out the very best investment banking firms to handle the offering.

You will be well advised to seek the very best investment banker to sell your company's stock.

## Deciding Whether to Work with an Investment Banking Firm In or Outside of New York City

The large investment banking firms, for the most part, have established their main underwriting offices in the Wall Street area in New York City. Most of these firms have branch offices throughout the country. As you consider a public offering for your company, you will want to keep in mind the need for working very closely with your underwriter. If your principal office, for example, is located on the West Coast, it might be more difficult to develop a public stock offering with an underwriter that has only one office in Wall Street in New York, as compared to working with a New York underwriter that has a strong West Coast branch office.

You will find as you work with an underwriter, that you will be in almost daily communication with the representatives of various departments of the underwriting firm. There will be numerous meetings with your underwriter which will require your presence as well as your attorneys and accountants. There will be considerable detailed information exchanged between the underwriter's representatives, your attorneys and your accountants. Time and cost can be saved if you work with an investment banker who has an office in your general vicinity. It certainly is not necessary that the main office of the underwriter be located in your city, but it is well to have a strong branch office of the underwriter in your area, so that much of the work can be done with the branch representatives rather than constantly having to go to New York for meetings with the underwriters, their attorneys, etc.

Normally, in your first contacts with an underwriter, the initial discussions may take place in a branch office if you are working with one of the larger investment banking firms. The resident partner or branch office manager will send on to the main office of the underwriter his general impressions of your company and its potential for a public stock offering. Generally, the recommendation of the branch office manager carries a great deal of weight but the final decision as to whether the bankers will accept your company for a public stock offering, normally rests with the partners who are usually resident in the principal office of the firm. In some firms all of the partners, whether in the principal office or in the branches, will consider and decide whether the firm should accept the underwriting of a particular issue.

If the principal office of the underwriter has a positive interest in your company, it normally will be necessary for you to meet with the partners and representatives of the firm in their principal office. Should an agreement be reached between you and the underwriter for a public stock offering, much of the preparatory work for the registration statement, prospectus, blue sky registrations, etc., can be done in the branch office of the underwriter. For these reasons, it is important for you to attempt to select an underwriter that has a major branch office either in your city or in an area adjacent to your own office.

### Deciding Whether to Work with a Local Underwriter or a National Firm

In every major city there are local investment banking firms that can effectively handle local underwritings. As you consider a public stock offering for your company you will want to determine whether you should work with a local firm or a national investment banker.

If an offering is small and primarily local in nature, it might be well to work with a local investment banking firm that is familiar with your company. If you wish to have widespread or national distribution of your company's stock, this can be accomplished by working with a local underwriter, but you should consider employing the services of a national firm of underwriters.

There are no hard and fast rules on this subject. Many local firms, while they do not have offices throughout the country do have facilities for syndicating an issue. On the other hand, if the issue is for 100,000 shares to sell at a minimum of $15, it would be advisable to also consult a large national investment banking firm, particularly if widespread distribution is desired.

Some national organizations will underwrite issues where there are fewer than 100,000 shares or the price is lower than $15. On the other hand there are some national investment banking firms with higher requirements. Some firms require as a condition to their underwriting an issue that the company have minimum sales and earnings above a specific level.

The underwriter that you select will quickly indicate to you whether the size of the issue that you contemplate falls within the framework of their company policy. In some situations the underwriter will revise his general requirements as to the size of an issue, if he sees substantial growth possibilities in the company as well as subsequent offerings.

You should give full consideration to a local underwriting if you do not operate your company on a national basis. Many companies contract with national underwriters because the company operates on a nation-wide basis and they want national distribution of their stock. If, for example, your company operates a chain of stores throughout America you might well want to have a national underwriter so that stock can be sold particularly in the communities in which you are located. If, on the other hand, your company's operations are purely local in nature, you may wish to have a local underwriter sell your stock issue.

There are many advantages in working with a local underwriter. You, the local underwriter, your counselors and advisors can meet easily and considerable time can be saved. There will be less travel costs—less time away from your desk with a local offering. Against this, you must weigh the advantages of having a large national investment banker as your underwriter. His prestige, selling organization, and ability to attract a strong selling group might well make it attractive for you to seek out a national firm. The selection of a local versus a national firm is one that should be made after thorough discussion between you, your attorneys, accountants, bankers and other consultants.

# 11

## Your Initial Discussions with an Underwriter

My best advice as to how to conduct your negotiations with an underwriter would be, "Be frank and completely honest." I think you should look upon your relationship with your underwriters in almost the same manner as you regard your dealings with your attorney or your accountant. "Kid him not" because to hold back the facts from your underwriters can bring about, in the days ahead, unhappiness for your underwriter and the public, and disappointment to you.

### Be Candid

Be candid, open and above board in all of your discussions with your underwriters. They know from experience, gained from many other corporate financings, that your company, also, has certain weaknesses as well as certain strengths. They will want to know your company's shortcomings, its "soft spots," and areas that require development. They must weigh carefully all of the minus factors as they analyze your company and its potential for a public stock offering. Keep in mind that if you fail to disclose facts to the underwriters, in all likelihood these facts will come out at a subsequent time.

Your initial discussions with your underwriter may well require numerous meetings, telephone calls, visits to your offices and plant. The underwriter will want to determine whether your company is ready for a public stock offering and whether the market is right. You will discuss the size of an issue, amount to be sold to the public, approximate price of stock, type of stock to be offered and timing.

Your underwriters will work very closely with your accountant, attorney, management team, and other persons in your organization. It is their business to analyze in detail the full nature and scope of your company operations. They are specialists in sifting out weaknesses and strengths. You will be well advised to point out the areas needing development, rather than wait for the underwriters to find them through their own investigations. They are thorough in their evaluation of your company. In all likelihood, the analyst for the underwriter will surprise you with the results of his "x-ray" of your company. Through a frank discussion of both the pluses and minuses in your business, your underwriters can very often assist you in evaluating your company weaknesses in the proper light. They often will make suggestions to bring about an improvement.

### Be Factual

Remember, "figures talk" to an underwriter. Give him facts—and not just estimates and conjectures.

Be sure that you have available in your discussions with your underwriters, the complete and accurate records of the operations of your business. Be careful of any projections that you might make to the underwriter. He will rely upon these as being your best "guesstimate" of the future sales and earnings of your business. The underwriter has the right to expect that you are giving him sound estimates based upon your experience, the knowledge of the business, and your understanding of the future of the industry. Be careful when you make estimates that you are basing them on the best source material available. Temper your predictions with good solid judgment.

### Be Frank about Weaknesses

If you do not have sufficient background to project every phase of your operations, be frank and tell your underwriter that you cannot come up with a sound prediction for a certain area of your company. If you are in a business that is relatively new and has had a spectacular growth, again, if you do not have a solid projection of the future, be candid in your talks with your underwriters and express yourself accordingly.

It is easy to make projections; it is not always as easy to come forth with the final result to back up and substantiate your original estimate. Your underwriters expect you to have confidence in the future, but they expect you to be realistic. They assume your projection will be based upon sound thinking and good judgment. Be extremely careful that you do not make wild predictions for the future of your business. Poorly conceived estimates and predictions can very easily haunt you in the years ahead.

### Don't "Shop Around"

You will find as you negotiate with an underwriter that it becomes increasingly more difficult to discuss your financing program with another investment banking firm. If you have presented your financing program to a top-flight investment banker, it may not be necessary for you to negotiate with a second or third firm.

If you are working with a local underwriter you may wish to discuss your proposed underwriting with a national firm also. I do not think it is wise, under any circumstances, to consult with more than two firms. If you do, you will quickly obtain the reputation as "shopping around" and all the major underwriting firms will quickly lose interest in your stock offering.

It is well, however, to discuss your financing with two top firms to be sure that you are developing the best possible underwriting program for your company. It is well to get two opinions as to marketability of your company's stock, price, underwriter's commissions, and extent of sales syndicate which will be formed.

Many companies negotiate with just one investment banker and proceed with him. Certainly there can be no objection to working with only one underwriter if the one selected is top-flight and has a proven record of integrity and success in selling new issues.

# 12

## Methods of Underwriting

In your discussions with your investment banker, you will want to consider his obligation to purchase your company's stock at the offering date. There are three methods of underwriting customarily used: fixed commitment, best efforts and all or nothing basis. It is important that you know the differences that exist between the three methods.

### Fixed Commitment Basis

The most desirable and most common method of selling your company's stock to an underwriter is on a fixed commitment basis. Under this method the underwriter or syndicate group of underwriters agrees to purchase the stock which your company or you wish to sell at a fixed price. This price is arrived at as a result of negotiations between you and the principal underwriter.

If your underwriter agrees to purchase stock from your company on this basis, you will receive a check in full for the stock, less the underwriter's commissions within a week after the public offering of your stock. If the underwriter has difficulty in selling the stock, this does not affect the obligation to purchase your company's stock, since the underwriter has made a firm commitment. The underwriter alone carries the risk of being able to sell the entire issue. It is important to keep in mind, however, that the underwriter, in a fixed commitment underwriting, has certain escape clauses and reserves the right to cancel the contract before the actual sale if certain contingencies arise. The likelihood of the underwriter cancelling the contract is remote since the time between the signing of the contract and the public offering is usually not longer than several days.

It is necessary to review the "escape" clauses in the contracts so that the seller knows exactly under what circumstances the underwriter can cancel their agreement. Normally underwriters will not enter into a fixed basis commitment unless they are quite certain that there will be a sufficient demand for the stock to justify its purchase.

## "Best Effort" Commitment

Where a stock is considered speculative, an underwriter may not wish to enter into a firm commitment to purchase stock. Instead, the underwriter will agree to use its "best efforts" to sell the company's securities. If the underwriter has difficulty in selling the full amount of stock offered to the public, the underwriter has no obligation to purchase the balance of the unsold stock. The underwriter on a "best efforts" basis is merely serving as an agent in attempting to sell as much of the stock as possible. It might be advisable to hold off a public stock offering if the underwriter will only sell the stock on a "best efforts" basis.

## Combined Firm Commitment and Best Efforts Basis

In some offerings, the underwriter agrees to purchase from the company a certain number of shares of stock and further agrees on a best efforts basis to sell the balance to be offered to the public. For example, the prospectus of Texas Research and Electronic Corporation states:

> The Company has entered into an underwriting agreement with Naftalin & Co., Inc., 207 South 6th Street, Minneapolis, Minnesota (the "Underwriter"), by which the Underwriter undertakes to sell for the Company the 1,000,000 shares of stock offered hereby, and in any event to purchase from the Company a minimum of 250,000 shares, subject to the terms and conditions of the Underwriting Agreement. Under the Underwriting Agreement the Underwriter is to offer the stock to the public for a period of thirty days, after which the Underwriter is obligated to purchase for its own account any of the shares not previously sold by the Underwriter up to at least 250,000 shares, which the Underwriter shall then attempt to sell to the public. The Underwriter is obligated to sell the stock to the public at a price of $1.15 per share and to pay the Company $1.00 for each share sold for or purchased from the Company.

## All or None Basis

Some underwriters, if they do not wish to enter into a firm commitment to purchase all of the stock to be offered, will sell an issue on an "all or none" basis. This means that if the stock cannot be sold to the public in its entirety, the underwriting will not become effective. Some recent examples of "all or none" basis, as shown in the prospectus are as follows:

> *Del Electronics Corp.* The obligation of the Underwriters is to cause to be purchased and sold either all or none of the 100,000 shares of Common Stock at the Closing Date, which (unless extended by mutual agreement)

is to be not later than 30 days following the effectiveness of the Registration Statement and State Qualifications with respect to the sale of the securities offered, but in the event that the sale of the said 100,000 shares is not so consummated, the Agreement may be terminated by the Company and the Underwriters shall refund to the subscribers for stock their entire purchase price.

*Chemtronic Corporation.* Under the terms and conditions of the Underwriting Agreement, the Company has employed Jay W. Kaufmann & Co. as exclusive agent to sell 200,000 shares of the Company's common stock (par value $.10 per share) for the account of the Company. No firm commitment has been made by the Underwriter to purchase or take down any of the shares of common stock offered hereby, but the Underwriter has agreed to use its best efforts to find purchasers for the shares offered hereby on an "all or none" basis. The Underwriter's commitment is subject to a "market out" in the Underwriter's sole discretion if market conditions are unfavorable.

*Lifetime Pools Equipment Corp.* On November 14, 1960 the Company entered into an agreement with Grant, Fontaine & Co. (the Underwriter), pursuant to which the Underwriter has been employed by the Company to sell and dispose of 175,000 shares of the Company's Common Stock at a public offering of $3.25 per share. There is no firm commitment by the Underwriter to purchase any of said shares. The agreement provides that unless the Underwriter has sold 87,500 shares within 60 days from the initial public offering date said agreement shall automatically be terminated and the Underwriter shall refund all moneys received from subscribers to the Common Stock in full.

*Aviation Employees Corporation.* While there is no firm commitment by the Underwriters to purchase the 2,500,000 shares of common stock offered hereby, the Underwriting Agreement provides that the Underwriters shall have ninety days, commencing the day after the date of this Prospectus, during which to find purchasers for at least 1,000,000 shares of said Common Stock and to deposit the full purchase price therefor in escrow with National Savings and Trust Company, Washington, D. C. If within such period an aggregate of at least $2,000,000 is deposited, the escrow agent not later than the tenth business day after such minimum aggregate of deposits has been completed, shall deliver the shares to the purchasers and pay the net proceeds thereof to the Corporation and the commissions due thereon to the Underwriters. If the Underwriters fail to find purchasers for at least 1,000,-000 shares within such period, the public offering shall terminate, the escrow agent shall refund in full all subscription payments, without interest, and the Underwriters shall be entitled to no commissions or options, except that the actual expenses of the Underwriters up to $50,000 shall be reimbursed by the Corporation.

# 13

## How to Determine the Offering Price of the Common Stock

In your initial discussions with your investment banker, you will ask, "How will the price be established on the stock that we offer to the public?"

### Why Is It a Difficult Task?

Naturally, you have a very definite interest in knowing the answer to this question. However, you will find it very difficult to obtain a firm answer to this question. You will be told by the underwriter that the offering price will be within a certain price range, but that the final price will not be determined until immediately before the SEC permits the registration statement to become effective. The price normally will be set the day before the sale of the stock to the public.

### Determining Factors

The underwriter will explain to you that there are many factors that must be taken into consideration in the final determination of the price.

1. *Timing.* An explanation will be given to you as to why the final price cannot normally be determined until the day before the stock is to be sold to the public.

As a seller of stock, you may not be completely satisfied with this answer; you would like to know at the outset in your negotiations what the final price will be. However, the price generally is not definitely fixed until the final sale and you may well have to be content to accept the underwriter's range of prices until the final price is established.

2. *Price Range.* You may want to obtain a written expression from your underwriter as to a range of prices for the offering of your stock. Keep in mind that the final price may be on the low side. You must be prepared to accept this if, in your final negotiations with your underwriter, it is determined that the stock

will have a better after market if it is offered at a price falling near or at the bottom of the range.

3. *Portion of Stock to Be Sold.* As you consider the sale of a portion of your company's common stock, you will inquire as to the formula that will be used in establishing the offering price of your company's stock.

Actually, there are no exact rules or guideposts that can be used in arriving at the price at which your stock will be offered to the market. Your investment banker will examine the market price of the companies that operate in a field similar to yours. Quite often there are no parallels than can be used. The underwriters will try then to find other companies which are in related areas. They will examine their price earnings ratio, capital, dividends, etc., and compare their operations with yours. They will weigh carefully your prospective earnings and dividends based upon past experience, and the amount of stock which will be available and the potential demand.

4. *"Seasoning" of Your Stock.* If your company is going to go public for the first time, there may be an entirely different reaction to your company than to one that has had its stock sold on an exchange for a period of years. Seasoning is an important factor in the price of new stock. Many buyers, in a cautious frame of mind, will want to wait and see how your company's stock behaves for a period of time before they acquire stock. If your company is not well known or operates on a local or regional basis, this again is a strong factor which must be weighed in setting the offering price.

5. *Price Earnings Ratio.* The price earnings ratio is the current price of the stock divided by the latest determinable annual earnings per share. If a particular stock is selling at $50 a share and its net income for the past year was $5.00 per share, the stock is selling for 10 times earnings. Price earnings ratios fluctuate widely.

6. *Growth Pattern.* It is also possible that in spite of the fact that your company is not well known in comparison to others in your industry, your growth pattern and future potential may be so great that the public will be willing to pay a greater price earnings ratio for your company's stock than for others that are more seasoned.

7. *Comparable Prices of Similar Issues.* Your underwriter will explain to you that in order for your issue to be successful, it must be priced somewhat lower than comparable issues that are currently on the market. These older issues have had seasoning, yours has not.

Quite naturally, you will want to get the top selling price for your company's stock, but your underwriter will explain to you that this might be a mistake. He will point out to you, that in order for your stock to be successful on the initial sale and as well as in the after market, the stock must be attractively priced. It will be pointed out to you that, while you may be getting somewhat less on the initial stock offering, you will find that by having sold at a proper price, the balance of your holdings will increase substantially over the years. In other words, your underwriter will urge you not to try to get the top dollar on the initial sale. Keep in mind that if you are retaining, for example, 75% of your stock, you want that 75% to gain in value over the years. If you overprice your stock at the initial offering, the stock might well drop in price after the initial sale and this would seriously affect the price of the stock which you still continue to hold.

### Don't "Second Guess" Your Underwriter

Since you have a relationship with your underwriter, similar to that of lawyer-client, you must for the most part, accept the advice of the underwriter in the pricing of your company's stock. You can make a serious mistake, in my opinion, in trying to "second guess" your underwriter. You would do well to accept his recommendations after discussing thoroughly with him all phases of the pricing problem.

When we sold 25% of our stock in Manpower, Inc., we had serious discussions with our underwriters as to the price to be established on the stock offering. Upon the recommendation of the underwriters, the price was established at $15 a share. Within six months the stock rose to $50 a share. We could have argued that our stock was underpriced as evidenced by the rapid increase in the selling price of the stock over the six month period. Conversely, it can be argued equally as well, that had our stock been initially offered at $20 a share instead of $15, the stock might have dropped materially in the after market and the confidence in our stock would have been lost.

While new issues are in great demand, there are many stocks that drop below the original offering price within a few months. Your investment banker is in the best position to advise you as to the proper offering prices.

Mr. Frederick W. Straus, partner in Straus, Blosser & McDowell, cautions against asking too high a price for your stock. His advice is as follows:

> It is only natural for each father to think that his child is the best, and for each business owner to think that his business is the best, and that his shares are entitled to the highest price. But remember one thing, we investment bankers are not geniuses; we are only merchants of securities. Securities are our inventory, exactly as your inventory might be merchandise, it might be steel, it might be raw materials, it might be manufactured products. Your inventory must be priced to compete in the open market in order to sell them. Your securities, just like a merchant's shirts, or a steel-maker's steel, cannot be sold at one cent higher than securities of competitive or comparable companies of the same type and the same quality, anymore than one

department store can sell an Arrow shirt for $6.95 if every other store in town is selling the same shirt for $5.95.

If you will keep in mind that we, the investment bankers, are merchants and not magicians, and that your shares of stock are our inventory, and that we know what the competitive price is for our merchandise, and at what price we can sell it, then your offering of securities is more likely to be successful.

### Determining Price Through Past Earnings

In establishing the price for your company's stock your underwriter will be influenced in the main by its price earnings ratios and its current book value. There is no magic formula for determining price. Normally the underwriters will examine the last 5 years' earnings and your projections for the coming years. The book value of your stock will be taken into consideration. This factor is not as important as your earnings record.

Should your stock be offered at $5 a share, $10, $15 or more? Your underwriter will guide you in establishing the price level at which your stock should be sold. Many investment bankers are of the opinion that a stock should not be offered for less than $10 a share. $15 to $20 a share seems to be the price that is most attractive at the initial offering. If the price is set too high, some potential investors will shy away from the stock even though the stock may well be worth the higher price.

What price will be established for your company's stock in relation to earnings? 10 times—15—20? Again, there is no hard and fast rule. The price will be the result of negotiations between you and the underwriter. It will be helpful to examine some recent offerings.

The following sales indicate offering price in relation to prior years' earnings.

| Company | Earnings Per Share—Year Ended in 1958 | | Earnings Per Share—Year Ended in 1959 | Earnings Per Share—Year Ended in 1960 | Price Per Share at Offering | Price Per Share in Relation to Earnings Last Year Ending |
|---|---|---|---|---|---|---|
| Adirondack Industries, Inc. | | .65 | 1.16 | 1.17 | 10.00 | 8.5 |
| Airport Parking Co. of America | (1) | .12 | .69 | | 10.00 | 14.5 |
| Ajax Magnethermic Corporation | (1) | .26 | .81 | | 11.00 | 13.6 |
| Alarm Device Mfg. Co. | (1) | .08 | .25 | | 4.00 | 16.0 |
| Allegri-Tech., Inc. | (1) | .01 | .25 | | 6.00 | 24.0 |
| American Foods, Inc. | | .11 | .26 | .49 | 3.00 | 6.1 |
| American-InterNtl Aluminum Corp. | | .07 | .39 | .45 | 5.00 | 11.1 |
| Bell Electronic Corp. | | .04 | .26 | .55 | 7.25 | 13.2 |
| Behlen Mfg. Co. | | 1.52 | 1.56 | | 15.50 | 9.9 |
| Brockway Glass Co., Inc. | | 2.12 | 2.85 | | 38.00 | 13.3 |

| Company | Earnings Per Share—Year Ended in 1958 | Earnings Per Share—Year Ended in 1959 | Earnings Per Share—Year Ended in 1960 | Price Per Share at Offering | Price Per Share in Relation to Earnings Last Year Ending |
|---|---|---|---|---|---|
| Buttrey Foods, Inc. | .72 | .80 | 1.09 | 12.25 | 11.2 |
| Byer-Rolnick Hat Corp. | .39 | 1.31 | 1.51 | 18.00 | 11.9 |
| Carolina Metal Prod. Corp. | .185 | .618 | .674 | 5.00 | 7.4 |
| Chicago Musical Instrument Co. | .95 | 1.62 | 1.97 | 20.00 | 10.2 |
| Cornet Stores | .61 | .77 | | 10.00 | 13.0 |
| Crawford Corporation | .86 | 1.13 | | 13.00 | 11.5 |
| Detroiter Mobile Homes, Inc. | (1) 1.25 | 1.85 | | 15.00 | 8.1 |
| Ennis Business Forms, Incptd. | .85 | .79 | 1.13 | 17.00 | 15.0 |
| Evans Rule Co. | .36 | .61 | 1.04 | 12.50 | 12.0 |
| Faultless Caster Corporation | (1) .52 | .82 | | 10.00 | 12.2 |
| Fitchburg Paper Co. | .65 | .92 | | 10.25 | 11.1 |
| Four Star Television | .34 | .63 | .66 | 15.00 | 22.7 |
| Gateway Sporting Goods Company | .99 | 1.22 | | 10.00 | 8.2 |
| General Drive-In Corp. | .88 | 1.07 | | 12.50 | 11.7 |
| The Green Shoe Mfg. Co. | 1.33 | 1.53 | | 20.00 | 13.1 |
| Gordon Jewelry Corp. | .77 | .64 | .85 | 9.50 | 11.2 |
| Harcourt, Brace and Co., Inc. | (1) .79 | 1.03 | | 23.50 | 22.8 |
| Hudson Vitamin Prod., Inc. | .26 | .79 | | 12.50 | 15.8 |
| Industrial Hose and Rubber Co., Inc. | (1) .16 | .35 | | 4.00 | 11.4 |
| Kingsport Press, Inc. | (1) 1.31 | 1.86 | | 22.50 | 12.1 |
| M & F Graphic Arts and Ind. Photographic Supply Co. | .26 | .53 | .59 | 8.25 | 14.0 |
| Premier Microwave Corp. | .16 | .23 | | 6.00 | 26.1 |
| The Puritan Sportswear Corp. | .28 | .54 | .92 | 9.50 | 10.3 |
| Rotron Mfg. Co., Inc. | .62 | .72 | .99 | 17.00 | 17.2 |
| Sampson-Miller Assoc. Companies, Inc. | .74 | 1.51 | 1.45 | 9.25 | 6.4 |
| Standard Pressed Steel Co. | (1) 1.43 | 1.92 | | 22.125 | 11.5 |
| Stop-Shop, Inc. | .89 | 1.24 | 1.64 | 31.25 | 19.05 |
| The Blue List Publishing Co., Inc. | .35 | .42 | .45 | 13.00 | 28.9 |
| The Technical Material Corporation | .42 | .72 | | 27.00 | 37.5 |
| Theil Publications, Inc. | .019 | .087 | .104 | 3.00 | 28.8 |
| Trans-Coast Inv. Co. | (1) 1.18 | 1.44 | | 15.00 | 10.4 |
| Wallace Press, Inc. | 1.44 | 1.36 | 1.52 | 16.75 | 11.0 |
| Waterman Products Co., Inc. | .21 | .24 | .35 | 5.00 | 14.3 |
| Win-Chek Industries, Inc. | .17 | .39 | .36 | 3.00 | 8.3 |

# 14

## Compensation to Underwriters

As you discuss your plans for a public stock offering with your underwriters, you will want to know how they are to be compensated for their work in connection with the proposed public offering. They will indicate the "gross spread" or commissions that are to be paid to them. The spread represents the difference between the price paid to the sellers and the price at which the securities are sold to the public at the offering.

On a "fixed" commitment underwriting basis, you must remember that the underwriter is compensated for the financial risks that he is taking by buying the complete issue as well as for his expenses in connection with the underwriting.

### Determining the Commission

In your early discussions with your underwriter, you will want to arrive at a formula for determining the underwriter's commission or discount. The underwriter will review with you the four factors which will determine, to a large degree, the compensation to be paid to the underwriter. These factors are:

1. The offering price of the stock.
2. The demand for the stock at the time of the public offering.
3. The size of the issue to be offered.
4. Prevailing market conditions.

Your underwriter will submit to you, if possible, an analysis of a large number of recent underwritings of companies that are similar to yours and have sold their stock in the same general price range. The analysis will show the offering price and the commission paid to the underwriter. You will notice a wide difference in commissions paid on other offerings. Some stocks are difficult to sell and require greater effort on the part of the underwriters. The risk is also higher and the spread will be on the high side.

## Some Recent Examples

An analysis of stock offerings during the past several years shows the following underwriting commissions paid:

| Name of Company | Price to Public | Underwriting Discounts | Proceeds to Seller | Per cent |
|---|---|---|---|---|
| American Duralite Corporation | $ 290,000.00 | $ 36,250.00 | $ 253,750.00 | 12.5 |
| BBM Photocopy Manufacturing Corp. | 300,000.00 | 45,000.00 | 255,000.00 | 15.0 |
| Cryogenics, Inc. | 350,000.00 | 52,500.00 | 297,500.00 | 15.0 |
| R.E.D.M. Corporation | 350,000.00 | 43,750.00 | 306,250.00 | 12.5 |
| Airport Parking Company of America | 425,740.00 | 41,722.52 | 384,017.48 | 9.8 |
| Sav-A-Stop, Incorporated | 450,000.00 | 45,000.00 | 405,000.00 | 10.0 |
| Win-Chek Industries, Inc. | 450,000.00 | 49,500.00 | 400,500.00 | 11.0 |
| Industrial Control Products, Inc. | 495,000.00 | 61,875.00 | 433,125.00 | 12.5 |
| Carolina Metal Products Corporation | 500,000.00 | 55,000.00 | 445,000.00 | 11.0 |
| General Bowling Corp. | 500,000.00 | 62,500.00 | 437,500.00 | 12.5 |
| Industrial Hose and Rubber Co., Inc. | 500,000.00 | 50,000.00 | 450,000.00 | 10.0 |
| Norwalk Company, Inc. | 500,000.00 | 75,000.00 | 425,000.00 | 15.0 |
| Waterman Products Co., Inc. | 500,000.00 | 50,000.00 | 450,000.00 | 10.0 |
| American Foods, Inc. | 501,000.00 | 60,120.00 | 440,880.00 | 12.0 |
| Alarm Devise Manufacturing Co., Inc. | 522,000.00 | 52,200.00 | 469,800.00 | 10.0 |
| Allegri-Tech, Inc. | 600,000.00 | 75,000.00 | 525,000.00 | 12.5 |
| American League Professional Football Team of Boston, Inc. | 600,000.00 | 60,000.00 | 540,000.00 | 10.0 |
| Americana Properties, Inc. | 600,000.00 | 75,000.00 | 525,000.00 | 12.5 |
| Dodge Wire Corporation | 600,000.00 | 75,000.00 | 525,000.00 | 12.5 |
| Premier Microwave Corporation | 600,000.00 | 60,000.00 | 540,000.00 | 10.0 |
| Navigation Computer Corporation | 608,508.00 | 58,315.35 | 550,192.65 | 9.6 |
| Ennis Business Forms, Inc. | 689,282.00 | 42,573.30 | 646,708.70 | 6.2 |
| Gateway Sporting Goods Company | 700,000.00 | 59,500.00 | 640,500.00 | 8.5 |
| Metcom, Inc. | 740,010.00 | 67,834.25 | 673,200.00 | 9.2 |
| Progress Industries, Inc. | 750,000.00 | 75,000.00 | 675,000.00 | 10.0 |
| Nissen Trampoline Company | 765,000.00 | 91,800.00 | 673,200.00 | 12.0 |
| Applied Research Inc. | 780,000.00 | 78,000.00 | 702,000.00 | 10.0 |
| Buttrey Foods, Inc. | 796,250.00 | 61,750.00 | 734,500.00 | 7.8 |
| Arco Electronics, Inc. | 850,000.00 | 93,500.00 | 756,500.00 | 11.0 |
| Rollins Broadcasting, Inc. | 880,000.00 | 69,650.00 | 810,350.00 | 7.9 |
| Clark Cable Corporation | 890,000.00 | 106,800.00 | 783,200.00 | 12.0 |
| Sampson-Miller Associated Companies, Inc. | 925,000.00 | 92,500.00 | 832,500.00 | 10.0 |
| Bell Electronic Corp. | 986,000.00 | 98,600.00 | 887,400.00 | 10.0 |
| Espey Mfg. & Electronics Corp. | 1,000,000.00 | 80,000.00 | 920,000.00 | 8.0 |
| General Bowling Corp. | 1,000,000.00 | 125,000.00 | 875,000.00 | 12.5 |
| Home Builders Acceptance Corporation | 1,000,000.00 | 150,000.00 | 850,000.00 | 15.0 |
| Movielab Film Laboratories, Inc. | 1,000,000.00 | 100,000.00 | 900,000.00 | 10.0 |
| The Puritan Sportswear Corp. | 1,140,000.00 | 96,000.00 | 1,044,000.00 | 8.4 |
| Texas Research & Electronic Corporation | 1,150,000.00 | 150,000.00 | 1,000,000.00 | 13.0 |
| Liberty Records, Inc. | 1,162,500.00 | 93,000.00 | 1,069,500.00 | 8.0 |
| Adirondack Industries, Inc. | 1,200,000.00 | 108,000.00 | 1,092,000.00 | 9.0 |
| American Playlands Corporation | 1,200,000.00 | 180,000.00 | 1,020,000.00 | 15.0 |
| Consolidated Marine Ind. Inc. | 1,200,000.00 | 120,000.00 | 1,080,000.00 | 10.0 |
| Glen Mfg. Inc. | 1,250,000.00 | 125,000.00 | 1,125,000.00 | 10.0 |
| Intercoast Companies, Incorporated | 1,320,000.00 | 132,000.00 | 1,188,000.00 | 10.0 |
| Jahncke Service, Incorporated | 1,333,200.00 | 119,988.00 | 1,213,212.00 | 9.0 |
| Cornet Stores | 1,500,000.00 | 105,000.00 | 1,395,000.00 | 7.0 |
| Reeves Broadcasting & Development Corporation | 1,500,000.00 | 105,000.00 | 1,350,000.00 | 10.0 |
| Indian Head Mills, Inc. | 1,548,000.00 | 144,000.00 | 1,404,000.00 | 9.3 |
| Talley Industries, Inc. | 1,550,000.00 | 150,000.00 | 1,400,000.00 | 9.7 |
| Victor Paint Company | 1,560,000.00 | 182,000.00 | 1,378,000.00 | 11.7 |

| Name of Company | Price to Public | Underwriting Discounts | Proceeds to Seller | Per cent |
|---|---|---|---|---|
| Pneumo Dynamics Corporation | 1,575,000.00 | 148,750.00 | 1,426,250.00 | 9.4 |
| Ajax Magnethermic Corporation | 1,650,000.00 | 142,500.00 | 1,507,500.00 | 8.6 |
| Warner Electric Brake & Clutch Company | 1,665,347.00 | 154,916.00 | 1,510,431.00 | 9.3 |
| Edgerton, Germeshausen & Grier, Inc. | 1,740,000.00 | 120,000.00 | 1,620,000.00 | 6.9 |
| Four Star Television | 1,800,000.00 | 162,000.00 | 1,638,000.00 | 9.0 |
| Evans Rule Co. | 1,812,500.00 | 174,000.00 | 1,638,500.00 | 9.6 |
| Cook Coffee Company | 1,825,000.00 | 125,000.00 | 1,700,000.00 | 6.8 |
| Howell Instruments, Inc. | 1,960,000.00 | 156,800.00 | 1,803,200.00 | 8.0 |
| United Electro Dynamics, Inc. | 1,974,500.00 | 157,960.00 | 1,816,540.00 | 8.0 |
| American-International Aluminum Corporation | 2,000,000.00 | 240,000.00 | 1,760,000.00 | 12.0 |
| Faultless Caster Corporation | 2,000,000.00 | 240,000.00 | 1,760,000.00 | 8.0 |
| Russell Stover Candies, Inc. | 2,000,000.00 | 150,000.00 | 1,850,000.00 | 7.5 |
| Crawford Corporation | 2,080,000.00 | 168,000.00 | 1,912,000.00 | 8.1 |
| Rotron Manufacturing Company, Inc. | 2,210,000.00 | 195,000.00 | 2,015,000.00 | 8.8 |
| Electro-Tec Corp. | 2,227,500.00 | 182,250.00 | 2,045,250.00 | 8.2 |
| General Drive-In Corporation | 2,250,000.00 | 168,750.00 | 2,081,250.00 | 7.5 |
| Hudson Vitamin Products, Inc. | 2,381,250.00 | 219,075.00 | 2,162,175.00 | 9.2 |
| Fotochrome Inc. | 2,420,000.00 | 220,000.00 | 2,200,000.00 | 9.1 |
| Interstate Finance Corporation | 2,475,000.00 | 202,500.00 | 2,272,500.00 | 8.2 |
| Standard Pressed Steel Co. | 2,561,190.00 | 178,270.40 | 2,382,919.60 | 7.0 |
| Restaurant Associates, Inc. | 2,695,000.00 | 242,550.00 | 2,452,450.00 | 9.0 |
| Infrared Industries, Inc. | 2,700,000.00 | 236,250.00 | 2,463,750.00 | 8.8 |
| Kingsport Press, Inc. | 2,722,500.00 | 193,600.00 | 2,528,900.00 | 7.1 |
| Albee Homes, Inc. | 2,760,000.00 | 224,250.00 | 2,535,750.00 | 8.1 |
| Microdot Inc. | 2,907,000.00 | 232,560.00 | 2,674,440.00 | 8.0 |
| Star Market Co. | 2,931,250.00 | 175,000.00 | 2,756,250.00 | 6.0 |
| Scantlin Electronics, Inc. | | | | |
| Minimum | 3,000,000.00 | 262,500.00 | 2,737,500.00 | 8.7 |
| Maximum | 3,300,000.00 | 288,750.00 | 3,011,250.00 | 8.7 |
| Wallace Press, Inc. | 3,089,286.25 | 248,987.25 | 2,840,299.00 | 8.1 |
| The Technical Material Corporation | 3,240,000.00 | 234,000.00 | 3,006,000.00 | 7.2 |
| Fitchburg Paper Company | 3,331,250.00 | 276,250.00 | 3,055,000.00 | 8.3 |
| Cannon Electric Company | 3,400,000.00 | 230,000.00 | 3,170,000.00 | 6.8 |
| Detroiter Mobile Homes, Inc. | 3,750,000.00 | 325,000.00 | 3,425,000.00 | 8.7 |
| Oxford Manufacturing Company, Inc. | 4,050,000.00 | 314,400.00 | 3,735,600.00 | 7.8 |
| Simplicity Manufacturing Company | 4,170,516.00 | 417,051.60 | 3,753,464.40 | 10.0 |
| Interstate Vending Company | 4,239,375.00 | 327,750.00 | 3,911,625.00 | 7.7 |
| American Rubber and Plastics Corporation | 4,350,000.00 | 350,000.00 | 4,000,000.00 | 8.0 |
| Chicago Musical Instrument Co. | 5,200,000.00 | 390,000.00 | 4,810,000.00 | 7.5 |
| The Hallicrafters Co. | 5,250,000.00 | 420,000.00 | 4,830,000.00 | 8.0 |
| Union Texas Natural Gas Corporation | 5,408,928.00 | 292,983.60 | 5,115,944.40 | 5.4 |
| Techno Fund, Inc. | 5,625,000.00 | 540,000.00 | 5,085,000.00 | 9.6 |
| Trans-Coast Investment Co. | 5,625,000.00 | 450,000.00 | 5,175,000.00 | 8.0 |
| Fischbach and Moore, Incorporated | 5,692,500.00 | 517,500.00 | 5,175,000.00 | 9.1 |
| Behlen Manufacturing Company | 5,735,000.00 | 444,000.00 | 5,291,000.00 | 7.7 |
| Brockway Glass Company, Inc. | 6,156,000.00 | 340,200.00 | 5,815,800.00 | 5.5 |
| Inland Container Corporation | 6,650,000.00 | 332,500.00 | 6,317,500.00 | 5.0 |
| MCA Inc. | 7,000,000.00 | 407,000.00 | 6,593,000.00 | 5.8 |
| Florida Capital Corporation | 7,600,000.00 | 760,000.00 | 6,840,000.00 | 10.0 |
| The Green Shoe Manufacturing Company | 8,400,000.00 | 504,000.00 | 7,896,000.00 | 6.0 |
| American Hospital Supply Corporation | 8,450,000.00 | 390,000.00 | 8,060,000.00 | 4.6 |
| The Franklin Corporation | 10,000,000.00 | 1,000,000.00 | 9,000,000.00 | 10.0 |
| Industrial Development Bank of Israel Limited | 10,000,000.00 | 550,000.00 | 9,450,000.00 | 5.5 |
| Harcourt, Brace and Company, Inc. | 11,595,487.50 | 754,940.25 | 10,840,547.25 | 6.5 |
| Western Publishing Company, Inc. | 15,208,788.00 | 760,439.40 | 14,448,348.60 | 5.0 |
| Harvey Aluminum (Incorporated) | 17,062,500.00 | 1,312,500.00 | 15,750,000.00 | 7.7 |
| The Brush Beryllium Company | 18,277,644.00 | 1,087,955.00 | 17,189,689.00 | 6.0 |
| Stop & Shop | 19,531,250.00 | 1,000,000.00 | 18,531,250.00 | 5.1 |
| Boston Capital Corporation | 22,500,000.00 | 2,175,000.00 | 20,325,000.00 | 9.7 |

In some stock offerings, the company as additional compensation agrees to sell the underwriter stock purchase warrants at a low price. For example:

*Del Electronics Corp.* The underwriters purchased 20,000 stock purchase warrants at a price of 1¢ per warrant, which warants expire Sept. 30, 1963 and entitle the holders to purchase 20,000 shares of common stock at the price of $4.00 per share.

*Aviation Employees Corporation.* The corporation has agreed to grant to the underwriters, without further consideration, transferable options covering a maximum of 150,000 shares of the Corporation's Common Stock on the basis of 6 options for each 100 shares of Common Stock purchased by the underwriters.

### Letter of Intent

While it is not standard practice, many investment banking firms will give a letter of intent, stating in general terms, the method to be used in setting the offering price and the underwriting discount. You may want a letter of this type after you have your preliminary discussions with your underwriter. Usually your underwriter, in arriving at a preliminary indication of an offering price, will not give you a fixed price but will establish a range. The underwriter will not normally make a commitment or set a firm price in the letter of intent but will try to indicate the earnings multiple which will be used in arriving at the offering price. The final price usually will be established immediately before the actual offering date and after the SEC Registration becomes effective.

The letter of intent will also establish a range for the underwriter's discount; for example, 7 to 8%—10 to 11%, etc. If the final price to the public will be $15 a share, a 7% discount would amount to $1.05 a share to be paid to the underwriter.

Analysis will be made of a large number of recent common stock offerings comparable to yours in the same general price range. Based upon this analysis, the underwriter will attempt to establish the discount formula for your offering.

In the letter of intent the underwriters will indicate that they have not made a firm commitment and that a reappraisal will be made immediately prior to the public offering based upon any changes that may exist in market and economic conditions. The offering price will be adjusted also if there are any substantial changes in the estimates of your corporate earnings, prospects for the future and other such considerations.

### Development of a Plan

After you have had your initial discussions with your underwriter and have determined to proceed with a public stock offering, it will be necessary for you to develop a financial plan with your underwriter. You will be asked to furnish considerable factual information, financial records, reports, etc., to the underwriter so that he can evaluate your company and make recommendations for you.

After thorough analysis by the underwriter you will receive his recommendations, estimates and a plan in the following areas:

1. Re-capitalization or stock split if necessary.
2. Number of shares to be authorized.
3. Number of shares to be sold to the public.
4. The range of price per share.
5. Par value or no par value.
6. Dividend policy.
7. Basis to be used in determining price for your stock.
8. Underwriting commissions.
9. Expenses.

Representatives of the underwriter, in all likelihood, will want to visit the main offices of your company and meet with executive groups to discuss the plans.

### Keeping Your Early Negotiations Quiet

One of the problems facing your company in the initial stages of a public offering will be, "How can we keep our negotiations with the underwriter secret?" It is possible that the underwriting will not go through, and if this is the case, you will not want it known that a public stock offering was under consideration. You will want to have as few people as possible know about your negotiations with the underwriter and it is important that you prevent any leaks during this period.

If word gets out that your company is considering a public stock offering, many questions will be raised by your employees who may have some fears as to their security within the company. You will not want them to know about the issue until such time as your plans are set and you can announce to them the program, if any, for the purchase of your company's stock. Also, if word gets out that you are considering a public stock offering, you will receive calls from numerous underwriters. They will want to talk to you about using their underwriting facilities.

It is best if you limit the number of people who are involved in the initial talks and that everyone recognize the confidential nature of the discussions. You can avoid embarrassment, rumors, and questioning by setting up safeguards so that there will not be leaks during the course of your talks with the underwriter. When the registration statement is filed, that will be the time to make the proper announcements to all who are interested.

# 15

## The Underwriter's Agreement

You would normally expect that at the time you complete your preliminary negotiations with your underwriter that you would enter into a written contract. This is not generally the case, since the signing of an underwriting contract or purchase contract takes place a day or so before the stock is sold to the public. In some cases the contract is signed on the day that the stock is sold.

You might well ask the question, "How do we know where we stand with the underwriter in the interim period if we do not have any written contract?" Actually, the answer is that you have, in effect, an informal understanding between your company and the underwriter, without having the contract reduced to writing. It would be a rare case where the underwriter would back out unless there was an important change of circumstances.

Immediately prior to the sale of your company's stock to the public you will be asked to enter into an underwriting contract with your investment banker. Here for the first time, the complete obligations of the parties are finalized in writing.

### The Basic Components

There are many variances in underwriting contracts depending upon the nature of the purchase commitment. It is important that you have an understanding of the customary clauses that will appear in the underwriting or purchase agreement.

1. *Purchase commitment.* The principal underwriters, acting on behalf of themselves and the other underwriters, enters into a purchase agreement with the sellers of the stock. Under this agreement the seller agrees to sell and each underwriter severally agrees to purchase a designated number of shares at the agreed price per share. The spread or commission deducted by the underwriter is set forth in the agreement. In many agreements, the sellers agree not to sell or dispose of stock other than the shares to be sold

under the agreement, for a period of 60 days up to 120 days after the date of the initial public offering without the consent of the principal underwriters.

2. *Method of offering.* The company authorizes the managing underwriter as representative of the several underwriters to manage the underwriting and the public offering of the shares. This authorization permits the underwriter to take any action that he deems advisable, including the termination of the time of the initial public offering of the shares, the initial public offering price, and the making of any change in the public offering price. The underwriter allocates shares to institutions and other retail purchasers, to dealers who are members of the National Association of Security Dealers, Inc., and foreign dealers. The other underwriters authorize the principal underwriter to fix the concessions and allowances in connection with any sales to dealers.

3. *Trading in the shares.* The underwriters authorize the principal underwriter to make purchases and sales of the company's stock in the over-the-counter market at such prices as the underwriter may determine. The underwriter is also authorized to arrange for sales to dealers, to overallot, and make purchases for the purpose of covering any over-allotment so made.

4. *Delivery and payment.* Provision is made for the payment of the full purchase price of the shares which the underwriter is obligated to purchase from the sellers. Generally payment is made at the office of the principal underwriter or at the offices of the transfer agent. Payment is made by certified or bank cashier's check against the delivery to the underwriters of certificates for the shares purchased.

5. *Representations and warranties.* The sellers make certain representations and warranties as to ownership of stock, marketable title, etc. The sellers also represent and warrant that the information contained in the registration statement or prospectus is true and that no material fact was omitted from the registration statement or prospectus.

6. *Statements.* In the agreement, the company frequently agrees to furnish to the principal underwriter, and to each of the other underwriters, as requested, a consolidated balance sheet and statements of income and surplus of the company.

7. *Expenses.* The company in selling its stock, generally agrees to pay all expenses in connection with the preparation, printing and filing of the registration statement, the preliminary prospectus, the final prospectus, the purchase agreement and all amendments. The company also generally agrees to pay for the registration or qualification of the shares under Blue

Sky Laws of the various states, as well as the expenses of the underwriters, including fees and disbursements of counsel in connection with the registration or qualification of the shares. Some contracts provide for a maximum dollar amount to be paid for this service.

In some contracts where the underwriting is on a "best efforts" basis, the company agrees to pay a fixed amount to cover the underwriter's expenses.

8. *Indemnification of underwriter.* The agreement generally provides that the issuer and the selling stockholders agree to indemnify the underwriters against liabilities under the Securities Act of 1933 which may arise as a result of misleading or untrue statements or through the omission of a material fact which should have been in the registration statement or the prospectus. The underwriters furnish indemnity to the seller with respect to material submitted by them for use in the registration statement.

9. *Obligation of underwriters.* The obligation of the underwriters to purchase the stock is conditioned upon receiving a favorable opinion from their counsel and counsel for the seller as to various corporate and legal matters and further conditioned upon the absence of a stop order from the SEC suspending the effectiveness of the registration. The obligation to purchase is further conditioned upon receipt of accountant's certificates, stockholder's certificates and there being no substantially adverse change in the financial condition of the issuer, or in the general market conditions.

See Appendix C for a sample copy of a fixed commitment underwriting agreement.

### Interim Financing

If your company is faced with the need for immediate financing, you may be frustrated and disappointed by the delays involved in a public stock offering. Try as you may to eliminate delays, there are many stumbling blocks that will be placed in your way before the final settlement is made with you by your underwriter. For example, the Securities Exchange Commission might require amendments to your registration statement which involves additional paper work and a further extension of time.

You must recognize that there are many delays that cannot be anticipated. If you have an immediate need for financing, discuss this in your initial talks with your underwriter. Very often he can assist you in interim financing through private placement, and then proceed later with a public offering.

### Underwriting Syndicate

In some situations, your underwriter may deem it desirable to select one or more investment banking firms to become part of the underwriting group. These firms become part of the group known as the "underwriting syndicate."

If the proposed issue is substantial, your underwriter will want to share the risk with others, and will invite a group of investment bankers and possibly a group of dealers to participate in the sale and distribution of the stock of your company. The number of underwriters forming the purchase group will vary depending upon the size of the issue. Some offerings have one underwriter; others have in excess of 250 underwriters. It is important to have maximum selling strength to cover all the types of investors—individuals, institutional, corporate, etc.

How are the underwriting firms which will become members of the underwriting syndicate selected? Normally your principal underwriter will make the selection based upon prior relationships. Your underwriter will want to be certain that those selected as part of the underwriting group have demonstrated in the past that they are able to sell your type of issue, and that they are highly regarded in their individual communities. Since the underwriting syndicate spreads the underwriting risk with the principal underwriter, it is also important that all members of the group have sufficient capital to carry the issue in the event there are delays in the sale.

In most cases, you will want to make certain that there is a proper geographical representation of underwriters so that your company's stock will be broadly distributed in all parts of the country. It is advisable that the members of the underwriter's group give you widespread distribution.

Your underwriter will discuss with you whether you wish to have any particular investment firms included in the underwriting syndicate. You may wish to invite a certain underwriter to participate and generally this will be arranged by your underwriter. When the group is established, your underwriter will serve as managing underwriter and will determine the amount of stock to be allocated to each member of the group. It is the responsibility of the managing underwriter to select the best group to sell the stock in your company.

You may receive many requests from investment banking firms to be included in the underwriting. It is recommended that you refer all of these requests to your underwriters for their decision.

If an underwriting syndicate is formed, your investment banker, serving as the managing underwriter, will enter into an agreement with other investment bankers who will serve as the underwriting group. The managing underwriter may also enter into an agreement with selected dealers who will purchase a portion of the stock for resale. Under the terms of the former agreement, the managing underwriter is given the authority by the other underwriters to act as agent for the group, to manage the offering and to determine the initial public offering price, as well as the time of the initial offering. The managing underwriter determines the membership of the buying group and the percentage of stock to be allocated to each member of the group.

# 16

## Expenses of Underwriting

It is difficult to ascertain in advance the exact expenses which your company will incur in completing its underwriting program. There is no rule of thumb to be used as a guide. In analyzing costs of a public stock offering it is necessary to keep in mind that the following costs will be incurred:

Underwriter's commissions
Accountant's fees
Attorney's fees
Blue Sky fees and expenses
Printing costs
Federal stamp taxes
State taxes and fees
Transfer agent fees
Registrar fees
SEC registration fees
Blue Sky registration fees
Travel expenses
Printing or engraving stock certificates
Miscellaneous

All of these costs will be discussed in the following chapters. The expenses of underwriting vary considerably. The following factors affect cost: size of issue, the underwriter, quality of issue, market conditions, accounting work and legal work required.

A review of some recent underwritings discloses the following *estimates* of expenses other than underwriters' commissions to be paid by the company and the selling stockholders:

## EXPENSES WHERE COMPANY SELLS ALL

| Company | Price to Public | Estimated Expenses Paid by Company |
|---|---|---|
| R.E.D.M. Corporation | $ 350,000.00 | $ 39,000.00 |
| Sav-A-Stop, Inc. | 450,000.00 | 29,000.00 |
| Industrial Control Prod., Inc. | 495,000.00 | 45,500.00 |
| General Bowling Corp. | 500,000.00 | 28,000.00 |
| Norwalk Company, Inc. | 500,000.00 | 17,500.00 |
| Waterman Products Co., Inc. | 500,000.00 | 29,500.00 |
| American Foods, Inc. | 501,000.00 | 35,000.00 |
| Americana Properties, Inc. | 600,000.00 | 50,000.00 |
| Allegri-Tech., Inc. | 600,000.00 | 30,500.00 |
| American League Professional Football of Boston, Inc. | 600,000.00 | 21,000.00 |
| Dodge Wire Corporation | 600,000.00 | 52,200.00 |
| Premier Microwave Corp. | 600,000.00 | 29,773.50 |
| Navigation Computer Corp. | 600,000.00 | 22,000.00 |
| Gateway Sporting Goods Co. | 700,000.00 | 19,000.00 |
| Nissen Trampoline Co. | 765,000.00 | 28,500.00 |
| Buttrey Foods, Inc. | 796,250.00 | 14,500.00 |
| Sampson-Miller Assoc. Cos., Inc. | 925,000.00 | 48,000.00 |
| Canaveral International Corporation | 1,000,000.00 | 60,000.00 |
| Texas Research & Electronic Corporation | 1,150,000.00 | 15,000.00 |
| Liberty Records, Inc. | 1,162,500.00 | 38,875.00 |
| Consolidated Marine Industries, Inc. | 1,200,000.00 | 50,000.00 |
| Portland Reporter Publishing Company, Inc. | 1,250,000.00 | 50,000.00 |
| Intercoast Companies, Inc. | 1,320,000.00 | 44,000.00 |
| Cornet Stores | 1,500,000.00 | 31,000.00 |
| Reeves Broadcasting & Development Corp. | 1,500,000.00 | 48,551.30 |
| Talley Industries, Inc. | 1,500,000.00 | 36,751.88 |
| Pneumo Dynamics Corp. | 1,575,000.00 | 40,000.00 |
| Four Star Television | 1,800,000.00 | 55,700.00 |
| Russell Stover Candies, Inc. | 2,000,000.00 | 56,500.00 |
| General Merchandise Co. | 2,025,000.00 | 29,000.00 |
| Interstate Finance Corp. | 2,475,000.00 | 40,000.00 |
| Albee Homes, Inc. | 2,760,000.00 | 49,000.00 |
| Detroiter Mobile Homes, Inc. | 3,750,000.00 | 50,730.00 |
| Techno Funds, Inc. | 5,625,000.00 | 54,687.50 |
| Inland Container Corp. | 6,650,000.00 | 58,125.00 |
| Florida Capital Corp. | 7,600,000.00 | 59,360.00 |
| American Hospital Supply Corp. | 8,450,000.00 | 54,000.00 |

| Company | Price to Public | Estimated Expenses Paid by Company |
|---|---|---|
| Industrial Development Bank of Israel Limited | 10,000,000.00 | 106,000.00 |
| Harvey Aluminum (Inc.) | 17,062,500.00 | 119,277.50 |

In many public stock offerings, part of the stock is sold by the company and a portion by some of the stockholders. A review of recent offerings indicates varying distribution of expense. The following figures were taken from various prospectuses.

## EXPENSES WHERE COMPANY SELLS PART AND BALANCE SOLD BY STOCKHOLDERS

| Company | Proceeds to Company | Estimated Expenses Paid by Company | Proceeds to Selling Stockholders | Estimated Expenses Paid by Selling Stockholders |
|---|---|---|---|---|
| Airport Parking Company of America | $  225,500.00 | $ 33,300.00 | $  158,517.48 | —— |
| Applied Research, Inc. | 351,000.00 | 12,500.00 | 351,000.00 | $12,500.00 |
| Evans Rule Co. | 452,000.00 | 37,500.00 | 1,186,500.00 | —— |
| Adirondack Industries, Inc. | 455,000.00 | 20,000.00 | 637,000.00 | 27,000.00 |
| Progress Industries, Inc. | 495,000.00 | 11,000.00 | 180,000.00 | 4,000.00 |
| Ajax Magnethermic | 502,500.00 | 15,000.00 | 1,005,000.00 | 30,000.00 |
| Metcom, Inc. | 545,000.00 | 51,010.75 | 127,175.75 | —— |
| Rollins Broadcasting, Inc. | 547,500.00 | 22,800.00 | 262,850.00 | 7,600.00 |
| Movielab Film Laboratories, Incorporated | 562,500.00 | 28,000.00 | 337,500.00 | 7,632.00 |
| Chicago Musical Instrument Company | 740,000.00 | 15,760.00 | 4,070,000.00 | 72,360.00 |
| Trans-Coast Investment Co. | 745,945.20 | 32,000.00 | 4,429,054.80 | 27,500.00 |
| Microdot, Inc. | 786,600.00 | 17,940.00 | 1,887,840.00 | 28,590.00 |
| The Green Shoe Mfg. Co. | 846,000.00 | 85,780.00 | 7,050,000.00 | 24,220.00 |
| Glen Mfg., Inc. | 900,000.00 | 29,500.00 | 225,000.00 | 3,300.00 |
| Simplicity Mfg. Co. | 945,000.00 | 20,000.00 | 2,808,464.40 | 20,000.00 |
| Crawford Corp. | 956,000.00 | 57,000.00 | 956,000.00 | 2,500.00 |
| Jahncke Service, Inc. | 982,982.00 | 77,000.00 | 230,230.00 | 327.87 |
| Victor Paint Co. | 1,007,000.00 | 27,000.00 | 371,000.00 | 11,000.00 |
| Rotron Mfg. Co. | 1,007,500.00 | 29,430.00 | 1,007,500.00 | 28,280.00 |
| Electro-Tec Corp. | 1,136,250.00 | 38,000.00 | 909,000.00 | 27,720.00 |
| Oxford Mfg. Co., Inc. | 1,245,200.00 | 82,000.00 | 2,490,400.00 | 41,000.00 |
| The Technical Material Corporation | 1,252,500.00 | 14,000.00 | 1,753,500.00 | 21,100.00 |
| Edgerton, Germeshausen & Grier, Inc. | 1,350,000.00 | 27,000.00 | 270,000.00 | 5,000.00 |
| Kingsport Press, Inc. | 1,463,000.00 | 38,000.00 | 1,065,900.00 | —— |
| General Drive-In Corp. | 1,503,125.00 | 75,000.00 | 578,125.00 | —— |
| The Hallicrafters Co. | 1,610,000.00 | 20,668.00 | 3,220,000.00 | 32,332.00 |
| United Electro Dynamics Incorporated | 1,679,920.00 | 49,500.00 | 136,620.00 | 3,740.00 |
| Infrared Industries, Inc. | 1,825,000.00 | 19,765.00 | 638,750.00 | 11,140.00 |
| Restaurant Assoc., Inc. | 1,951,950.00 | 52,000.00 | 500,500.00 | 12,000.00 |
| Fotochrome, Inc. | 2,000,000.00 | 44,500.00 | 200,000.00 | 2,500.00 |
| Fitchburg Paper Co. | 2,039,800.00 | 57,000.00 | 1,015,200.00 | —— |
| Interstate Vending Co. | 3,431,250.00 | 105,528.45 | 480,375.00 | 17,179.05 |
| Brockway Glass Co., Inc. | 4,667,000.00 | 62,000.00 | 1,148,800.00 | —— |

| Company | Proceeds to Company | Estimated Expenses Paid by Company | Proceeds to Selling Stockholders | Estimated Expenses Paid by Selling Stockholders |
|---|---|---|---|---|
| The Foxboro Co. | 5,000,000.00 | 39,600.00 | 3,440,000.00 | 5,400.00 |
| Western Publishing Co., Inc. | 5,985,000.00 | 36,470.00 | 8,463,348.60 | 27,550.00 |
| The Brush Beryllium Co. | 10,270,000.00 | 33,900.00 | 6,919,689.00 | 18,100.00 |

## What Are the Printing Costs?

It is customary, in a public stock offering, that the following documents be printed:

(a) Registration statement
(b) Preliminary prospectus
(c) Final prospectus
(d) Agreement between principal underwriter and seller
(e) Agreement between underwriters (costs are generally paid by the underwriters)
(f) Opinion on state registrations—Blue Sky opinion
(g) Stock certificates

The printing costs of each underwriting vary, depending upon the number of copies to be printed, the length of the documents, the number of changes to be made, etc. It is important that good clean copy be given to the printers to cut down the costs, since corrections are costly.

In setting a reserve for printing costs for a company going public for the first time, it is well to set $7,000 to $13,000 as a range. In many offerings, the printing costs will exceed the top point of this range. There is no relationship between printing costs and the dollar amount of the issue. The companies that print the documents referred to above are generally specialists in this field and are equipped to give rapid, overnight service.

Again time is very much of the essence and a considerable number of the corrections are made during the night at higher printing rates.

If it is intended that the company will be listed on the New York Stock Exchange, engraved certificates are required at the time of listing. The cost of engraving certificates in quantities of 20,000 to 50,000 would be approximately 11¢ to 13¢ per certificate.

*Cost of Maintaining A Stockholder's Account.* In considering the costs of going public, don't overlook the expense of maintaining a stockholder's account. You will find that your company will incur continuing costs each year for the work involved in the payment of dividends, preparation of quarterly reports, annual reports, annual meeting notices, etc.

W. J. Rockwell, Jr., president of the Rockwell Manufacturing Company, determined that the cost to his company for servicing a stockholder's account for one year was $2.904. Mr. Rockwell reported that there were 31 measurable items of cost. He stated:

> Nine are involved in the payment of quarterly dividends, ranging from the obvious sixteen cents for postage to $.004 for imprinting dividend checks. Payment of stock dividends creates seven items of cost. Three quarterly reports cost $.069 per shareholder, plus $.03 for addressing. After the Annual Report is printed, three separate costs are involved in getting it to each stockholder. Annual Meeting notices create four separate charges, plus the $.007 for the notice itself. The total is $2.904 per stockholder, per year.

## Who Pays the Cost of Underwriting If the Offering Is Abandoned?

Some companies, due to change in market or business conditions, agree with their underwriters to postpone the offering of their stock to the public. There are many changes that can take place between the time when a decision is reached to have a public stock offering and the final date of sale. The market can be on a downward swing or the public's appetite for your company's stock may not be as good as originally thought. There are many reasons why your issue may not be completed.

The question will then arise, "Who will pay the costs incurred for attorneys, accountants, printing, etc.?" Usually there is no contractual understanding on this subject. In these cases the company normally will pay its own accounting fees, attorney's fees, printing costs, and filing fees. The underwriter will pay for its own attorney fees and its out-of-pocket expenses incurred in investigation time, telephone calls, etc.

# 17

## Who Will Sell Stock?

In most offerings, the company is the sole seller of stock. In other cases, both the company and certain of its stockholders sell stock. In the latter case, the company and the selling stockholders will each receive a portion of the proceeds. For example:

> *Victor Paint Co.* Of the shares offered hereby, 95,000 are being issued and sold by the Company, and 35,000 are being sold by the stockholder of the Company, named herein under the caption "Principal and Selling Stockholder." The Company will receive no part of the proceeds of the sale of shares by the Selling Stockholder.

> *Andersen Laboratories, Inc.* Of the 150,000 shares offered hereby 40,000 are being purchased by the Underwriters from the Company and 110,000 from stockholders of the Company. (See "Selling Stockholders" herein.) The Company will receive no part of the proceeds of the sale of any of the shares not purchased by the Underwriters from the Company.

In many offerings, the company is not a seller, and all of the net proceeds from the sale of the stock are paid to the selling stockholders. Some recent examples of stock offerings where the stock was sold solely by the individuals are as follows:

> *Yardney Electric Corporation.* The securities being offered hereby are a portion of the currently issued and outstanding common stock of the Company, representing 25% of the total number of shares issued. No portion of the proceeds to be derived from the sale of these securities is to be realized by the Company, all of such proceeds being for the account of the selling stockholders.

> *Sunset House Distributing Corp.* The 150,000 shares of Common Stock to which this prospectus related are issued and outstanding shares which are owned by Mr. Leonard P. Carlson, one of Sunset House's two stockholders

(see "Principal Shareholders" and "Selling Shareholder" herein). The Selling Shareholder will receive all of the net proceeds from the sale of the shares offered hereby for his own use and no part of such proceeds will be received by Sunset House.

The decision as to who will sell stock will be reached between the company and/or certain of its large stockholders and the underwriter. Each situation must be considered separately. If the corporation has need for additional funds, it alone may be the seller. Should certain stockholders wish to sell a portion of their holdings, they may join in or be the sole sellers of stock. A competent underwriter and your attorney will guide you in this area.

## How Much Stock Should Be Sold to the Public?

It is natural that you will want to retain more than half of the stock in your corporation. You have been conditioned to the fact that owning a majority of the stock in your company gives you certain protections and a continuity of management. Is this necessarily important?

Frederick W. Straus, partner of Straus, Blosser & McDowell, in a speech before the American Management Association stated:

> Far too many people when deciding to "go public," have a fear that unless they retain at least 51% of the voting stock of their company, they shall be in a position to lose control of their company either to raiders or to a competitor who wants to gobble them up and throw out the management.
>
> Control does not require any magic percentage or fraction of the stock outstanding. Any management that has a substantial stake in a company and is earnestly applying itself to the job at hand need not worry about control of its corporation. At the same time, if these worries or fears about control exist they may hamper the development of a satisfactory market for the company's securities. Too few shares in the hands of the public are bound to mean large price fluctuations. And this lack of stability not only will reduce the attractiveness of the stock for long term investors, but it will hamper the liquidity of persons with large holdings in the company. In other words, the fear of losing control can defeat some of the very reasons that bring about management's decision to "go public."

Unless there are urgent needs for the capital, it would seem that the initial offering should be for 25% to 33⅓% of the outstanding stock. This will assure management of control at all times.

# 18

## Selection of Attorneys and Accounting Firm

The question will arise as to whether you should retain a New York attorney, a local attorney, or one located in an adjacent metropolitan area. New York is by all odds our foremost financial center and it sometimes appears as if all the financing matters are conducted there. On the other hand, there are many very competent investment banking firms and well-qualified legal firms in Chicago, Philadelphia, Boston, Los Angeles, etc. Selection of New York attorneys is often unnecessary and can create delays. In fact, often times, there are many advantages in having security issues prepared and marketed close to the business headquarters where the company is better known. Of course, the smaller the community the fewer investment banking and legal firms will be found that have the necessary experience and recognition. It is frequently necessary for a company operating in these communities to turn to the nearest major financial center.

### His Skill in Public Stock Offerings

Of major importance is the selection of a well-qualified attorney—one skilled in public stock offerings. You must recognize that this work is highly specialized and your attorney must be completely experienced in the field of securities registration.

It is important to keep in mind that the Securities Act of 1933 provides for criminal penalties and civil actions where the registration statement contains an untrue statement of a material fact or fails to state a fact necessary in order that statements made will not be misleading. You may be subjected to penalties and civil suit if your attorney mishandles the registration proceedings. Your general lawyer, whom you have used for many years, may not have the experience that is required in preparing a registration statement, prospectus, state registrations, etc. You would be well advised to get the most competent lawyer in this field. You will save endless delays, amendments, conferences, etc. A skillful attorney will also be of great value to you in your negotiations with your investment banker. Don't try to save costs by selecting an attorney who has not had the proper experience—even though he will do the job for less money.

### The Attorney's Role

The role played by the company's counsel in arranging the financing varies enormously from situation to situation and it is extremely difficult to generalize. At one extreme, a large company that does public financing with any regularity is likely to have a department headed by an experienced financial officer who handles negotiations himself. In such a situation the role of the lawyer in negotiations with investment bankers and their counsel is limited to technical matters. At the other extreme, a corporation that is marketing securities for the first time is unlikely to have a financial officer with such specialized experience, and must rely much more heavily on counsel in negotiating substantive, as well as technical, points. Stated another way, the issuer's counsel is likely to have a major role in negotiating technical aspects of the underwriting arrangements in any case, and whether or not he will have a major role in substantive negotiations depends largely on the degree of experience within the management itself.

After tentative arrangements with the underwriter are complete, your company attorney will play an important role as he carries the laboring oar in preparing the registration statement, prospectus, recapitalization, etc. You will work closely with your attorney continuously throughout the registration proceedings with the SEC. Your attorney also can assist you greatly in presenting the proper image of your company in the prospectus.

The legal opinions are ordinarily expressed in rather standardized or "boiler plate" wording, but needless to say, in view of the great weight attached to the opinions, the lawyers must be satisfied that the underlying facts fully support the legal conclusions expressed. As a practical matter, this means that, for example, when a lawyer expresses the conclusion that the corporation is duly and validly organized and the stock is or will be fully paid and nonassessable, he must carefully review the corporate records and, if necessary, recommend changes to cure any defects. Furthermore, a first public issue is frequently preceded by a recapitalization or reorganization, and the role of the lawyer giving the opinion usually includes recommending, formulating and effectuating an appropriate recapitalization or reorganization, in collaboration with the underwriters and their counsel.

### Relationship Between Your Company's Attorney and Your Underwriter's Attorney

The relative roles of issuer's counsel and underwriters' counsel vary to some extent, but in general the former takes the lead in preparing the corporate documents and the Registration Statement, whereas the latter takes the lead in preparing the underwriting agreement. If the issuer's counsel is not adequately experienced in this field, the underwriters' counsel, of course, plays a relatively larger role in the original preparation of the corporate documents and Registration Statement. In any case the two sets of counsel normally review and approve each other's documents. In larger stock offerings, underwriters' counsel is paid by the underwriters out of the total underwriting fee and the amount is usually not known or of concern to the issuer. One slight exception is that the underwriters' counsel frequently, although not invariably, handles State Blue Sky qualifications and is paid for this work by the seller rather than the underwriters. In smaller issues, the underwriter may require the seller to pay all of the underwriter's legal expenses. This is a matter of negotiation between the parties.

## FUNCTIONS OF YOUR ACCOUNTING FIRM

It is of utmost importance that you employ a well-qualified accountant or accounting firm to assist in your company's public financing program. It is not sufficient that your accountant be an expert in auditing and tax work. Experience in SEC work is most important. There are many rules and regulations issued by the SEC that must be followed. An accountant with experience in this area can save many hours of work, errors and omissions. Also, by submitting well-prepared financial statements, your accountant can speed up the processing of the registration statement by the SEC.

Your accountants should play an active role in the preparation of the registration statement, prospectus and financial statements to be submitted to the SEC. They should be consulted every step of the way where financial matters are involved. It is important that they be brought into the preparation of the time table (see Chapter 21) as it will be necessary for your accountant to furnish a great deal of the financial information. Be sure that sufficient time is allowed for your accountants to prepare financial statements, audits and schedules.

Your accountant should also review carefully the registration statement before it is submitted to the SEC because there are many portions of the registration that contain financial information. Your accounting firm will assist in the preparation of the registration statement, prospectus and the financial statements. Detailed schedules must be filed with the SEC showing balance sheets, statement of earnings, etc. Your accountants must certify as to the accuracy and correctness of the financial material to be included in the registration statement.

The Security Exchange Commission in 1940 promulgated regulation S-X. This regulation relates to the financial statements that must be filed under the

SEC Act. Your accountant will be familiar with the provisions of regulation S-X and will discuss with you many of the items to be included in the financial statement. It is important that all information that is filed with the Security Exchange Commission be accurate and true. Even though your independent public accountants certify as to the correctness of statements filed with the SEC, there is a primary responsibility placed upon management for the accuracy of the statements and information which are filed with the SEC.

# 19

## Capitalization

In most family corporations, the capitalization consists only of common stock, with a relatively modest number of shares issued—perhaps no more than 1,000. The common stock represents the ownership of the corporation. Each share of stock must be considered as a fractional share of ownership.

But now that your company is going public, your underwriters will propose, for example, that your company sell 150,000 shares. That number of shares, they explain, can be made to represent 25% of the outstanding common stock, which they propose increasing from 1,000 to a total of 600,000 shares.

How do you create 600,000 shares from 1,000?

The solution is a stock split, achieved through approval of your existing stockholders. Each of 1,000 issued shares is split into 600 new shares. A stock split is merely a means of slicing the corporate ownership into thinner portions. The proportion of ownership is not changed. If you owned 800 shares of the original 1,000, or 80% of the total, after the split you will own 480,000 shares, or 80% of the 600,000 shares outstanding.

The following are examples of recapitalizations prior to the public stock offering as shown in the prospectus of these companies.

> *Del Electronics Corp.* Prior to July, 1960, the authorized and issued capital stock of the Company consisted of 900 shares of Common Stock, no par value. In July, 1960 Del Electronics Corp., by an Amendment to its Certificate of Incorporation, reclassified each share of issued Common Stock, no par value, into 227,777 shares of Common Stock, par value 10¢ per share, and the authorized capital of the Company was increased to 1,000,000 shares of Common Stock, 10¢ par value.

> *Victor Paint Co.* On September 29, 1960, the authorized capitalization of the Company was changed from 500 shares of $100 par value Common Stock, 370 shares of which were issued and outstanding, to 400,000 shares

of $1.00 par value Common Stock, of which 205,000 shares were issued and outstanding by September 30, 1960.

*Hudson Vitamin Products, Inc.* By amendment to the Certificate of Incorporation which has been approved by its stockholders and will become effective prior to delivery of any of the shares offered hereby, the Company's presently authorized capital stock of 375 shares, no par value, will be reclassified into 1,125,000 shares of Common Stock, $1 par value, and, accordingly, each of the 225 outstanding shares of capital stock will become 3,000 shares of Common Stock, or an aggregate of 657,000 shares.

It might be necessary in preparation for your stock offering to eliminate stockholder agreements, buy and sell agreements, restrictions on dividends, pre-emptive rights, etc. Your underwriter and your counsel in discussing your future stock offering with you, will give you their recommendations as to the stock restrictions that should be eliminated upon your recapitalization and other changes in your Charter which may be desirable. The attorneys for your company will amend the articles of incorporation of your company to increase the amount of authorized stock. In order to permit future sales of stock or to have stock available for acquisition or for stock options, it would be well to provide for a larger amount of authorized stock than currently needed. For example, if the outstanding stock after the split will be 600,000 shares, it would be advisable to have an authorized stock of 1 million shares. In calculating costs of an underwriting, compute the State taxes which must be paid on increasing the authorized shares.

It is important to keep in mind that the "authorized" common stock of a corporation is the total number of shares approved for issuance under terms of the corporate charger. Stock that is sold is called "issued" stock; the shares not issued are called "unissued stock."

Unissued and "treasury" stock are not the same thing. The latter is fully paid issued stock which a corporation has reacquired by purchase, or perhaps by donation. Treasury stock has no voting power and receives no dividends. It can be held by the corporation indefinitely or it can be retired. It can be sold at any price, or it can be distributed to officers or employees as bonus payments, and thereafter is no longer treasury stock.

When financial people speak of "outstanding" stock, their reference is to the total issued stock less any issued stock which has been reacquired; that is, treasury stock.

As your company enters into a recapitalization plan as a prelude to a public offering, you and your associates also must decide, with the advice of your financial and legal counsel and underwriters, what par value—if any—you will place on each share.

## Par Value Stock

The par value is the face or stated value of each share. In years past, it was customary practice to place a par value on a share of stock—say $100. This sum was supposed to reflect the equivalent value of cash, services or property of the issuing company. The par value figure, however, had little relationship to what the stock was sold for initially or later.

Consequently, par value came to have little meaning except as it is shown on a corporate balance sheet; that is, 1,000 shares of $100 par is entered as $100,000. It has no importance to the investing public in evaluating securities.

Over the years, the practice of stating a par value has changed vastly. There are scores of variations, from 10 cents a share up to $100, with the most common being $1, $5, $10 and $25.

There also developed, especially in the 1920's, the practice of issuing "no par" value stock. No par stock carries no face value. It is carried on the corporate balance sheet at a value fixed by the Board of Directors, or at a specified minimum, such as $1.

## No Par Value Stock

Stock without a par value is termed "no par" value stock and can be sold at any price set by the Directors of the company.

There is one disadvantage which has tended to reduce the practice of issuing no par value stock. A higher tax is imposed in transactions in no par stock, and as a corporation pays the original issue tax, it thus submits itself to an increased cost.

## Class A and Class B Stock

Some corporations have two classes of stock, namely, Class A and Class B common stock. Generally the stock designated as Class A is sold to the public, whereas the Class B stock is owned by the controlling stockholders of the company. Often there are differences in the voting rights between the two classes of stock, and it is also possible that there may be differences in the dividend rights. Beyond these two differences, normally the stock, regardless of classification, has the same rights.

## Reincorporations in Another State

As you give consideration to recapitalizing your company and issuing more shares of stock, you might well discuss with your attorney the advisability of reincorporating your company in another state. Possibly when you originally organized your corporation, you obtained a license from your own state to operate as a domestic corporation. Now as you consider a public offering, you might find that the cost of increasing your capital stock will be considerably higher in your state than in some other state.

You might also welcome the flexibility that another state will give to you in place of meetings, calling of meetings, stockholders' rights, etc. In considering reincorporation in another state, you might give consideration to the laws of the state of Delaware. Many advantages exist in organizing a corporation under the laws of Delaware. Other states also offer certain advantages. If you are recapitalizing your company, this would appear to be the proper time to give consideration to another state in which you might reincorporate.

# 20

## Reserving Stock for Your Employees and Customers

One of the important considerations in a public stock offering is that your employees will have an opportunity to acquire stock in your company. There are two ways in which they can obtain stock at the time of a public stock offering.

(a) One method of acquisition is through granting of options to your employees to purchase stock. This plan is discussed in Chapter 32.

(b) The other method is through the reservation of a certain amount of stock by the underwriters for sale to the company employees.

### Granting Options

Let us assume that your company is going to sell 150,000 shares of stock to the public. You will want to make certain that the underwriters will have enough stock to sell to your employees. The best way to accomplish this is through an understanding in advance with the underwriters that they will reserve, for example, 15,000 shares of stock for your employees. This means your underwriter will offer 135,000 shares to the public out of the full 150,000 shares, the balance of 15,000 to be offered to your employees.

This plan does not require that the stock be offered to your employees at a bargain price. You are protecting them so that they can be certain that they will be able to purchase stock through the underwriters. They will not find themselves in a position of being unable to buy stock on the open market the day the stock is offered. Since many of your employees will not have any prior relationship with a stock broker, they might not be able to obtain stock at the initial stock offering unless you have protected them through an understanding with the managing underwriter.

### Beware of Oversubscription

Even though the underwriter sets aside stock for the employees, you might well be faced with an oversubscription by your employees. This again may create some ill-will when you must tell an employee that the underwriter can only sell him 50 shares instead of the 200 requested. However, if all employees are treated fairly, they should have no cause for complaint.

In notifying the employees of your company of the proposed stock offering, enclose a copy of the preliminary prospectus. Keep a record of the names of all persons to whom a prospectus is furnished.

Employees will naturally want to know the price at which the stock will be offered. It is impossible to state a price at the time you present the initial material to the employees as market conditions change. Point out to the employees that if they purchase stock it must be paid for in cash on a certain day.

### Avoid "Sales" Flavor

I would add a strong word of caution at this point. Be sure you are not in a position where you are attempting in any way to influence your employees to buy stock in your company. You are in a very tenuous position when stock is offered to your employees. If the stock increases in value, your employees might criticize you for not having urged them to buy the stock. If, on the other hand, you have urged your employees to buy stock and the stock declines in value, quite naturally the employees will be unhappy with the fact that you recommended an unfavorable purchase.

It is best to make no statements of any kind that could be construed either in favor or against the purchase of stock in your company. Through your letter to your employees, make it clear that the stock is available and that you are making no representations of any type. The decision as to whether the employee will buy or not buy must rest solely with the employee.

Suggest to the employees who wish to purchase stock, that they buy it from the managing underwriter. Keep away from discussing with your employees the pros and cons of the purchase. This can be subjected to misinterpretation and possibly cause hard feelings later. When the stock is sold to the employees by a representative of the managing underwriter, they will bill the employees for the stock and will make the collections from them. It might be well to advise your employees of the rules of the underwriters requiring payment be made within 5 days from date of purchase of the stock. Some of your employees might not be familiar with this requirement.

### Making Loans for Employee Purchase

You might be asked by some of your employees whether the company will make loans to the employees to assist them in the purchase of stock. You will have to answer this question as the circumstances require. It would be my general feeling that if an employee can not afford to pay cash for his stock, he should not purchase stock at the time of the offering. In all likelihood, most employees earning average compensation need most of their money for necessities, insurance, taxes, etc. They should purchase stock only after they have adequately provided for their family needs. Even though you might be willing to loan the money to an employee, this may put pressure on the employee. If the stock should decline later in value, you might find it difficult to obtain repayment of the loan from an unhappy employee.

As soon as the registration statement becomes effective the employees of the company who have expressed an interest in purchasing stock should be notified and they should receive a copy of the final prospectus. The employees should be given the name of the representative of the underwriter to contact for the completion of the purchase of stock.

It might be advisable to have such representative of your underwriter present in your office to complete the purchase and sale of the stock to your employees. Provide a private room for the underwriter's representative so that he can meet with the employees and consummate the purchase of the stock in privacy.

## Sale of Stock to Employees of the Company

The prospectus generally sets forth the plan of offering stock to employees. The following are examples of stock offerings to employees:

*Scott, Foresman & Company.* Of the shares offered by this Prospectus, 50,000 are being offered by the Underwriters to employees, including officers, of the Company (other than Selling Stockholders), at the price per share set forth under "Price to Employees" on the cover page of this Prospectus, subject to the condition that no employee purchasing shares will resell such shares within 60 days of the commencement of the offering by the Underwriters without the consent of Smith, Barney & Co. Incorporated. Sales will be made only for cash. If employee subscriptions exceed the number of shares offered to employees, the Underwriters will make allocations in accordance with the directions of the Chairman of the Board and the President of the Company. Any portion of the shares not subscribed for by employees by 3:00 P.M., Chicago Time, on the second business day following the effective date of the Registration Statement will be offered by the Underwriters to the public at the price per share set forth under "Price to Public" on the cover page of this Prospectus.

*Crown Photo, Inc.* The Company proposes to offer 10,000 shares of Common Stock directly to its employees (other than officers and directors). Any shares not subscribed for by such employees will be offered to officers and directors. If the offering to employees is oversubscribed, the Company will in its discretion make allocations with regard first to employees who owned the Company's First Preferred Stock and then to employees based on salary and length of service.

The offering price will be $7.36 per share. Employees will be allowed either to make full payment at the time of purchase or to make payment under a payroll deduction plan over a period not to exceed twelve months.

## Reserving Stock for Customers

As word gets out that your company is planning an offering of stock to the public, the phone will ring continuously. The party on the other end of the line will be saying, "Hello, this is Joe out in Bay City. We're one of your good customers and we'd like to get in on the ground floor. How can we get some of your stock?"

You again have a public relations problem, in meeting these requests. Your best answer is, "I'm sorry I can't give you a definite answer, Joe. We have agreed to sell the entire issue to our underwriters. They are taking indications of interest from prospective investors and I suggest you call them to ask them to reserve some stock for you." It will be helpful to your underwriter if you will indicate how important the customer is, so that he can cooperate in setting aside some stock.

Again, it may be necessary to allocate the available stock, particularly if your company operates on a national basis with many interested customers throughout the country. Your underwriter will be familiar with the best methods for handling these requests and will certainly cooperate with you in making a fair distribution. If there is to be any reservation of stock for customers it should be definitely stated in the prospectus. You will be in a better position with your customers if you let your underwriter handle all the details.

# 21

# A Timetable for a Public Offering

"Time is of the essence" in any public stock offering. Once you have agreed with your underwriter to proceed, it is important to establish a timetable to assist you in the completion of your program. You will find that normally when your registration statement is pending before the SEC, amendments must be prepared quickly, printed, and returned to the SEC for review. Actually, split second timing is involved once your registration statement has been declared effective by the SEC.

Your attorneys will establish a comprehensive timetable for you, your advisors, the underwriters, and their advisors. The timetable will set out the work that is to be performed by each group and the time in which the work is to be completed.

### SAMPLE TIMETABLE

The following is a sample timetable to be used as a guide in a public stock offering:

*Tentative Agenda and Time Schedule*

| | |
|---|---|
| July 18 | Meeting of Board of Directors to receive and act upon proposals for stock offering. |
| July 29 | Prepare Registration Statement and other corporate documents hereinafter referred to. |
| August 10 | Financial Statements made available by accountants. Send Registration Statement to printer. |
| August 14 | Execute Registration Statement and mail to SEC. |
| August 17 | Registration Statement filed with SEC. |
| August 17–21 | Meeting of Board of Directors of (the "Company") at which following action is taken: |

    (a) Adopt Amendment to Articles reclassifying stock;

    (b) Authorize execution of Agreement and Plan of Reorganization between the Company and its stockholders;

91

(c) Adopt Amended by-laws. Increase number of directors;

(d) Ratify preparation and filing of Blue Sky applications;

(e) Elect additional officers.

Mail notice of special meeting of stockholders of Company to be held August 27.

Prepare and file Blue Sky applications.

| | |
|---|---|
| August 24–28 | Tax ruling received. |
| August 27 | Special meeting of stockholders of Company is to be held approving the matters previously adopted or approved by the Board of Directors, and electing new directors. |
| | File certificate of amendment to articles of incorporation. |
| September 4–8 | Deficiency memorandum received from SEC. |
| September 4–10 | Note: This is predicated upon receiving the deficiency memorandum at the end of 20 days. This date varies depending upon the time schedule of the SEC at the time of filing. |
| | Prepare and file Amendment No. 1 with the SEC. |
| September 8 | Due diligence meeting of underwriters. |
| September 14 | Issue new temporary stock certificates evidencing the stock recapitalization. |
| | Procure, affix and cancel Federal documentary issuance and transfer tax stamps. |
| | File report of issuance of shares. |
| | Execute agreement among stockholders. |
| | Special meeting of Board of Directors of Company authorizing execution of Underwriting Agreement, fixing price and authorizing appointment of transfer agent and registrar. |
| | Execute Underwriting Agreement. |
| | Prepare and send price amendment to SEC. |
| | Complete Blue Sky qualification. |
| September 15 | Price amendment is filed and Registration Statement becomes effective. |
| September 16 | Public offering of stock by Underwriters. |
| | Release press release on notice of receipt of order of Commission. |
| | Underwriters' counsel mails 25 copies of Prospectus to SEC (Rule 424(c)). |
| | Managing Underwriter informs Sellers as to names, denominations in which shares are to be issued, with copy to transfer agent. |
| September 23 | Closing date. |

# 22

# The Role of the Securities and Exchange Commission in Your Company's Stock Offering

*General*

In 1933, Congress passed the Securities Act to correct certain abuses that existed prior to that time. It was the purpose of the Securities Act of 1933 to provide, through a registration statement and a prospectus, for a full, fair and accurate disclosure of the character of securities that are offered publicly for sale and sold in interstate commerce or through the mails. The act was passed to prevent any fraudulent practices in the sale of securities, whether registered or not.

The Act of 1933, also known as the "truth-in-securities" Act, provides for information to be given to potential investors so that they might judge whether new security offerings provide good investment opportunities. The Act requires a complete disclosure. However, an investor must realize that the Securities and Exchange Commission, which administers the Act, does not pass upon the merits of the securities. It does not advise an investor whether to buy or not to buy. The Commission's position is to determine whether the disclosures made in the registration statement and the prospectus are adequate and accurate to inform the buyer.

It is important to keep in mind that the Securities and Exchange Commission does not have the power to either approve or disapprove any security that is registered with the Commission. Congress decided that it was important that no federal agency be given the responsibility of passing judgment upon any issue that was registered with the agency. It was intended through the Securities Act, that even though the Commission permits a registration statement to become effective at a specific time, this is not in any way to be considered an endorsement by the Commission that the statements made and the registration are true or accurate. It was determined by Congress that the Securities Act provide for disclosure of the important facts in connection with a registration. Disclosure is

93

made through a registration statement and the prospectus. "Caveat emptor"—let the buyer beware—applies to new issues even though registered with the SEC.

Basically, the Securities Act of 1933 was designed to give the potential investor an opportunity and a basis on which to form a judgment as to whether a particular offering represents a good investment. When one purchases securities that have been registered with the SEC, he has the assurance that the securities were registered with the Securities and Exchange Commission in accordance with their regulations. The purchaser is also assured that if there are misrepresentations or fraud in the issuance of the security, the SEC under such conditions has the power to take appropriate steps against the selling stockholder or selling corporation. If the registration statement does not present all of the facts to the Securities and Exchange Commission, it may place a "stop order" and suspend the effectiveness of the registration statement until the deficiency is corrected by an amendment. The Act also provides for civil and criminal liabilities where there have been materially false representations or omissions.

## Organization of the Securities and Exchange Commission

It is important that you understand the function of the Securities and Exchange Commission and the work that it performs. Historically, the SEC was not created under the Securities Act of 1933. Congress in 1934 passed the Securities Exchange Act which created the Securities Exchange Commission, an independent agency of the United States. This act also provided for the regulation of stock exchanges, functions of members, brokers, dealers, registration of listed securities, filing of reports, proxy rules, etc. The President of the United States appoints, with the advice and consent of the Senate, the five members to serve on the Securities and Exchange Commission. The President designates the Chairman. The principal office of the Commission is located in Washington, D. C.

The SEC maintains regional and district offices, which serve as the investigation and enforcement arm of the Commission. The regional offices are located in New York, Chicago, Boston, Atlanta, Denver, San Francisco, Seattle and Fort Worth. The Commission also maintains branch offices in Detroit, Cleveland, St. Paul, Los Angeles and Salt Lake City. The Commission maintains public reference rooms in its offices in Washington, New York, and Chicago. Copies of all public information filed with the SEC are available for inspection in the public reference room of the SEC in Washington, D. C.

The Commission functions through a staff of lawyers, accountants, financial analysts, engineers, administrative and clerical employees. The staff of the SEC is organized into the following divisions:

Executive Division—Division of Administrative Management
Division of Corporation Finance

Division of Trading and Exchange
Division of Corporate Regulation
Regional Offices
Office of General Counsel
Office of Chief Accountant
Office of Opinion Writing
Office of the Secretary
Office of Hearing Examiners
Executive Assistant to the Chairman

A corporation seeking to register its securities with the SEC will be in close contact with the Division of Corporation Finance. It is the primary responsibility of this division to seek to prevent fraudulent offerings of securities to the public. Standards of information, including financial and economic are established by this division. Auditing procedures and priorities are also established. This division also prescribes types of information which must be included in proxy statements, proxies, and proxy soliciting statement.

The Division of Corporation Finance examines all registration statements, prospectuses, financial statements, appraisals, engineering reports, proxy statements, etc., which are filed with the SEC to assist the Commission in its functions.

Each regional office of the SEC maintains a file of all prospectuses of companies that have registered securities under the Securities Act of 1933. These documents are available for public inspection. If photo copies of registration statements, prospectus, etc. are required, these may be obtained from the Administrative Division of the SEC in Washington.

# 23

## What Issues Are Exempt from SEC Regulations?

The first question asked by one interested in public stock offering is, "Will we be required to file a registration statement with the SEC?" This question must be answered by your attorney as there are a number of exemptions provided for in the SEC regulations. However, generally speaking, it is necessary first to determine whether the company will become "an issuer" within the provisions of the Securities Act of 1933.

The "issuer" of securities is required to file a registration statement with the SEC. It is necessary to look to the definition of the word "issuer" contained in Sec. 2(4) of the Securities Act of 1933. With certain exceptions, the Act defines the term "issuer" to be every person who issues or proposes to issue any security.

It is possible that the sale of the securities may be exempt from the registration provisions of the SEC if the offering does not involve a "public offering," if the aggregate amount of the offering to the public does not exceed $300,000, or the issue is to be sold on an intra-State basis.

*Private Sale*

The regulations are specific as to what constitutes a public offering as distinguished from a "private offering." Generally speaking, if the sale of the stock to be made is to a specific person or is purely an isolated transaction, it is exempt from registration if the purchasers take for investment and not with a view to distribution. However, if it is contemplated that there are to be sales of stock to the public in general, the sale would be subject to the registration provisions of the Securities Act. In considering whether a sale of a security is exempt as a transaction not involving any public offering, the following factors are to be considered:

1. Number of offerees and their relationship to each other and to the issuer;
2. The number of units offered;

3. The size of the offering;
4. The management of the offering;
5. The intention of the offerees to acquire the shares for investment.

There is no magic number of persons to whom a private placement can be offered before it is considered a public offering. As a general rule a greater number of persons may be approached in connection with the placement of a security of high investment merit (a high grade debenture, for example) than in the case of a more speculative security. Also, a larger number may be approached where the placement involves a greater amount of money. Probably the most important consideration is the character of the purchaser. If those approached fall fairly into the category of informed or sophisticated investors, the SEC is less likely to challenge a placement than if a more general group is approached. Informed or sophisticated investors usually means insurance companies, pension funds, mutual funds or other institutional purchasers with ample research facilities but also includes individual professional investors of substance. The latter category would however be more carefully scrutinized and with such investors the number of purchasers should be substantially smaller than with institutional investors.

In private placements the so-called investment letter is generally employed. The investment letter is a warranty on the part of the purchaser that the security is being purchased for investment and not with a view to resale or distribution. However, the SEC looks upon the investment letter with a jaundiced eye and presently takes the position that the value attached to it depends upon the performance of the purchaser after the letter is given—have the purchasers held the security long enough to justify the original investment intent? Holding for six months is not enough, the real question is whether there was an intent to resell sometime or an intent to hold indefinitely subject to a right to resell if conditions change. Sales to individuals under "investment letters" are generally eyed more suspiciously than sales to institutional investors.

Since determination of what constitutes a public offering is essentially a question of fact and law in which all the circumstances must be considered, your attorney is in the best position to advise you as to whether your company's stock offering will be considered an exempt transaction not involving any public offering.

### Issues of $300,000 or Less

Many corporations limit the amount of their public offering to $300,000 to take advantage of the limited filing requirements of the SEC. In 1945, the SEC was permitted by Congress to exempt securities offerings not exceeding $300,-000. It is important to note that the exemption from registration in this case does not offer complete exemption from all of the provisions of the SEC Act. The liabilities of the Act may be still invoked in the event of the use of mails to defraud.

Regulation A, issued by the Commission, provides for the exemption of certain classes of Domestic and Canadian securities where the aggregate offering to the public does not exceed $300,000. While a registration statement need not be filed with the SEC under Regulation A, notification and reports are required. This regulation requires that offering circulars containing information prescribed by the Commission must be furnished to buyers. The circular must contain the following statement on the outside of the front cover page:

> These securities are offered pursuant to an exemption from registration with the United States Securities and Exchange Commission. The Commission does not pass upon the merits of any security nor does it pass upon the accuracy or completeness of any offering circular or other selling literature.

Generally, the offering circular must furnish prospective investors with basic information as to the company, including financial statements, and must be filed with the Regional office of the SEC in which the Company's principal business operations are conducted at least ten days before the stock is offered to the public. The Commission will examine the material furnished on Form 1-A to determine whether the necessary facts have been disclosed. Semi-annual reports of the progress of the offering must be filed with the Commission.

Although filing under Regulation A is not as difficult or time consuming or expensive as a registration, it still does involve expense and labor. Your attorney can advise you as to the costs involved for registration, legal and accounting fees.

*Intrastate Issues*

Many companies today wish to sell their stock exclusively within the confines of a state since costs, fees and time can be saved. Quite often the savings in filing fees, printing, etc. may bring the cost down to 25 per cent of the expenditures that are incurred in an SEC registration. Certain states are in a position to qualify an issue within a week if it is presented properly as compared to the six weeks or more that are normally required in filing with the SEC.

It is necessary to determine whether an issue is exempt from registration with the SEC under the provisions of Section 3A (11) of the Securities Exchange Act of 1933 which provides:

> Any security which is a part of an issue offered and sold only to persons resident within a single State or Territory, where the issuer of such security is a person resident and doing the business within, or, if a corporation, incorporated by and doing business within such State or Territory.

The Securities and Exchange Commission has issued a series of interpretations relating to intrastate offerings. The Commission has emphasized that the Federal Law exempts only issues which in reality represent local financing by local industry. The SEC suggested that any dealer proposing to participate in the distribution of an issue claimed to be exempt should examine the character of the transaction and the proposed or actual manner of its execution by all persons concerned with it with the greatest care to satisfy himself that the distribution will not violate the Federal law. The Commission has pointed out that a dealer acting contrary to the above interpretation may subject himself to serious risk of civil liability under the Securities Act of 1933 for selling without prior registration a security not in fact entitled to exemption from registration. The SEC can ask the courts to enjoin a securities offering being made in violation of the 1933 Act. The company issuing the security and the security dealer as well can be named as defendants.

The Commission has advised dealers to examine all aspects of a proposed intrastate issue to make sure that it does not become an interstate distribution through resales. The Commission has suggested to dealers that they obtain assurances from each purchaser of an intrastate offering that purchases are not made with a view to resale to non-residents.

In *Stadia Oil & Uranium Co. vs. Wheelis,* 21 F (2d) 269,275, sales of securities to residents of the state followed shortly thereafter by resale to non-residents, were held to be a circumvention of the law.

A single sale or offer of an unregistered security to a non-resident was held sufficient to destroy the exemption and render the entire issue illegal. The exception provided for intrastate issues was designed to apply only to such types of distributions that are *genuinely* local in character.

While it may be easier and less costly to qualify an issue under the state laws as compared to filing with the SEC, many investment bankers shy away from intrastate offerings, and prefer that the issue be registered with the SEC.

State laws differ as to registration of intrastate issues. If your company's issue can be sold within the confines of a state, it would be well to consider with your attorney the advantages and disadvantages of this type of registration.

# 24

## The Registration Statement

After determining that the issue of stock is subject to the Securities Act of 1933, the next step in moving forward with a public offering is the registration of the securities with the Securities and Exchange Commission. Generally speaking, the issuer is required to file a registration statement with the SEC to provide full and fair disclosure of the character of the securities sold in interstate commerce and through the mails. This is accomplished by filing a Registration Statement which will be examined by the Commission.

The preparation of the registration statement requires great care, skill and a full knowledge of the Securities Exchange Act. Full information concerning the company's business, its financial position, securities, and indemnity agreements must be disclosed to enable the investor to determine whether he wishes to purchase the securities.

Form S-1 has been created by the SEC and contains the information required in a registration statement. This form is used by all registrants of securities for which no other form is authorized or prescribed.

Normally, the registration statement is printed, but this is not a requirement of the SEC. Under Rule 403 the statements may be printed, lithographed, mimeographed or typewritten. The statements must be signed by the registrant, its principal executive officer, the principal financial officer, its principal accounting officer and by the majority of the Board of Directors.

The registration statement, after it is approved by the Board of Directors, must be filed in triplicate in Washington. The address of the Securities and Exchange Commission is 425 Second Street N.W., Washington 25, D. C. All financial statements that accompany the registration statement must be prepared in accordance with Form S-1, Regulation S-X. On filing the registration statement, a fee must be paid to the Security and Exchange Commission equivalent to one hundredth of 1 per cent of the maximum aggregate price for which the securities are to be offered. The minimum fee that is payable is $25. Rule

458 requires that fees be paid in cash, U.S. Postal Money Order, Certified Check, or by bank cashier's check.

The registration statement cannot become effective—that is, stock cannot be sold—until the twentieth day after the filing of the registration statement or any amendment thereto. The SEC may reduce the 20 day period if, in its discretion, it determines it is in the public interest to shorten the period. The date of filing is considered to be the date on which the registration statement and fees are received by the Commission. In recent years, relatively few registration statements have become effective in less than 30–60 days after filing with the SEC.

### Preparation of the Registration Statement

Get out the midnight oil—you will be using plenty of it in the preparation of a registration statement and prospectus, particularly if this is the first public stock offering. Remember, you are not preparing an advertising piece or a sales manual. However, you are creating a public document which will establish an "image" of your company. When you prepare the registration statement, you will measure every word, check it carefully with your advisors, and be sure that the final result complies 100 per cent with the regulations of the SEC. The registration statement must include complete facts about your company, and its business and the property of the company. It will also contain many financial statements prepared by your certified public accountants.

Form S-1 specifically points out the exhibits that must accompany the registration statement. These exhibits include copies of your company's by-laws and charter, copies of all material agreements of the company, underwriting agreements, stock option plans, etc.

The actual preparation of the registration statement and prospectus is done by you, your attorneys, the managing underwiter and underwriter's counsel. Prepare for many hours of discussion with your underwriters, their advisor and your advisors. Each word and statement will be weighed carefully to be sure that they are correct and your prospectus gives complete information about your company.

### Forming a Thinking Team

You will want to have the best thinking of the group of people both in and outside of your organization. The following should form your team in preparing the registration statement and the prospectus:

1. *The president of the company.* He should serve as coordinator. He will put his signature on the registration statement and he will want to be certain that all the material contained in the statement is true and accurate. By working closely with the team in the preparation of the statement, the president will

have the assurance that the material is being presented properly to the Securities and Exchange Commission.

2. *The chief financial officer of the company.* He will work closely with the independent Public Accountants for the company in gathering together the information that is required in the financial statements.

3. *Vice president in charge of marketing.* A great deal of information is required in the prospectus showing the company's sales programs, marketing plans, competition, etc. This material should be submitted by the Sales Department with a word of caution—the prospectus is not an advertising piece. The attorneys will take out of the prospectus any of the "puff" in setting forth the marketing program of the company.

4. *The attorneys for the company.* Since the preparation of the registration statement and the prospectus must comply strictly with the Securities Act of 1933 and the rules and regulations of the Securities and Exchange Commission, your attorneys will and must play an important role in the preparation of the statement and prospectus. They will literally dot every "i" and cross every "t." Each word will be weighed carefully in light of the Securities and Exchange Commission regulations. The attorneys will be guided by their responsibility to make certain that the registration statement and prospectus contain a complete and full disclosure and that the registrant has not omitted any material information.

5. *Certified Public Accountant.* Since the independent public accountants for the company must certify most if not all of the financial statements that are to be included in the registration statement and prospectus, they will want to make certain that all the financial information contained in the statement and in the prospectus is 100 per cent accurate and that there are no omissions of material information. The accountants, as well as lawyers, engineers named in the Registration Statement will be required to furnish a written consent to the Securities and Exchange Commission stating that they are agreeing to the inclusion of their certificate in the registration statement.

6. *Investment banker.* One of the important roles that your investment banker plays in the public offering is the assistance which he furnishes in the preparation of the registration statement and prospectus. He is skilled in this area; experience has taught him many important lessons. He, too, will want to make doubly certain that the statement is clear and concise and that there are no omissions. While the attorneys for the investment banker might not assist in the detailed preparations of the statement and prospectus, they will be in on the various drafts, again lending the value of their background and experience.

7. *Engineers.* Certain outside engineering firms possibly should be consulted to assist in the preparation of the registration statement and the prospectus.

While each member of the team has a specific responsibility, everyone work-ing on the preparation of the registration statement and the prospectus should review all portions of these documents. The narrative section should be consistent with the financial statements and the accountants and attorneys should work closely together on all phases of this work.

Your underwriter's attorneys will examine the corporate records such as char-ter, by-laws, minute books, contracts, patents, leases, etc. They will work closely with your legal counsel during the initial stages and will review carefully all of the documents submitted to the SEC.

### Contents of Registration Statement

Your attorneys together with your accountants and underwriters will prepare the registration statement to comply with the SEC rules.

The registration statement consists of two parts, as follows:

*Part 1*—contains items of information that must be included in the prospectus which forms a part of the registration statement.

*Part 2*—includes information which, while it must be included in the registration statement, need not be included in the prospectus.

Under Rule 404(a) the registrant is permitted to file a copy of the proposed prospectus in place of furnishing all of the item by item answers required in prescribed Form S-1.

The following undertaking must be included in every registration statement:

> Subject to the terms and conditions of Section 15(d) of the Securities Ex-change Act of 1933, the undersigned registrant hereby undertakes to file with the Securities and Exchange Commission such supplementary and pe-riodic information, documents and reports as may be prescribed by any rule or regulation of the Commission heretofore or hereafter duly adopted pur-suant to authority conferred in that section.

### Financial Statements

Your accountant will prepare the financial statements that are required by Form S-1. Basically, the registration statement must contain financial statements, supporting schedules and summaries of earnings. Subject to certain exemptions all of the financial data must be certified by an independent public accountant. The accountant must sign his certificate in the registration statement and must also sign a consent to including his certificate in the registration statement.

It is important to remember that the financial statements are the representa-tions of management and not the accountants. The primary responsibility for the accuracy of the information contained in the financial report rests on man-agement. You cannot discharge your responsibilities by "passing the buck" to your accountants. In completing the registration statement on Form S-1, it is important that close attention be paid to the rules of the Securities and Exchange Commission as to financial statements which are as follows:

### Balance Sheets of the Registrant

(a) The registrant shall file a balance sheet as of a date within 90 days prior to the date of filing the registration statement. This balance sheet need not be certified. If all of the following conditions exist, this balance sheet may, however, be as of a date within six months prior to the date of filing.

(1) The registrant files annual and other reports pursuant to Section 13 or 15(d) of the Securities and Exchange Act of 1934;

(2) The total assets of the registrant and its subsidiaries, as shown by the latest consolidated balance sheet filed, less any valuation or qualifying reserves, amount to $5,000,000 or more, exclusive of intangibles; and

(3) No long-term debt of the registrant is in default as to principal, interest or sinking fund provisions.

(b) If the balance sheet required by paragraph (a) is not certified, there shall be filed in addition a certified balance sheet as of a date within 90 days prior to the date of filing, in which case the certified balance sheet may be as of the end of the preceding fiscal year.

The registrant shall file a profit and loss statement for each of the three fiscal years preceding the date of the lastest balance sheet filed, and for the period, if any, between the close of the latest of such fiscal years and the date of the latest balance sheet filed. These statements shall be certified up to the date of the latest certified balance sheet filed.

There are numerous instructions provided for special situations in preparing Form S-1. Your accountant will be familiar with these provisions of the regulations and will guide you accordingly.

### Inspection of Registration Statement

In filing the registration statement with the Securities Exchange Commission, it is important to keep in mind that the statement will be available for public inspection at the offices of the SEC in Washington. Rule 120 of General Rules and Regulations under the SEC Act of 1933 provides as follows:

Except for material contracts or portions thereof accorded confidential treatment pursuant to Rule 485, all registration statements are available for public inspection, during business hours, at the principal office of the Commission in Washington, D.C.

# 25

## How to Prepare the Prospectus

In filing a registration statement with the Securities and Exchange Commission, it is required that the registrant submit a copy of the proposed prospectus or selling circular to the Commission.

What is a "prospectus"? This word as defined in Section 2 (10) of the Securities Act of 1933 as amended, includes any notice, circular, advertisement, letter or communication, written or by radio or television which offers any security for sale or confirms the sale of any security, except that a communication sent or given after the effective date of the registration statement shall not be deemed a "prospectus" if it is proved that prior to or at the same time with such communication, a written prospectus, meeting the requirements of Section 10 (a) was sent or given to the person to whom the communication was given.

Said in another way, where securities must be registered with the SEC, it is illegal under the Act to publicly offer a security prior to the filing of a registration statement with the SEC. A security may be offered after the statement is filed but before it becomes effective—if and only if—the prospectus meets the standards of Sec. 10 of the Securities Act of 1933. This section spells out the information required in the prospectus and will be discussed in detail in this chapter.

Keep in mind that the prospectus must be designed to be read by people who are making business judgments. If the prospectus is too long and cumbersome, it will not be effective. It should not be written in legalistic language. Excerpts from contracts should be avoided in the preparation of the prospectus. Statements should be brief and may incorporate particular sections of Exhibits by reference.

It is important to bear in mind that the purpose of the prospectus is to inform investors. The prospectus must be carefully prepared in clear and concise language.

In presenting the information in the prospectus, you will be guided by Rule

421 of General Rules and Regulations under the Securities Act of 1933 which provides as follows:

(a) The information required in a prospectus need not follow the order of the items or other requirements in the form. Such information shall not, however, be set forth in such fashion as to obscure any of the required information or any information necessary to keep the required information from being incomplete or misleading. Where an item requires information to be given in a prospectus in tabular form, it shall be given in substantially the tabular form specified in the item.

(b) All information contained in a prospectus shall be set forth under appropriate captions or headings reasonably indicative of the principal subject matter set forth thereunder. Except as to financial statements and other tabular data, all information set forth in a prospectus shall be divided into reasonably short paragraphs or sections.

(c) Every prospectus shall include in the forepart thereof a reasonably detailed table of contents showing the subject matter of the various sections or subdivisions of the prospectus and the page number on which each such section or subdivision begins.

(d) All information required to be included in a prospectus shall be clearly understandable without the necessity of referring to the particular form or to the General Rules and Regulations. Except as to financial statements and information required in tabular form, the information set forth in a prospectus may be expressed in condensed or summarized form. Financial statements included in a prospectus are to be set forth in comparative form if practicable, and shall include the notes thereto and the accountants' certificate.

It is important as stated above to keep in mind that the SEC Act is a "Disclosure Act"—and that the Commission does not approve or disapprove of any security registered with it.

Therefore, in preparing the prospectus, it is necessary to set forth in bold type on the front cover the following statements in accordance with Rule 425:

These securities have not been approved or disapproved by the Security and Exchange Commission, nor has the Commission passed upon the accuracy or adequacy of this prospectus. Any representation to the contrary is a criminal offense.

The prospectus, in some instances, contains the following statements:

Except where otherwise indicated, this Prospectus speaks as of its date of issue. Neither the delivery hereof nor any sales made hereunder shall under any circumstance create any implication that there has been no change in the affairs of the Company since the date hereof.

In addition, the prospectus generally contains the following statements:

> No dealer, salesman or any other person has been authorized to give any information or to make any representations other than those contained in this Prospectus, and if given or made such information and representations must not be relied upon as having been authorized by the Company or the Underwriters. This Prospectus does not constitute an offer to sell or a solicitation of an offer to buy any of the securities offered hereby in any state to any person to whom it is unlawful to make such offer in such State.

## CONTENTS OF PROSPECTUS

### Item 1. *Distribution Spread*

In preparing Item 1 of the prospectus, a tabulation must be presented on the outside front cover of the prospectus giving the distribution spread which includes the price to the investing public—the commission paid and net proceeds to the registrant and the selling stockholders, if any. If the stockholders are also selling stock, the distribution spread may be shown separately.

The following tabular form is used:

|  | *Price to Public* | *Underwriting discounts and commissions* | *Proceeds to registrant or other persons* |
|---|---|---|---|
| Per unit ............ | | | |
| Total ............ | | | |

If it is impractical to state the price, the prospectus should explain the method used in determining the price. Reference is also made at this point to warrants and options to underwriters, expenses, etc.

### Item 2. *Plan of Distribution*

If the securities being registered are to be offered through underwriters, it is necessary to include
  (a) the names of the principal underwriters,
  (b) the respective amounts underwritten,
  (c) the application of any underwriter having a material relationship to the registrant, and
  (d) the nature of the underwriter's obligation to take the securities.
The registrant must state briefly the discounts and commissions to be allowed or paid to dealers, including all cash, securities, contracts or other consideration to be received by any dealer in connection with the sale of the securities. The

regulations also require that the registrant outline briefly the plan of distribution of any securities being registered which are to be offered otherwise than through underwriters.

The prospectus contains a listing of underwriters. The following is an example:

SCANTLIN ELECTRONICS

The names and addresses of the several Underwriters and the respective numbers and percentages of shares to be purchased by each of them are as follows:

| Underwriter | Address | Number of Shares to be Purchased from Company | Number of Shares to be Purchased from Selling Stockholders | Percentage of Total Shares to be Purchased from Paul M. Davis on Exercise of Option |
|---|---|---|---|---|
| Carl M. Loeb, Rhoades & Co. | 42 Wall St. New York 5, N.Y. | 65,625 | 28,125 | 37½% |
| Paine, Webber Jackson & Curtis | 25 Broad St. New York 4, N.Y. | 65,625 | 28,125 | 37½% |
| Merril Lynch, Pierce, Fenner & Smith Incorporated | 70 Pine St. New York 5, N.Y. | 43,750 | 18,750 | 25% |
| | TOTAL | 175,000 | 75,000 | 100% |

At this point in the prospectus, reference should be made to the purchase agreement between the registrant and the underwriter. The following are examples of various types of commitments:

*Victor Paint Co.* Subject to certain conditions set forth in the Underwriting Contract, the commitment of the Underwriters is to purchase all of the shares of Common Stock, if any are purchased.

*Caroline Metal Products Corp.* Attention is directed to the fact that the Underwriting Agreement with respect to the shares offered hereby permits the initial 45 day period during which the Underwriter is to use its best efforts to find purchasers for such shares to be extended, by mutual agreement of the Company and the Underwriter, without limit. Should such period be extended, purchasers of shares the purchase price of which is deposited with the escrow agent will lose the use of, and will not receive a return on, the funds so deposited, and the Company will be unable to utilize funds so deposited in its business, until the completion of the financing.

## Item 3. *Use of Proceeds to Registrant*

The registrant is required to state the principal purposes for which the net proceeds from the securities to be offered are intended to be used, and the approximate amount intended to be used for each such purpose. It is not necessary to present a detailed explanation of the proposed use of the proceeds. Only a brief outline is required.

The following are explanations of the use of proceeds that have been obtained from prospectuses:

*The Stephan Company.* Net proceeds to the Company, after payment of expenses, will be approximately $482,000.00. Of such sum the Company intends to use aprpoximately $63,000 for packaging equipment and modification of bottling machines. It is intended to use approximately $225,000 for sales promotion and $25,000 for advertising, primarily for the new products described herein under BUSINESS. The balance of $169,000 will be added to working capital and used to finance an increased finished products inventory.

*Chemtronic Corporation.* The net proceeds to the Company on the sale of the 200,000 shares offered herein, assuming all the shares are sold, will be approximately $324,000 after deducting certain expenses of approximately $13,500 payable by the Company. Of this total $52,225 will be used to repay bank loans. $33,000 of these bank loans were incurred within the twelve month period ending May 31, 1960—$9,000 to increase inventories, $11,000 increased accounts receivable, and $13,000 to purchase new equipment. Over a two-year period $70,000 of the net proceeds of this issue will be used to add two engineers and one technician to the Company's present research staff. To complete automation of production facilities the Company plans to spend $75,000 of the proceeds of this issue, and $100,000 will be used to finance increased inventories and accounts receivable. The balance of $26,-775 will be used for general corporate purposes or as required by any of the uses referred to above.

## Item 4. *Sales Otherwise than for Cash*

If any of the securities being registered are to be offered otherwise than for cash, it is necessary to state briefly:
1. the general purposes of the distribution,
2. the basis upon which the securities are to be offered,
3. the amount of compensation and other expenses of distribution,
4. and by whom they are to be borne.

Sales of this type are rare, but if contemplated, must be reported as indicated above.

## Item 5. *Capital Structure*

It is necessary to furnish information concerning each class of the registrant's securities other than those securities owned by the registrant or its totally-held subsidiaries.

The corporation is to furnish a tabular form as follows:

| Title of Class | Amount authorized or to be authorized | Amount outstanding as of a specified date within 90 days | Amount to be outstanding if all securities being registered are sold |
| --- | --- | --- | --- |

### Item 6. *Summary of Earnings*

The registrant is required to furnish in comparative columnar form a summary of:

1. each of the last five fiscal years or for the life of the registrant and its immediate predecessors, if less than five years, and
2. for any period between the end of the latest of such fiscal years and the date of the latest balance sheet furnished, and
3. for the corresponding period of the preceding fiscal year.

In connection with such summary, the registrant, whenever necessary, must reflect information or explanation of material significance to investors in appraising the results shown, or refer to such information or explanation elsewhere in the prospectus. The material that is set forth under this heading is the same as that generally contained in the profit and loss statements of the company.

In some offerings, the results of the operations for a three-, six- or nine-month period are set forth in the prospectus. If an unaudited summary for an interim period is included in the prospectus, a statement should be made that all adjustments necessary to a fair statement of the results of the interim period or periods have been included. For example, the following statement was made in the prospectus of:

> *Navigation Computer Corporation.* Sales, income before income taxes, and net income for the three months ended May 31, 1960, based on unaudited financial statements, amounted to $161,367, $13,621 and $10,046, respectively. In the opinion of the Company, such figures include all adjustments, consisting only of normal recurring accruals, necessary to present fairly the results of operations for that period.

Explanations are sometimes included in the summary. For example: Liberty Records, Inc. made the following statements in its prospectus:

> Liberty attributes the variances in its profit margins over the past five years to the following circumstances. In its initial years, Liberty was under-financed and had to resort to costly factoring of its accounts receivables. It had to seek out suppliers who would extend substantial credit, and was not in a position to obtain more favorable prices for pressing records and making

jackets. Liberty did not have an adequate Artists and Repertoire Staff to enable it to be selective in its earlier recordings, resulting in production of a number of recordings which could not be sold and which had to be scrapped.

## Item 7. *Organization of Registrant*

It is necessary for the registrant to state the year in which it was organized, its form of organization (such as a corporation, an unincorporated association or other appropriate statement) and the name of the State or other jurisdiction under the laws of which it was organized. It is customary to include additional information in this item as to the historical background of the company, mergers, successions, change of names, etc.

## Item 8. *Parents of Registrant*

The registrant must list all parents showing the basis of control and, as to each parent, the percentage of voting securities owned or other basis of control by its immediate parent, if any.

## Item 9. *Description of Business*

A great deal of thought and effort will go into a proper description of the registrant's business. The material included in this does not relate to the powers and objects specified in the Charter, but the actual business done and intended to be done. This includes the business of the parent company and its subsidiaries, if any. It would be well to renew the requirements of Form S-1 on this very important subject, which are as follows:

(a) Briefly describe the business done and intended to be done by the registrant and its subsidiaries and the general development of such business during the past five years. If the business consists of the production or distribution of different kinds of products or the rendering of different kinds of services, indicate, insofar as practicable, the relative importance of each product or service or class of similar products or services which contributed 15% or more to the gross volume of business done during the last fiscal year.

(b) Indicate briefly, to the extent material, the general competitive conditions in the industry in which the registrant and its subsidiaries are engaged or intend to engage, and the position of the enterprise in the industry. If several products or services are involved, separate consideration should be given to the principal products or services or classes of products or services.

A review of some recent prospectuses will be helpful in determining the material to be included under Item 9.

## A. *General*

*The Paddington Corporation.*   Since 1937 the Company has had the exclusive right to import J & B products for resale in the United States. For the terms of the present contract, which expires in 1975, see Contract with Justerini & Brooks, Ltd. under Business. The Company knows of no reason why its contractual arrangements with J & B will not be continued after the present contract expires, but the terms of future contracts cannot be determined at the present time.

## B. *Acquisitions*

*Western Publishing Company, Inc.*   In July, 1957 the Company acquired Kable Printing Company, a printer of magazine and catalogs by rotogravure and letterpress located at Mount Morris, Illinois, for a total of $3,948,932 in cash and 5% serial notes of the Company. In April, 1958 the Company at Aurora, Illinois, manufacturers of toys and educational items marketed under the name of "Magic Slate," a registered trademark.

## C. *Awards*

*Movielab Film Laboratories, Inc.*   In a poll of television commercial producers conducted in 1957 by Billboard Magazine, the Company received the last Billboard Award given, as the highest ranked East Coast laboratory in quality, speed and economy.

## D. *Backlog*

*Del Electronics Corp.*   As of July 21, 1960, the Company had a backlog of orders of approximately $80,000 as compared with a backlog of approximately $138,000 on July 31, 1959. This decrease in the backlog resulted from a lull in the electronics industry. The Company's business is not dependent upon patents to any extent.

## E. *Competition*

*MCA Inc.*   All the branches of the entertainment business in which the Company is engaged are highly competitive. The business of representing artists is extremely speculative. A large number of firms and individuals are engaged in this business; therefore, the Company's business can decrease or increase in significant proportions at any time.

## F. *Customers*

*ARCO Electronics, Inc.*   During the past two years the Company's customer coverage was extremely varied, no one customer accounting for more than 3% of its combined sales. During said period a total of less than 3% of the Company's combined sales were made directly to United States Government and Military agencies, through numerous small individual sales. None of said sales is subject to renegotiation.

### G. *Employee Relations*

*Interstate Finance Corporation.* The business of the Company requires experienced personnel. The Company conducts various types of training programs designed to teach the business to qualified personnel and to train them in handling increased responsibility. Employee relations have been excellent and the Company has made an effort to foster a continuing interest of its employees in the business by promoting qualified personnel within the organization to management positions in existing and newly-opened or acquired offices rather than hiring persons from outside the organization.

### H. *Foreign Sales*

*The Foxboro Co.* Foreign sales are significant. In 1959, sales (on a consolidated basis) for ultimate delivery outside of the United States amounted to roughly one-third of the consolidated sales of the Company and its subsidiaries. Of this one-third of sales outside of the United States, approximately one-third was made by the Company's British subsidiary, one-fifth by the Canadian subsidiary and the balance directly by the Company, except for a small amount by its recently organized Dutch subsidiary.

### I. *Government Contracts*

*Andersen Laboratories, Inc.* Substantially all of the Company's sales of delay lines have been made under contracts for or sub-contracts with contractors for the United States Government. As is usual in contracts of this type they are terminable at the convenience of the Government or of the parties with whom the Company contracts, or both. In the event of any such termination (not due to any default by the Company) the Company is entitled to receive payment of its costs and some profit. Government sales have not yet exceeded the statutory minimum and hence have not been subject to renegotiation under the Renegotiation Act of 1951.

### J. *Growth of Company*

*American Hospital Supply Corporation.* The growth of the business of the Company and its subsidiaries over the years is attributable to a number of factors, principally (a) the expanding demand for their products and services because of steadily increasing utilization of medical and hospital services by the public in the United States and abroad; (b) the addition of new lines of products and services to meet growing hospital needs, including supplies and equipment for use in connection with new techniques and therapies; (c) the development by the Company of an efficient sales organization composed of carefully recruited personnel who are schooled in hospital requirements, together with aggressive sales policies and methods and intensive market coverage; (d) the establishment by the Company of regional sales and distribution centers at strategic points throughout the nation; and (e) increasing emphasis on research.

## K. *Recent Developments*

*Movielab Film Laboratories, Inc.*  Increasing public interest in the use of sound for 8mm color and black and white movies has opened up an apparently significant new field. In order to serve its professional customers, the Company is presently adapting its mechanized equipment to process 8mm sound color and black and white film for home, educational and commercial use.

## L. *Seasonal Trends*

*Liberty Records, Inc.*  While Liberty was not in existence during a war, experience in the industry has indicated that shortages of materials, rationing and restrictions on distribution methods in a wartime economy would adversely affect Liberty's business. Similarly, its business would probably be adversely affected during periods of regional and/or nationwide economic depression because its products are not classifiable as necessities.

## M. *Trade Names*

*Sunset House Distributing Corp.*  The Company uses the name "Sunset House" in over 99% of its national advertising and catalogs, and management believes that this name is of substantial value to the business of the Company. The name "Sunset House" is not a registered trademark and is used by other businesses throughout the United States.

## Item 10. *Description of Property*

The registrant is required to state briefly the location and general character of its principal plants, offices, sales headquarters, warehouses, etc., as well as those of its subsidiaries. If any property is not held in fee or is held subject to any major encumbrance, it is necessary to explain the basis of the company's holdings. It is not necessary to describe the property in detail by legal descriptions. It is intended that the investor be reasonably informed as to the suitability, adequacy, productive capacity and extent of utilization of the facilities used in the enterprise.

## Item 11. *Organization within Five Years*

If the registrant was organized within the past five years, it is necessary to furnish the following information, as required in Form S-1:

(a) State the names of the promoters, the nature and amount of anything of value (including money, property, contracts, options or rights of any kind) received or to be received by each promoter directly or indirectly from the registrant, and the nature and amount of any assets, services or other consideration therefor received or to be received by the registrant. The term "promoter" is defined in Rule 405.

(b) As to any assets acquired or to be acquired by the registrant from a promoter, state the amount at which acquired or to be acquired and the principle followed or to be followed in determining the amount. Identify the persons making the determination and state their relationship, if any, with the registrant or any promoter. If the assets were acquired by the promoter within two years prior to their transfer to the registrant, state the cost thereof to the promoter.

## Item 12. *Pending Legal Proceedings*

The registrant is required to briefly describe any material pending legal proceedings, other than ordinary routine litigation incidental to the business, to which the registrant or any of its subsidiaries is a party or of which any of their property is the subject. The registrant must include the name of the court or agency in which the proceedings are pending, the date instituted and the principal parties thereto. Similar information must be furnished as to any proceedings known to be contemplated by governmental authorities. It is not necessary to give information with respect to any proceeding which involves primarily a claim for damages, if the amount involved, exclusive of interest and costs does not exceed 15% of the current assets of the registrant and its subsidiaries.

MCA Inc. in its prospectus reported:

In January, 1959, one of the Company's then affiliates, Music Corporation of America, was requested by the United States Department of Justice to make its files available for examination in connection with an investigation of alleged violations of the federal antitrust laws by talent agencies. Since that time, the Department of Justice has been investigating the Company's activities and those of its prior affiliates, predecessors and subsidiaries to determine whether there has been any such violations by the Company or by such affiliates, predecessors or subsidiaries. In the opinion of the Company and its counsel, no such violations have existed or do exist.

Item 13. *Capital Stock Being Registered*

Form S-1 requires the registrant to include in its prospectus the following information:

If capital stock is being registered, state the title of the class and furnish the following information:

(a) Outline briefly (1) dividend rights; (2) voting rights; (3) liquidation rights; (4) pre-emptive rights; (5) conversion rights; (6) redemption provisions; (7) sinking fund provisions; and (8) liability to further calls or to assessment by the registrant.

(b) If the rights of holders of such stock may be modified otherwise than by a vote of a majority or more of the shares outstanding, voting as a class, so state and explain briefly.

(c) Outline briefly any restriction on the re-purchase or redemption of shares by the registrant while there is any arrearage in the payment of dividends or sinking fund installments. If there is no such restriction, so state.

Only a brief summary of the provisions which are pertinent from an investment standpoint need be included. A complete legal description is not required. The following are examples taken from various prospectuses:

*Del Electronics Corp.* The holders of the Common Stock are entitled to one vote per share and have no pre-emptive, conversion, subscription, or redemption rights. In the event of liquidation, they are entitled to share ratably in the remaining net assets of the Corporation after the payment of all of its debts and obligations. The Common Stock is entitled to receive such dividends and at such times as are declared by the Board of Directors. All issued and outstanding shares of the Corporation are fully paid and non-assessable and the shares of Common Stock covered by this Prospectus, when issued in accordance with the terms set forth herein, will be fully paid and non-assessable. Section 71 of the Stock Corporation Law of the State of New York provides, however, that stockholders of a stock corporation shall be severally and jointly liable under certain circumstances for unpaid debts, wages and salaries to any laborers, servants and employees.

*Standard Motor Products, Inc.* The shares of Class A and Class B Capital Stock of the Company have non-cumulative voting rights which means that the holders of more than 50% of the shares voting for the election of directors can elect 100% of the directors if they choose to do so, and, in such event, the holders of the remaining less than 50% of the shares voting for the election of directors will not be able to elect any person or persons to the Board of Directors.

*Ginn and Company.* Holders of the Common Stock are not subject to call or assessment, but under certain circumstances stockholders of a Massachusetts business corporation are subject to liability for money due to operatives for services rendered within 6 months before demand made upon the corporation and its neglect or refusal to make such payment.

*Cook Coffee Co.* Holders of Common Stock are entitled to dividends when and as declared by the Board of Directors. In the agreement relating to the Term Bank Loan, the Company has agreed not to pay cash dividends or purchase or redeem any of its stock or make other distribution to its shareholders if, after giving effect thereto, the aggregate of all such dividends, purchases, redemptions or distributions from January 4, 1959 to the date of the transaction in question would exceed the aggregate of the Company's available earnings (consolidated net earnings, as defined, in excess of $500,000 per year) cumulated from January 4, 1959 to the close of the last preceding accounting period of the Company. At September 10, 1960, retained earnings were unrestricted to the extent of $213,962.00.

*American Title Insurance Company.* The Common Stock is non-assessable; however, under Florida law the Board of Directors is permitted in certain circumstances, but not required, to call upon stockholders for additional payments. A stockholder who fails to comply with the Board's request may have his stock interest proportionately reduced, but in no event can he be required to make any additional payments on his Common Stock. See caption "Description of the Company's Common Stock."

## Item 14. *Long-Term Debt Being Registered*

Form S-1 requires the following to be included in the prospectus:

(a) Provisions with respect to interest, conversion, maturity, redemption, amortization, sinking fund or retirement.

(b) Provisions with respect to the kind and priority of any lien securing the issue, together with a brief identification of the principal properties subject to such lien.

(c) Provisions restricting the declaration of dividends or requiring the maintenance of any ratio of assets, the creation or maintenance of reserves or the maintenance of properties.

(d) Provisions permitting or restricting the issuance of additional securities, the withdrawal of cash deposited against such issuance, the incurring of additional debt, the release or substitution of assets securing the issue, the modification of the terms of the security, and similar provision.

(e) The name of the trustee and the nature of any material relationship with the registrant or any of its affiliates; the percentage of securities of the class necessary to require the trustee to take action, and what indemnification the trustee may require before proceeding to enforce the lien.

(f) The general type of event which constitutes a default and whether or or not any periodic evidence is required to be furnished as to the absence of default or as to compliance with the terms of the indenture.

## Item 15. *Other Securities Being Registered*

If securities other than capital stock or long-term debt are being registered, it is necessary to outline briefly the rights. If subscription warrants or rights are being registered, it is necessary to state the title and amount of securities called for, the period during which and the price at which the warrants or rights are exercisable.

## Item 16. *Directors and Executive Officers*

This item requires the registrant to list the names of all directors and executive officers of the registrant and all persons chosen to become directors or executive officers. It is necessary to indicate all positions and offices held by each person named in the company and the principal occupations during the past five years of each executive officer and each person chosen to become an executive officer.

If any person chosen to become a director or executive officer has not consented to act as such, it is necessary to state this fact.

## Item 17. *Remuneration of Directors and Officers*

Form S-1 requires the following of the registrant:

(a) Furnish the following information in substantially the tabular form indicated below as to all direct remuneration paid by the registrant and its subsidiaries during the registrant's last fiscal year to the following persons for services in all capacities:

(1) Each director, and each of the three highest paid officers, of the registrant whose aggregate direct remuneration exceeded $30,000, naming each such person.

(2) All directors and officers of the registrant as a group, without naming them.

| (A)                                           | (B)                                                | (C)                                      |
| --------------------------------------------- | -------------------------------------------------- | ---------------------------------------- |
| *Name of individual or identity of group*     | *Capacities in which remuneration was received*    | *Aggregate direct remuneration*          |

This item applies to any person who was a director or officer of the registrant at any time during the period specified. The information is to be given on an accrual basis, if practicable.

Form S-1 also requires the registrant to:

Furnish the following information, in substantially the tabular form indicated below, as to all pension or retirement benefits proposed to be paid under any existing plan in the event of retirement at normal retirement date, directly or indirectly, by the registrant or any of its subsidiaries to each director or officer named in answer to the paragraph above:

| (A) | (B) | (C) |
|---|---|---|
| | Amounts set aside or accrued during registrant's | Estimated annual benefits upon |
| Name of individual | last fiscal year | retirement |

The term "plan" includes all plans, contracts, authorizations or arrangements, whether or not set forth in any formal document.

The following material obtained from prospectuses indicates how remuneration of officers and directors is described:

Item 18. *Options to Purchase Securities*

Under the requirements of Form S-1, the registrant must:

Furnish the following information as to options to purchase securities from the registrant or any of its subsidiaries, which are outstanding as of a specified date within 30 days prior to the date of filing.

(a) Describe the options, stating the material provisions including the consideration received and to be received for such options by the grantor thereof and the market value of the securities called for on the granting date. If, however, the options are "restricted stock options" as defined in Section 421 of the Internal Revenue Code of 1954 only the following is required:

(i) a statement to that effect,

(ii) a brief description of the terms and conditions of the options or of the plan pursuant to which they were issued, and

(iii) a statement of the provisions of the plan or options with respect to the relationship between the option price and the market price of the securities at the date when the options were granted, or with respect to the terms of any variable price option.

(b) State (i) the title and amount of the securities called for by such options; (ii) the purchase prices of the securities called for and the expiration dates of such options; and (iii) the market value of the securities called for by such options as of the latest practicable date.

(c) Furnish separately the information called for by paragraph (b) above for all options held by (i) each director or officer named in answer to paragraph (a) (1) of Item 17 naming each such person, and (ii) all directors and officers as a group without naming them.

The following is an example of options to purchase securities as described in a prospectus:

*Cook Coffee Co.* While the Company does not have a stock option plan, the Board of Directors from time to time has granted stock options to key employees. During the last five years options covering a total of 78,030 shares of Common Stock were granted to 41 employees. The options with respect to 18,500 of these shares were canceled by reason of terminations of employment. The only officers or directors of Cook Coffee Company who received options were Charles G. Roth, Herbert F. McVay, Ralph R. Luffler and Mae Hoffman, and Edward E. Ornstein, who was an officer and director at the time options were granted to him.

The purpose of the options was to offer key employees benefits comparable to those which would be available to them in other employment and to enable and encourage them to acquire a proprietary interest in the Company through investment in its stock. The Company believes that these options have increased the continuity of employment and that they have provided key employees additional incentive for increasing the Company's profit.

## Item 19. *Principal Holders of Securities*

Form S-1 requires the registrant to:

Furnish the following information as of a specified date within 90 days prior to the date of filing in substantially the tabular form indicated:

(a) As to the voting securities of the registrant owned of record or beneficially by each person who owns of record, or is known by the registrant to own beneficially, more than 10 per cent of any class of such securities. Show in Column (3) whether the securities are owned both of record and beneficially, of record only, or beneficially only, and show in Columns (4) and (5) the respective amount and percentages owned in each such manner:

| (1) | (2) | (3) | (4) | (5) |
|---|---|---|---|---|
| | *Title of* | *Type of* | *Amount* | *Percent of* |
| *Name and Address* | *Class* | *Ownership* | *Owned* | *Class* |

(b) As to each class of equity securities of the registrant or any of its parents or subsidiaries, other than directors' qualifying shares, beneficially owned directly or indirectly by all directors and officers of the registrant, as a group, without naming them.

## Item 20. *Interest of Management and Others in Certain Transactions*

It is necessary to describe briefly, and where practicable to state the approximate amount of any material interest, direct or indirect, of any of the following persons in any material transactions during the last three years, or in any material proposed transactions, to which the registrant or any of its subsidiaries was, or is to be, a party:

(a) Any director or officer of the registrant;
(b) Any security holder named in answer to Item 19 (a);
(c) Any associate of any of the foregoing persons.

The name of each person whose interest is described in any transaction should be included as well as the nature of the relationship. Form S-1 spells out numerous cases where information need not be given in answer to this item.

## Item 21. *Financial Statements*

Form S-1 requires the registrant to:

Include in the prospectus all financial statements called for by the Instructions as to Financial Statements for this form, except as provided in paragraphs (a) and (b) below:

(a) All schedules to balance sheets and profit and loss statements may be omitted from the prospectus except (1) those prepared in accordance with Rules 12–16 and 12–32 of Regulation S-X which are applicable to balance sheets and profit and loss statements included in the prospectus, and (2) those prepared in accordance with Rule 12–27 in Regulation S-X which are applicable to a company's latest balance sheet included in the prospectus. All historical information required by Part E of the Instructions as to Financial Statements may also be omitted from the prospectus.

(b) If either the profit and loss or earned surplus statements required are included in their entirety in the summary of earnings required by Item 6, the statements so included need not be otherwise included in the prospectus or elsewhere in the registration statement.

Reference to some recent prospectuses indicates the following qualification and explanation relating to the financial statements:

*Chicago Musical Instrument Co.* We observed and tested the physical inventories of Chicago Musical Instrument Co. as of April 30, 1960 and 1959, but we were not present to observe the physical inventories taken as of April 30, 1958 and 1957, as those dates were prior to our initial engagement as auditors for the company. We did, however, test check the pricing and clerical accuracy of those inventories and we made tests of the quantities of certain selected items by tracing receipts and shipments. We also made certain over-all analytical and statistical tests of operating data. Nothing came to our attention in the course of making these tests which caused us to question the credibility of those inventories.

*Win-Chek Industries, Inc.*   Inventories on January 31, 1959, 1958, and 1957 were not based upon physical counts but were computed by the gross profit percentage method. This procedure may have produced variations in the profit reported as between the respective periods. However, based upon the auditing procedures that we applied, nothing came to our attention which would lead us to believe that the aforementioned inventories are not fairly stated.

*Victor Paint Co.*   Because we were not engaged as auditors of the company until 1960, we were not present to observe the taking of physical inventories at the beginning and end of each period in the two years and eleven months period ended November 30, 1959. Moreover, records are not available with respect to the physical inventories at December 31, 1957. We did, however, observe the taking of physical inventories on September 30, 1960. The inventories at the beginning and end of each period in the two years and eleven months period ended November 30, 1959 were tested by us by means of statistical and other data, and, although there may be variations which would affect the reporting of earnings among the aforementioned periods, such inventories do not appear to be unreasonable.

Items 22–31 are not required in the Prospectus. It is important, however, to review them carefully. For complete details, reference should be made to Form S-1.

## Item 22. *Marketing Arrangements*

It is necessary to describe any arrangement to limit or restrict the sale of other securities of the same class as those to be offered, to stabilize the market and to withhold commissions.

## Item 23. *Other Expenses of Issuance and Distribution*

Under this item, the registrant furnishes a reasonably itemized statement of all expenses in connection with the issuance and distribution of the securities being registered, other than underwriting discounts and commissions. If any of the securities being registered are to be offered by stockholders, it is necessary to indicate the portion of such expenses to be borne by such stockholders.

## Item 24. *Relationship with Registrant of Experts Named in Registration Statement*

If any expert named in the registration statement as having prepared or certified any part thereof was employed for such purpose on a contingent basis or had a substantial interest in the registrant or was connected with the registrant as a promoter, underwriter, voting trustee, director, officer or employee, it is necessary to furnish a brief statement of the nature of such contingent basis, interest or connection. This applies to subsidiaries as well as the parent corporation.

## Item 25. *Sales to Special Parties*

It is necessary to name each person, other than underwriters or dealers, to whom any securities have been sold within the past six months, or are to be sold, by the registrant or any security holder for whose account any of the securities being registered are to be offered, at a price varying from that at which securities of the same class are to be offered to the general public pursuant to the registration. The registrant is required to state the consideration given or to be given by each such person or class.

## Item 26. *Recent Sales of Unregistered Securities*

It is necessary to furnish the following information as to all securities of the registrant sold by the registrant within the past three years, which were not registered under the Securities Act of 1933.

(a) The date of sale and the title and amount of securities sold.
(b) The names of the principal underwriters, if any.
(c) As to securities sold for cash, the aggregate offering price and the aggregate underwriting discounts of commissions.
(d) The section of the act under which exemption from registration was claimed.

## Item 27. *Subsidiaries of Registrant*

In completing this item, the registrant must furnish a list or diagram of all subsidiaries of the registrant, and as to each such subsidiary indicate: (1) the State or other jurisdiction under the laws of which it was organized, and (2) the percentage of voting securities owned or other basis of control, by its immediate parent.

### Item 28. *Franchises and Concessions*

The registrant at this point sets forth briefly the general effect of all material franchises and concessions held by the registrant and its subsidiaries.

### Item 29. *Indemnification of Directors and Officers*

The registrant outlines the general effect of any charter provision, by-law, contract, arrangement or statute under which any director or officer of the registrant is insured or indemnified in any manner against any liability which he may incur in his capacity as such.

### Item 30. *Treatment of Proceeds from Stock Being Registered*

If capital stock is being registered and any portion of the consideration to be received by the registrant for such stock is to be credited to an account other than the appropriate capital stock account, it is necessary to state as to what other account such portion is to be credited and the estimated amount per share. If the consideration from the sale of par value shares is less than par value, the registrant is to state the amount per share involved and its treatment in the accounts.

### Item 31. *Financial Statements and Exhibits*

This item requires the listing of all financial statements and exhibits filed as a part of the registration statement. This includes:

(a) Financial statements, indicating those included in the prospectus.
(b) Exhibits.
(c) Statement of eligibility and qualification of each person designated to act as trustee under an indenture to be qualified under the Trust Indenture Act of 1939.

### Additional Information

The prospectus normally has a section which provides for general information which is not included in the major portions of the prospectus. For examples of additional information, see the following excerpt from the Simplicity Manufacturing Company prospectus which provides:

This Prospectus omits certain information contained in the Registration Statement on file with the Securities and Exchange Commission. For further information, reference is made to the Registration Statement and to the exhibits and financial statements filed therewith. Statements contained in this Prospectus as to the contents of any contract or other document referred to are not necessarily complete and where such contract or other document is an exhibit to the Registration Statement, each such statement is deemed to be qualified and amplified in all respects by the provisions of the exhibit.

## The "Red Herring" Prospectus

In your early discussions with your underwriter, you will hear the term "red herring" prospectus used very often. It is important that you have an understanding of the "red herring" prospectus, how it came about and the part that it plays in underwriting.

Under the Securities Act of 1933, a registration statement becomes effective on the twentieth day after the filing of the statement. Congress, in this Act, provided for a waiting period between the filing date of the registration statement and the effective date, to give the public and dealers every opportunity to study the proposed offering.

During the waiting period it is unlawful to make any sales or offers to sell the stock about to be offered to the public. Since the public does not have access to the registration statement, it became necessary to have a preliminary prospectus to give the public information about the stock that was to be offered at the end of the waiting period. Consequently, the "red herring" prospectus was devised, and it was provided that the "red herring" should be a summary of the material that was contained in the registration statement.

The "red herring" prospectus must not contain any material that could be construed to be an offer to purchase stock. Actually, the term "red herring" came about from the fact that there must be printed on the front cover of the preliminary prospectus, a statement, in red ink, which clearly points out that the prospectus is not an offer to sell nor is it a solicitation of an offer to buy any security.

On the cover page of each Preliminary Prospectus or "Red Herring" Prospectus, the following or similar statements are printed in red ink:

A Registration Statement relating to these securities has been filed with the Securities and Exchange Commission but has not yet become effective. Information contained herein is subject to completion or amendment. These securities may not be sold nor may offers to buy be accepted prior to the time the Registration Statement becomes effective. This Prospectus shall not constitute an offer to sell or the solicitation of an offer to buy, nor shall there be any sale of these securities in any State in which such offer, solicitation or sale would be unlawful prior to registration or qualification under the Securities Laws of any such State.

When the initial or preliminary "red herring" prospectus is printed and distributed to the public in general, it does not generally contain the offering price, the discounts to be paid to the underwriters or any other matters pertaining to the offering price. This information is contained in the final prospectus after the registrant has filed a price amendment with the SEC. The final prospectus must be sent to anyone who received a copy of the "red herring" prospectus.

# 26

## Letters of Comment

The Securities Exchange Commission reviews the registration statement, prospectus and financial material submitted to determine whether the disclosures made are adequate. The SEC will also review the material submitted to determine whether there are any statements included that may be misleading. The review work is carried out by the Division of Corporation Finance through its Division accountants, lawyers and analysts. Quite often the Division confers with engineers, other branches of the government, etc. It is possible to have conferences with the Division of Corporation Finance, should it be necessary to do so.

No sales may be made until the SEC advises that the registration is effective. Occasionally the Commission will not raise any question about the information submitted and will permit the registration to become effective as originally filed.

If the registration statement is not complete the Commission will mail a letter of comment to the person designated as "agent for service." In this letter, the SEC will request additional information and ask for explanations and substantiation of information previously given. These letters are sometimes referred to as "deficiency letters."

It is quite unusual that the registration statement will be permitted to become effective without need for amendments other than a price amendment. While great care and attention is given to the preparation of the statement and prospectus, it is only normal that the letter of comment will request some changes, further explanation or additional financial information.

It is necessary that immediate steps be taken to comply with the suggestions made in the letter of comment. If the amendments are not made, the Commission will refuse to accelerate the effective date of the registration. Upon receipt of a letter of comment, the representatives of the underwriter, the accountants and the lawyers should meet immediately with representatives of the company to discuss the amendments that must be made. Speed is essential, and there should be specific assignments to the various advisors to complete the amendments.

Quite often it will be necessary for your attorneys to contact the SEC by telephone for a further discussion of the amendments required. In certain instances it might even be necessary for them to arrange a personal conference with the representatives of the SEC as a meeting may readily clarify the points raised in the letter of comment.

If some or all of the stock is to be sold by stockholders, the Commission asks for a statement signed by the selling stockholders disclosing the reasons why they are disposing of a portion of their holdings and whether they know of any matters which might adversely affect the business and income of the company.

At the time the registration statement and the "deficiency" amendment are filed with the Security and Exchange Commission, generally no fixed agreement exists between the underwriter and the seller of the Securities as to the public offering price or the underwriter's discounts or commissions. Conditions change daily and the final price determination is not usually made until the day before the stock is to be offered to the public. Immediately prior to the offering date, a "price" amendment will be prepared by the attorneys for the company and the underwriters. The amendment will be filed with the SEC and will contain the final offering price and the commissions to be paid to the underwriters.

This will be the price and the commission that you have negotiated on the final day with your underwriter. When the price amendment is filed, a request for acceleration should be made to the Commission so that there will be no further delay in offering the issue to the public.

*Effective Date.* The Commission will review the amendments and if there are no further deficiencies, the Commission will permit the registration statement to become effective and will advise the person designated as agent for service by telegram that the registration statement as amended is effective as of the date of the telegram. The underwriters are then permitted to sell the securities to the public.

The Secretary of the Security and Exchange Commission will send to the agent for the company a copy of the order of the Commission fixing the effective date of the registration statement. The order will contain the following statements:

> Attention is directed to Rule 424(b) of the General Rules and Regulations under the Securities Act of 1933, and amended, relating to the requirement for the filing of twenty-five copies of the actual prospectus used.

> Attention also is directed to the provisions of Sec. 23 of the Securities Act of 1933, as amended, which follows: "Neither the fact that the registration statement for a security has been filed or is in effect nor the fact that a stop order is not in effect with respect thereto shall be deemed a finding by the

Commission that the registration statement is true and accurate on its face or that it does not contain an untrue statement of fact or omit to state a material fact, or be held to mean that the Commission has in any way passed upon the merits of, or given approval to, such security. It shall be unlawful to make, or cause to be made, to any prospective purchaser any representation contrary to the foregoing provisions of this section."

### Withdrawal of the Registration Statement

Circumstances may arise during the "waiting period" where the issuer decides to withdraw the registration statement. How can the statement be withdrawn? The SEC, through its rules, has made provision for the withdrawal of a registration statement or amendment upon application to the Commission. A review of the application and the grounds for withdrawal will be made by the SEC. If the Commission permits the withdrawal, it will not, however, refund the fees paid upon registration. If the registration statement has become effective and securities have been sold to the public, the Commission will not permit a withdrawal of the registration statement.

# 27

## Sanctions under the Securities Act of 1933

There are four principal types of sanctions which may be invoked under the Securities Act of 1933. They are stop orders, injunctions, criminal penalties and civil liabilities. It is important that every registrant be familiar with the penalties and liabilities which may be imposed in the event that there is a violation of any part of the Act.

### Stop Order

The SEC, if it determines that there are any untrue statements or any omissions of material fact in the registration statement after notice and an opportunity for a hearing, may enter a "stop order" suspending the effectiveness of the registration statement. This prevents the sale of the security through the mails or other channels of interstate commerce.

It would be well to refer to section 8(d) of the Securities Act of 1933 which provides as follows:

> If it appears to the Commission at any time that the registration statement includes any untrue statement of a material fact or omits to state any material fact required to be stated therein or necessary to make the statements therein not misleading, the Commission may, after notice by personal service or the sending of confirmed telegraphic notice, and after opportunity for hearing (at a time fixed by the Commission) within fifteen days after such notice by personal service or the sending of such telegraphic notice, issue a stop order suspending the effectiveness of the registration statement. When such statement has been amended in accordance with such stop order the Commission shall so declare and thereupon the stop order shall cease to be effective.

The SEC has suspended many registration statements over the years. For example, in one case, suspension was on the following grounds:

   a. Failure to state that five underwriters had been named to distribute the securities.

130

 b. Inconsistent statements concerning the proposed use of the proceeds from the sale.

 c. Failure to state that the registrant had no experienced personnel to participate in its proposed management of companies in which it would invest.

 d. Non-disclosure of the highly competitive nature of the business in the area where registrant proposed to operate.

 e. Misleading statements concerning stock options and membership on the Board of Directors.

In another case the Commission suspended the effectiveness of a registration statement on the following basis:

 a. Failure to disclose that no market study had been made and that the product which registrant planned to produce presented difficulties and higher costs in production.

 b. Misleading representations concerning the registrant's estimated costs of building its plant.

 c. Misleading representation concerning raw material deposits.

 d. Failure to disclose the liquidation and dividend rights of the stock.

 e. Failure to accurately report experience of the company officers.

In some instances the registrant attempts to correct the deficiencies by amendments. However, the Commission might well refuse the amendment in view of the material nature of the deficiencies.

## Injunction

If the SEC determines that a person is engaged or is about to engage in a violation of the Act or the rules of the SEC, it may apply to the Federal Court to seek an injunction to prevent further violation of the law.

## Criminal Proceedings

The law, Section 24 of the Securities Act of 1933, provides that any person who willfully violates the Act or the rules of the SEC or who willfully makes any untrue statement of a material fact or omits to state any material fact required in a registration statement, is guilty of a crime. The law further provides that upon conviction the violator may be fined not more than $5,000 or imprisoned for not more than five years, or both.

## Civil Liability

The Securities Act of 1933 provides in Section 11 that after the registration is effective, civil actions may be brought under certain conditions by persons acquiring securities against every signer of the registration statement, directors, accountants, engineers, underwriters, etc.

It is important that you have a complete understanding of the law and its implications. The following provisions shall be carefully studied.

Section 11(a) of the Act provides:

> In case any part of the registration statement, when such part became effective, contained an untrue statement of a material fact or omitted to state a material fact required to be stated therein or necessary to make the statements therein not misleading, any person acquiring such security (unless it is proved that at the time of such acquisition he knew of such untruth or omission) may, either at law or in equity, in any court of competent jurisdiction, sue—
>
> 1. every person who signed the registration statement;
>
> 2. every person who was a director of (or person performing similar functions) or partner in, the issuer at the time of the filing of the part of the registration statement with respect to which his liability is asserted;
>
> 3. every person who, with his consent, is named in the registration statement as being or about to become a director, person performing similar functions, or partner;
>
> 4. every accountant, engineer, or appraiser, or any person whose profession gives authority to a statement made by him, who has with his consent been named as having prepared or certified any part of the registration statement, or as having prepared or certified any report or valuation which is used in connection with the registration statement, with respect to the statement in such registration statement, report, or valuation, which purports to have been prepared or certified by him;
>
> 5. every underwriter with respect to such security.

A different set of rules applies after one year. Section 11(a) states:

> If such person acquired the security after the issuer has made generally available to its security holders an earning statement covering a period of at least 12 months beginning after the effective date of the registration statement, then the right of recovery under this sub-section shall be conditioned on proof that such person acquired the security relying upon such untrue statement in the registration statement or relying upon the registration statement and not knowing of such omission, but such reliance may be established without proof of the reading of the registration statement by such person.

Under the provisions of Sec. 11(b) of the Securities Act of 1933, a person sued, except the issuer, may absolve himself from liability if he can sustain the burden of proof that

1. before the effective date of the part of the registration statement with respect to which his liability is asserted (A) he had resigned from or had taken such steps as are permitted by law to resign from, or ceased or refused to act in, every office, capacity, or relationship in which he was described in the registration statement as acting or agreeing to act, and (B) he had advised the Commission and the issuer in writing that he had taken such action and that he would not be responsible for such part of the registration statement; or

2. if such part of the registration statement became effective without his knowledge, upon becoming aware of such fact he forthwith acted and advised the Commission, in accordance with paragraph (1), and, in addition, gave reasonable public notice that such part of the registration statement had become effective without his knowledge; or

3. (A) as regards any part of the registration statement not purporting to be made on the authority of an expert, and not purporting to be a copy of or extract from a report or valuation of an expert, and not purporting to be made on the authority of a public official document or statement, had, after reasonable investigation, reasonable ground to believe and did believe, at the time such part of the registration statement became effective, that the statements therein were true and that there was no omission to state a material fact required to be stated therein or necessary to make the statements therein not misleading; and (B) as regards any part of the registration statement purporting to be made upon his authority as an expert or purporting to be a copy of or extract from a report or valuation of himself as an expert, (i) he had, after reasonable investigation, reasonable ground to believe and did believe, at the time such part of the registration statement became effective, that the statements therein were true and that there was no omission to state a material fact required to be stated therein or necessary to make the statements therein not misleading, or (ii) such part of the registration statement did not fairly represent his statement as an expert or was not a fair copy of or extract from his report or valuation as an expert; and (C) as regards any part of the registration statement purporting to be made on the authority of an expert (other than himself) or purporting to be a copy of or extract from a report or valuation of an expert (other than himself), he had no reasonable ground to believe and did not believe, at the time such part of the registration statement became effective, that the statements therein were untrue or that there was an omission to state a material fact required to be stated therein or necessary to make the statements therein not misleading, or that such part of the registration statement did not fairly represent the statement of the expert or was not a fair copy of or extract from the report or valuation of the expert; and (D) as regards any part of the registration statement purporting to be a statement made by an official person or purporting to be a copy of or extract from a public

official document, he had no reasonable ground to believe and did not believe, at the time such part of the registration statement became effective,
that the statements therein were untrue, or that there was an omission
to state a material fact required to be stated therein or necessary to make
the statements therein not misleading, or that such part of the registration
statement did not fairly represent the statement made by the official person or was not a fair copy of or extract from the public official document.

*Note:* In determining, for the purpose of paragraph (3) of subsection (b)
of this section, what constitutes reasonable investigation and reasonable ground for belief, the standard of reasonableness shall be that required of a prudent man in the management of his own property.

In no case shall the amount recoverable exceed the price at which the security
was offered to the public.

The issuer or other persons sued may also limit the damages recovered by the
buyer by proving that there were other circumstances beside the registration
statement that lowered the value of the stock.

Under Section 12 of the Act, a person may be held liable in a civil suit if he
sells or offers to sell through the mail or in interstate commerce a security that
is non-exempt or non-registered. Section 12 provides that any person who:

1. offers or sells a security in violation of section 5, or
2. offers to or sells a security (whether or not exempted by the provisions of
   section 3, other than paragraph (2) of subsection (a) thereof), by the
   use of any means or instruments of transportation or communication in
   interstate commerce or of the mails, by means of a prospectus or oral
   communication, which includes an untrue statement of a material fact
   or omits to state a material fact necessary in order to make the statements, in the light of the circumstances under which they were made, not
   misleading (the purchaser not knowing of such untruth or omission),
   and who shall not sustain the burden of proof that he did not know, and
   in the exercise of reasonable care could not have known, of such untruth or omission, shall be liable to the person purchasing such security
   from him, who may sue either at law or in equity in any court of competent jurisdiction, to recover the consideration paid for such security
   with interest thereon, less the amount of any income received thereon,
   upon the tender of such security, or for damages if he no longer owns
   the security.

## Limitation of Actions

The Securities Act of 1933 provides for a limitation of civil actions. Sec. 13
provides:

No action shall be maintained to enforce any liability created under section 11 or section 12 (2) unless brought within one year after the discovery of the untrue statement or the omission, or after such discovery should have been made by the exercise of reasonable diligence, or, if the action is to enforce a liability created under section 12 (1), unless brought within one year after the violation upon which it is based. In no event shall any such action be brought to enforce a liability created under section 11 or section 12 (1) more than three years after the security was bona fide offered to the public, or under section 12 (2) more than three years after the sale.

# 28

## Advance Publicity and Speeches

*SEC Restrictions*

The Securities and Exchange Commission, through periodic releases, has defined the rules as to the publication of information both prior to and after the effective date of a registration statement. It is important that everyone in your company interested in a public stock offering be familiar with the rules. The consequences, if you deviate, can be very serious.

Generally speaking, while certain publicity may be properly released by the company, the Commission examines the content to determine if the company is intending to artificially stimulate the market. The Commission will want to know whether the release is part of a sales campaign designed to create a favorable attitude towards the securities to be offered.

The Commission, in a release issued October 8, 1957, #3844, stressed the limitations imposed upon persons engaged in the sale of securities and pointed out that the publicity and public relations activities under certain circumstances may involve violation of the securities laws and the imposition of civil suit and criminal liability.

A security may be offered legally after filing the registration statement and before the effective date of a registration statement provided the prospectus meets the standards of Section 10 (a) of the Act. In general, after the filing of the registration statement and before the effective date of the registration, no communication relating to a security may be transmitted through the mails or in interstate commerce other than a prospectus authorized or permitted by the statute.

An underwriter or issuer may not legally begin a public stock offering or initiate a public sales campaign prior to the filing of a registration statement. Publicity efforts, even though not containing an offer to sell securities, made in advance of a proposed offering may raise a question whether the publicity is not in fact part of the selling effort.

Similarly, a release of publicity between the filing date and the effective date of a registration statement often raises a question whether the publicity is not in fact a selling effort through an illegal means.

## Preparation of Press Releases

At the outset, it is important that you clear all press releases with your attorneys, public relations director, and underwriter, whether you issue the release prior to filing a registration statement or during the waiting period.

The Securities and Exchange Commission normally does not object to the announcement of a dividend, the receipt of a contract, a settlement of a strike, the opening of a plant, or any similar event of interest to the community in which the company operates. On the other hand, the Commission might well object to news items which play up the company's securities or discuss the financial aspects of the company ordinarily associated with the sale of securities. It is well to clear all these releases, routine as they may seem, with your legal advisors.

Another word of caution: Have your advisors meet with the executives of your company and review with them what may or may not be said publicly about your company before and during the registration period. This is a new problem for your executives, and it is important that they be thoroughly briefed.

Edward N. Gadsby, former Chairman of the Securities and Exchange Commission, Washington, D.C., in an address before the Central States Group of The Investment Bankers Association in Chicago, Illinois, explained the limitations on publicity as follows:

> An issuer or its officials or employees cannot legally begin to offer a security to the public prior to the filing of a registration statement, nor, as we see it, can they engage in a publicity campaign prior to the filing which is part of an effort or plan having for its purpose the sale to the public of a non-exempt security. This does not mean, of course, that a corporation which is planning to bring an issue to market must close its advertising department, dismiss its public relations people and gag its officials and employees.

> Most certainly an issuer may continue the normal conduct of its business and may communicate with its security holders and customers prior to the filing of a registration statement or during the so-called "waiting period." Thus, it may continue to publish advertisements of its products and services without interruption. It may send out its quarterly, annual and other periodic reports to its security holders. It may publish its proxy statements, send out its dividend notices and make routine announcements to the public press and to employees without objection from the Commission. Indeed, we do not normally regard these activities as any of our business nor do we wish to

be concerned with them. But when, shortly before the filing of a registration statement or during the pre-effective period, public communications of various sorts begin to appear which discuss such aspects of a business as its finances, its earnings or its growth prospects in glowing and optimistic terms, stressing the favorable over the unfavorable, I think we may be pardoned if we are so unkind as to suspect that this activity may not be entirely concerned with the sale of soap or machine tools or what have you.

Your publicity will be held up to the test, "Is the publicity part of a selling effort or an item of legitimate disclosure to investors unrelated to such an effort?" These are the words that were used by the SEC in the matter of Carl M. Loeb, Rhoades & Company and Dominick & Dominick, in a release dated February 9, 1959. The Commission stated:

> In the normal conduct of its business, a corporation may continue to advertise its products and services without interruption, it may send out its customary quarterly, annual and other periodic reports to security holders, and it may publish its proxy statements, send out its dividend notices and make routine announcements to the press.
>
> This flow of normal corporate news, unrelated to a selling effort for an issue of securities, is natural, desirable and entirely consistent with the objective of disclosure to the public which underlies the federal securities laws.

However, an issuer who is a party to or collaborates with underwriters or prospective underwriters in initiating or securing publicity must be regarded as participating directly or indirectly in an offer to sell or a solicitation of an offer to buy prohibited by Section 5 (c) of the Act.

The Commission in commenting on the reasons for the prohibition in the Carl M. Loeb, Rhoades & Co. case stated:

> The Congress in 1954 adopted a carefully worked out procedure to meet the problem. It is essentially as follows: (1) the strict prohibition of offers prior to the filing of a registration statement was continued: (2) during the period between the filing of a registration statement and its effective date offers but sales may not be only documents prescribed or processed by the Commission; and (3) sales continued to be prohibited prior to the effective date. In permitting, but limiting the manner in which pre-effective written offers might be made, the Congress was concerned lest inadequate or misleading information be used in connection with the distribution of securities. We were directed to pursue a vigorous enforcement policy to prevent this from happening. In obedience to this mandate we have made clear our position that the statute prohibits issuers, underwriters and dealers from initiating a public sales campaign prior to the filing of a registration statement by means

of publicity efforts which, even though not couched in terms of an express offer, condition the public mind or arouse public interest in the particular securities. Even if there might have been some uncertainty as to the Congressional intent with regard to pre-effective publicity prior to 1954, none should have existed thereafter. The Congress has specified a period during which, and a procedure by which, information concerning a proposed offering may be disseminated to dealers and investors. This procedure is exclusive and cannot be nullified by recourse to public relations techniques to set in motion or further the machinery of distribution before the statutory disclosures have been made and upon the basis of whatever information the distributor deems it expedient to supply. We accordingly conclude that publicity, prior to the filing of a registration statement by means of public media of communication, with respect to an issuer or its securities, emanating from broker-dealer firms who as underwriters or prospective underwriters have negotiated or are negotiating for the public offering of the securities of such issuer, must be presumed to set in motion or to be a part of the distribution process and therefore to involve an offer to sell or a solicitation of an offer to buy such securities prohibited by Section 5(c). Since it is unlawful under the statute for dealers to offer to sell or to offer to buy a security as to which registration is required, prior to the filing of a registration statement, dealers who are to participate in a distribution likewise risk the possibility that employment by them of public media of communication to give publicity to a forthcoming offering prior to the filing of a registration statement constitutes a premature sales activity prohibited by Section 5(c).

The Commission, in Release No. 3844, gave the following examples of prohibited public relations activities:

*Example.* An underwriter-promoter is engaged in arranging for the public financing of a mining venture to explore for a mineral which has certain possible potentialities for use in atomic research and power. While preparing a registration statement for a public offering, the underwriter-promoter distributed several thousand copies of a brochure which described in glowing generalities the future possibilities for use of the mineral and the profit potential to investors who would share in the growth prospects of a new industry. The brochure made no reference to any issuer or any security nor to any particular financing. It was sent out, however, bearing the name of the underwriting firm and obviously was designed to awaken an interest which later would be focused on the specific financing to be presented in the prospectus shortly to be sent to the same mailing list.

The distribution of the brochure under these circumstances clearly was the first step in a sales campaign to effect a public sale of the securities and as such, in the view of the Commission, violated Section 5 of the Securities Act.

*Example.* An issuer in the promotional stage intended to offer for public sale an issue of securities the proceeds of which were to be employed to explore for and develop a mineralized area. The promoters and prospective underwriter prior to the filing of the required registration statement or notification under Regulation A arranged for a series of press releases describing the activities of the company, its proposed program of development of its properties, estimates of ore reserves and plans for a processing plant. This publicity campaign continued after the filing of a registration statement and during the period of the offering. The press releases, which could be easily reproduced and employed by dealers and salesmen engaged in the sales effort, contained representations, forecasts and quotations which could not have been supported as reliable data for inclusion in a prospectus or offering circular under the sanctions of the Act.

It is the Commission's view that issuing information of this character to the public by an issuer or underwriter through the device of the press release and the press interview is an evasion of the requirements of the Act governing selling procedures, a violation of Sections 5 and 17(a) of the Act, and that such activity subjects the seller to the risk of civil and penal sanctions and liabilities of the Act.

*Example.* An issuer filed a registration statement for an issue of securities to be offered through underwriters. Following the effective date of the registration statement, efforts to market the issue were not wholly successful and a substantial amount of the securities remained in the hands of the underwriters and dealers. At this point the issuer published an advertisement which received wide newspaper and magazine circulation and which included data purporting to show reserves of raw materials in terms of estimated future dollar realization per share. The advertisement took the conventional form of a product advertisement except for the inclusion of calculations of per-share asset values.

The Commission brought an action to enjoin further publication of the advertisement on the theory that its content and use, at a time when the existence of unsold allotments in the hands of underwriters and dealers indicated clearly that the distribution of the registered securities had not been completed, involved a violation of Sections 5 and 17(a) of the Securities Act.

## Press Release on Filing Date

At the time that your company files its registration statement with the Securities and Exchange Commission, consideration should be given to preparing a simple release which can be given to the newspapers. The material contained in the release and the legality of preparing such a release should be carefully checked with your attorneys and the underwriter to be sure that there is complete compliance with the law.

The release will normally make reference to such matters as the filing of the registration statement with the SEC, the business of the company, the number of shares to be sold, the identity of the seller (company or stockholders), purpose of the proposed sale and the name of the principal underwriter.

# 29

## Due Diligence Meeting

Prior to the effective date of the SEC registration, your principal underwriter usually will arrange for a meeting between the representatives of the company and the underwriting firms who will participate in the public offering. This get-together, referred to as either a "Due Diligence" or "Underwriters Meeting" is called to give the members of the underwriting group an opportunity to make a reasonable investigation of the company to protect themselves from the sanctions imposed under Sec. 11 (a) of the Securities Act of 1933.

*Participants*

It would be well for the company accountants and attorneys as well as the principal officers of the company to be present at the meeting. The company's background, present operations, future plans, competitive position, financial matters, etc., will be discussed. The representatives of the underwriters should be given ample opportunity to ask questions about the company as well as the material contained in the registration statement and the prospectus. Some questions should be answered by the attorneys or the accountants for the company. These meetings are very important and preparation should be made in advance as to the method of presentation, material to be included, etc. Look upon the meeting as an opportunity to fully present the complete story of your company to the underwriters who will be marketing the stock to the public. Answer the questions asked of you fairly and completely. The impression that is formed of you and the other members of your management group will play an important role in the future success of your company's public stock offering.

The managing underwriter will arrange the meeting and will invite all of the underwriters who are participating in your issue. These firms will send one of their representatives to the meeting. The president of the company will be introduced to the group by the managing underwriter. It is suggested that the president make a 15 to 20 minute presentation and that his business associates also participate. The officers and directors of the company who are in attendance should also be introduced.

### Presentation

Plan your presentation carefully. Discuss the subjects to be presented with your Public Relations Counsellors, your attorney and your accountants. Remember, this is not a sales meeting in the ordinary sense where you introduce a new product or service. At the Due Diligence meeting, you are presenting in effect your company, its past, present, future and its growth potential. Be certain that all the facts and figures which you use are completely accurate. If your presentation is well made, the representatives of the underwriters will sell your company's stock with confidence and pride.

### Post Presentation Discussion

After the formal presentation, the representatives of the underwriters, through questioning, will want to get further information about some items discussed or omitted. They will have the "red herring" prospectus before them and normally they will want to have a further discussion of some of the points made in the prospectus. Again, it is of utmost importance that you be candid in your presentation. Keep in mind that normally the groups you are addressing are sophisticated and knowledgeable. They want facts and figures. They do not want wild statements that obviously cannot be substantiated. They want to receive from your presentation, sufficient information about your company so that they will develop a confidence in your company. If they are to sell your stock wisely and well, they must be informed through facts and figures of the values your company has

It is of great importance at this meeting that you be able to satisfy the representative of the underwriters that you and your associates are men of ability, integrity, sincerity, and will provide solid leadership to your company in the years ahead. It is highly desirable that the underwriters' representatives leave the meeting completely convinced not only of the growth potential of your company but of the executive capacity of your group.

### BLUE SKY LAWS

In your talks with your underwriters and attorneys, you will be told about the need to qualify the proposed stock issue under various state "Blue Sky Laws." This refers to the various state statutes which regulate the registration of securities to prevent promoters from making wild claims—"the sky is the limit."

Most states today require underwriters or dealers to register securities before sales may be made in their state. Even though your company has filed a registration statement with the SEC, it must comply with the various laws of the states where stock will be sold. The SEC Act does not interfere with the State Blue Sky Laws. Your attorney and the underwriter are in the best position to advise you as to the need for registration of securities in various states. State registration procedures vary. In some states it is only necessary to notify the state authorities of the intention to sell in the state while in other states it is necessary to qualify through a registration statement.

Where it is necessary to register in order to qualify in a state, an application must be made to the proper authorities in the state. Exhibits, statements, copies of the prospectus, financial information, etc. must be furnished in detail. After an examination of the files, the state agency, if satisfied, will grant a permit to sell the securities within the state. Until such a permit is granted, the securities may not be sold in the state.

In a few states, including New York, it is not necessary to qualify before the securities are to be offered to the public in the state. However, in these states, the Attorney General can bring an action to restrain the sale if he is of the opinion that there is fraud in the sale of the securities.

Your attorney, at the time of your SEC registration, together with attorneys for the underwriter, will advise you on the necessity of "blue skying" securities in various states. Generally, the attorneys for the underwriter, as part of the underwriting agreement, will furnish a memorandum setting forth the states in which the stock has been qualified for sale.

The attorneys set forth in this survey their advice as to the requirements that must be satisfied under the various security laws of the states before offers and solicitations of offers to buy the stock may be made orally or by means of written material. The survey will set forth the action required when the sales are made to the public generally.

The survey also will spell out the various state requirements on sales to certain classes of purchasers such as banks, savings institutions, trust companies, insurance companies, etc. It is customary that the seller pay the underwriters for the services of their attorneys in connection with the Blue Sky Survey and the filings under the various state laws.

Bear in mind that each state provides for sanctions in the event that its administrative agency determines that the sale of the securities in the state is fraudulent.

# 30

# "D Day," Speaking Engagements, Tombstone Ads and Stabilizing

Let's designate the day when the registration statement becomes effective as "D Day"—that is an important day in your corporate financing and one that you will want to be well prepared for.

Suppose September 15 is your company's "D Day"—the day when the price amendment is filed and the registration statement becomes effective. On September 14, "D minus 1," you and your advisors and underwriters will be busy getting set for "D Day." On that day, you and the underwriters will reach an informal agreement as to the public offering price and underwriting discounts. On September 15, D Day, these terms will be finalized and your Board of Directors will hold a special meeting, authorizing the execution of the Underwriting Agreement. On that day you will finally execute the Underwriting Agreement. The price amendment will be filed with the SEC, and the Blue Sky State qualifications will be completed.

On September 15, "D Day," the registration statement will become effective and you will receive your telegram from the SEC advising accordingly. The underwriters on "D Day" will release the tombstone ad for publication. The printer will commence the printing of the final prospectus so that distribution can be made to the underwriters the following morning.

On September 16, "D plus 1," the day after the registration becomes effective, the tombstone ad appears. This is the day the stock normally will be offered to the public. The underwriters and selling group members are released by the managing underwriter to commence selling the stock to the public. Frequently the sale is completed almost immediately because the stock offered has been oversubscribed. In such event, a press release announcing that the issue is oversubscribed is often forwarded to the financial press. On the other hand, if the stock does not sell readily, the books may be kept open for a longer period of time.

### Speaking Engagements

In planning your speaking engagements prior to the filing of a registration statement and during the pre-effective period, you should be guided by the comments of Edward N. Gadsby, former Chairman Securities and Exchange Commission, who stated in an address before the Central States Group of The Investment Bankers Association:

> Fairly frequent inquiry is made to us concerning the status of speeches by corporate officials before groups of financial analysts or similar trade organizations. We understand that such an address is usually scheduled by the societies some time in advance at a time when there may be no contemplation of an offering. It sometimes happens that the date so scheduled for the speech is sufficiently close to a proposed filing of a registration statement as to cause some concern to counsel for the issuer or underwriter.

> I do not believe that the Commission has ever expressed the view that such a speaking engagement made in advance with a financial analysts' society should be cancelled or even rescheduled. We think it is incumbent upon the executive, however, not to phrase his talk in such a manner as to constitute a selling effort, and we have from time to time expressed the view that any public distribution of the speech and of the material sometimes employed in connection therewith might well raise a serious problem under Section 5.

> Perhaps I can point up the latter observation to some extent. I think you would all agree that an issuer or an official of an issuer could not properly distribute to the public, or to a group of people who might redistribute to the public, copies of a draft of a Securities Act prospectus with the old red-herring legend prior to the filing of a registration statement. The parallel is, to my mind, perfectly clear. And it is generally conceded, I hope, that a person should not be permitted in this field to do indirectly that which he should not do directly.

After your Company's stock offering it will be necessary to maintain a continuing public relations program. In all likelihood you will need a more dynamic public relations program than you had prior to becoming a publicly-held corporation.

### Tombstone Ads

During your discussions with your underwriter, reference will be made frequently to the placement of "tombstone ads." While it is an ominous sounding term, it is one that is commonly used to describe the announcement of the issue in the press. The information to be included in the ad is limited. It is possible under SEC Regulations to place an ad containing the name of the issuer of the security, full title of the security, the amount being offered, the price that the security will be offered at, and the name of the underwriters.

Remember that these "tombstone ads" are not intended to be selling ads and must be carefully prepared to conform to the rules of the SEC. Their purpose is to advise anyone that is interested in purchasing the stock where the copy of the prospectus may be obtained.

Your underwriter will place these tombstone ads in various papers throughout the country. The ad will appear on the offering date in the business or financial section of leading financial and certain local newspapers, especially the *Wall Street Journal, The New York Times,* etc.

Generally the cost of the ad is borne by your underwriter. He normally will discuss with you the placement of these ads prior to the effective date of your registration.

The following is a sample of a tombstone ad:

> This announcement is not an offer to sell or a solicitation of an offer to buy any of these securities. The offering is made only by the prospectus.

NEW ISSUE

150,000 Shares

CARCO INDUSTRIES INC.

COMMON STOCK

(Par Value $.10 Per Share)

Price: $5.00 per share

A copy of the Prospectus may be obtained from the undersigned and from such other dealers as may lawfully offer these securities in this state.

Myron A. Lomasney & Co.
New York 4, N. Y.

Hallowell, Sulzberger, Jenks, Kirkland & Co.
Philadelphia 7, Penn.

| Robinson & Company | Kesselman & Co., Inc. | J. R. Holt & Co. |
| Philadelphia 2, Penn. | New York 5, New York | Denver 2, Colorado |
| Courts & Co. | P. De Rensis & Co., Inc. | Moran & Co. |
| Atlanta 1, Georgia | Boston 9, Mass. | Newark 2, N. J. |

*Stabilizing*

In your discussion with your investment banker, you will be told that at the initial sale of your company's stock, there will be some buyers who purchase shares with the intention of getting in for a fast rise and then selling. Your underwriters will try to limit the number of free riders—but try as they might, there will be those who will sell several days after acquiring stock at the initial offering price. This stock will get back into the open market and it could have an adverse effect on the balance of the unsold stock. The market price under such conditions could fall below the initial public offering price. In order to stabilize the market and prevent or retard a decline in the market price, the principal underwriter, acting on behalf of the syndicate, may enter bids to buy the stock offered by those wishing to sell in the early stages of the offering. Stabilization can not begin at a price above the then current bid price and, in any event, cannot occur at a price above which the security is currently distributed. The stabilizing purchases by the syndicate may run to 10 to 15 per cent of the issue.

Stabilizing, which in effect can be considered a form of manipulation, is permitted under the regulations of the Securities Exchange Commission—provided, of course, certain requirements are met. Stabilization is a highly technical practice and is accomplished on an infrequent basis.

The Securities and Exchange Commission has provided in Rule 426 of its General Rules and Regulations under the Securities Act of 1933 as follows:

> (a) If the registrant or any of the underwriters knows or has reasonable grounds to believe that there is an intention to over-allot or that the price of any security may be stabilized to facilitate the offering of the registered securities, there shall be set forth, on the outside front cover page of the prospectus, a statement in substantially the following form, subject to appropriate modifications where circumstances require. Such statement shall be in capital letters, printed in bold face roman type at least as large as 10-point modern type and at least 2 points leaded.
>
> IN CONNECTION WITH THIS OFFERING, THE UNDERWRITERS MAY OVER-ALLOT OR EFFECT TRANSACTIONS WHICH STABILIZE OR MAINTAIN THE MARKET PRICE OF (Identify each class of securities in which such transactions may be effected) AT A LEVEL ABOVE THAT WHICH MIGHT OTHERWISE PREVAIL IN THE OPEN MARKET. SUCH TRANSACTIONS MAY BE EFFECTED ON (Identify each exchange on which stabilizing transactions may be effected. If none, omit this sentence). SUCH STABILIZING, IF COMMENCED, MAY BE DISCONTINUED AT ANY TIME.

The SEC also requires the filing of detailed reports setting forth all stabilizing operations to facilitate the offering.

# 31

# Selection of Transfer Agent and Registrar

Your past experience with a transfer agent and a registrar may have been casual, and possibly you have had no previous reason to use the services of these corporate agents. If you are considering "going public," it would be a good idea to get better acquainted with these organizations—usually they are banks or trust companies—and develop an understanding of what they can do for your company.

A company whose stock is not listed on a stock exchange can perform its own stock transfer and registration operations. There is no legal requirement that an independent organization be appointed. Under this arrangement, the company keeps its own stockholders' certificate ledger and a transfer journal showing the day by day itemization of each transaction. The secretary's office is responsible for the original issuance of the stock, reissues of certificates, and conversion of certificates into smaller denominations.

*Appointing the Transfer Agent*

Most companies however, as they plan to go public, will appoint a transfer agent and a registrar. As a publicly owned corporation with a moderately small issue, your company may have 500–1,000 or 1,500 shareholders—most of them probably unknown to you. And very shortly after your public stock offering, some of these new shareowners are going to sell their stock; for whatever reason, it doesn't particularly matter. Regular trading in your company's shares is going to develop, meaning there will be changes of share ownership to record on your stock ledgers, practically daily.

Absolute accuracy is a "must" in handling transfers because any errors could lead to claims against the company and possible financial liability. With only a small group of stockholders, the chances are fewer that a mistake could be made. These chances are multiplied many times when the stockholder list grows to

149

hundreds or thousands. The transfer agent assumes the responsibility of making sure that mistakes in stock transfers do not occur.

### Steps in the Transfer

There are specific steps a transfer agent takes in transferring ownership of shares from one person to another. Let's follow the procedure.

1. The transfer agent checks to determine whether the transfer stamps, if required, are affixed in the proper amount. The federal government and the states hold the corporation responsible for seeing that these stamps are affixed. If inspectors find that transfers are entered on a corporation's stock ledger without proper stamps, the corporation can be held liable for the penalty if it handles its own transfers.

2. The seller of securities must endorse the stock certificate at the time of the sale. Furthermore, the seller must endorse the certificate just as his or her name appears on the face of the certificate. The transfer agent checks to determine that the signature is proper, and also that it is not a forgery. The broker or dealer handling the transaction, or banks, are responsible for guaranteeing that the signature is genuine.

3. It is the transfer agent's duty to make sure there is no "stop order" against a transfer of a certificate. The agent does this by maintaining a file of stock certificates that may have been lost, stolen or destroyed, or that may be subject to a court proceeding.

4. Most states require a corporation to ascertain that inheritance taxes are paid as they apply to the corporation's securities. When the certificate presented for transfer was owned by a deceased person, the transfer agent checks for compliance with state laws that might be involved. Furthermore, the transfer agent establishes that the transfer of any stock held in the name of an executor, trustee, guardian or other fiduciary is fully authorized.

5. After the agent is satisfied that all requirements are met, he issues a new stock certificate. He also, of course, makes a full record of the transfer, of the new owner, number of shares issued and number cancelled.

The Banker's Trust Company of New York in outlining its functions as a transfer agent has stated:

> Stock certificates are received by the Transfer Agent endorsed over to new owners, the old certificates are cancelled and new certificates issued in the owner's name. These transactions are then recorded on ledger cards, commonly called the stock books, where the cancelled shares are debited off the transferor's account and credited to the account of the transferee. The importance of properly maintaining a company's stock books cannot be exag-

gerated because here we have the official record of the names and addresses of the company's owners.

It is to the stock books that we refer when called upon to perform any one of a number of collateral functions such as disbursing a cash dividend, mailing annual reports and proxies, issuing rights to subscribe to additional shares and distributing a dividend payable in stock. All of these represent duties which the transfer agent is in a position to perform only if he also maintains the stock books, in which case he is known as the Principal Transfer Agent. Other agents may have the responsibility of transferring stock and reporting to the principal agent, and they are referred to as Co-Transfer Agents.

## The Registrar's Function

The stock transaction is now ready to go to the registrar, which is generally another bank or trust company. The registrar's work is routine, but it is important because it is intended to insure that only the same number of new shares are issued as the number of old shares to be cancelled.

A registrar is appointed to assure the stockholders that there will not be an over-issue of the stock. The stock certificates are countersigned by the registrar. It is the responsibility of the independent registrar to limit the issuance of stock to the authorized common stock provided by the charter of the company. The registrar has no responsibility for the validity of the transfer but does keep a very active record of all the shares that are outstanding. The registrar keeps records of the certificates that have been cancelled, lost or destroyed as well as those that have been issued, so that the registrar has the exact record of stock outstanding at any given moment.

This careful double check was instituted to make sure that a corporation could not dilute the equity of its shareholders by issuing stock indiscriminately —a practice that was followed on occasion a good many years ago.

Normally, the corporation appoints a transfer agent and a separate registrar. In some offerings, the company appoints the same trust company to serve as transfer agent and registrar.

## Effects of Stock Exchange Listing

If you wish to have your company's stock listed on a stock exchange, the requirements concerning transfer agents and registrars become more stringent. The New York Stock Exchange, for instance, specifies that a company must have a transfer agent and a registrar located within the financial district of New York City.

The New York Stock Exchange reserves the right to approve the transfer agent. In some cases it may be the company itself, but in most instances a commercial bank or stock company is appointed as the transfer agent. If the company serves in the position of its own transfer agent, it must have an office in New York. Many companies maintain more than one transfer agent, but if the stock is listed on the New York Stock Exchange, one of the transfer agents must be located in New York. Under the agreements with the New York Stock Exchange, the company must also maintain a registrar in the financial district of New York. The registrar cannot be the same as the transfer agent.

## Handling Your Own Transfers

A company, if it wishes to handle its own stock transfers, can establish a company office to meet the transfer requirement, but it must have an independent registrar. Opening, staffing and maintaining a transfer office is expensive, which is why all listed companies with the exception of only a few of the biggest in the country employ banks or trust companies as transfer agents.

It is possible, also, to employ co-transfer agents. Suppose that your company has a transfer agent elsewhere than in New York at the time it seeks an exchange listing on the New York Stock Exchange. It is not necessary to abandon the existing agent. A New York bank or trust company can be named co-agent, and the two transfer organizations then correlate their operations.

Banks and trust companies that serve as transfer agents also provide related services, at the option of the corporation.

For example: The Chase Manhattan bank offers the following services as transfer agent:

1. Keeping custody of unissued stock certificates and guarding them under a rigid system of accounting and auditing control against theft, misuse, and unauthorized issuance.
2. Replacing stock certificates which have been lost, stolen or destroyed, after obtaining from the stockholder adequate bond against future reappearance of the securities.
3. Maintaining detailed records of stock ownership.
4. Disbursing dividends and handling correspondence concerning dividends, and replacing checks reported lost or undelivered.
5. Preparing and filing information returns of dividends paid, as required by the Federal Government. Preparing information returns of dividends paid to, or stock held by, residents of various states.
6. Furnishing lists of stockholders for annual and special meetings, or furnishing selective lists of stockholders for special purposes.
7. Addressing and mailing to stockholders the reports, statements, notices,

proxies and other material that may have to be sent to the shareowners.

8. Tabulating proxies for stockholders' meetings.

## Fees to Transfer Agent

If your company utilizes the services of a transfer agent, it is well that you know the charges that will be made for these services. The following fees, which serve as a guide, are charged by a New York bank for serving as the principal transfer agent.

Minimum Charge Per Annum covering issuance of 500 certificates and maintenance of 500 accounts .......................... $500.00

For issuance of each certificate in excess of 500 ............ .45

For maintenance of each of the next 5,000 accounts in excess of 500 ......................................................... .45

For maintenance of each of the next 15,000 accounts in excess of 5,500 ......................................................... .40

For maintenance of each account in excess of 20,500 ........ .35

For each out-of-town certificate posted, debit or credit .......... .12½

For posting out certificates on the retirement of stock, per debit certificate ...................................................... .15

For opening up new ledger accounts on exchanges of stock etc., per account opened ........................................... .15

For furnishing reports of transfers:

$100.00 per annum an all agencies with stockholders up to 5,000
$200.00 per annum on all agencies with stockholders in excess of 5,000

DOCUMENTARY TRANSFERS:

For the examination of Wills, Trust Agreements, etc., in connection with transfers by Trustees or estate representatives, each $ 2.50

DIVIDEND DISBURSEMENTS:

Minimum for each dividend disbursement .................... $ 50.00

Each of the first 250 checks .............................. .30

Each of the next 250 checks .............................. .25

Each of the next 9,500 checks ........................... .15

Each check over 10,000 .................................. .12½

For each enclosure with dividend checks .............. $5.00 per M

STOCKHOLDERS' LISTS:

For each 1,000 accounts .................................. $ 25.00

For additional copies of lists, each 1,000 accounts ............. 12.50

SPECIAL SERVICES:

For stenciling envelopes, per 1,000 ......................... 12.50

For addressing envelopes, making one enclosure and mailing, per 1,000 .............................................. 22.50

For addressing envelopes, making more than one enclosure and mailing, per 1,000 ...................................... 27.50

> If duplicate names of holders of more than one class of stock
> are eliminated an extra charge of 25% will be made.
> If enclosures are inserted by hand rather than machine an
> extra charge of 25% will be made.

For preparation of certificates of distribution required by Stock
Exchanges, $20 per 1,000 ledger sheets analyzed.

For issuance of subscription warrants, stock dividends and other
special services not covered by the above schedule, charges
will be based upon an analysis and appraisal of the services
rendered.

It is important to note that the cost of all stationery, such as binders and ledger sheets, transfer and registration sheets, window receipts, checks, paper used for lists, etc., and disbursements such as postage, taxes and insurance, are to be added to the regular charges.

## Registrar Fees

While the charges for performing registrar services vary, the following are some sample rates charged by a New York bank.

| | |
|---|---|
| Minimum Charge Per Annum covering registration of 500 certificates | $250.00 |
| For registration of each certificate in excess of 500 | .15 |
| Annual charge for exchanging advices with each Co-Registrar | $125.00 |
| For posting out certificates on the closing of a registration agency or retirement of stock, per debit certificate | .07½ |

The cost of all stationery, such as binders and ledger sheets, transfer and registration sheets, window receipts, checks, paper used for lists, etc., and disbursements such as postage, taxes and insurance, are to be added to the regular charges.

# 32

## Stock Options to Employees

Many corporations create stock option plans for their top management and key personnel. Stock options of this type are generally created for many reasons, including the following:

    a. To attract new employees.

    b. To keep present employees who may be looking for another job.

    c. To supplement present compensation arrangements.

    d. To give executives an incentive to earn more for themselves and produce greater profits for the company.

*How It Works*

Generally, the plans work this way: An employee is given the right to buy a given number of shares of stock in his company at some future date at 95 per cent of the price prevailing when the option is granted. If he buys the stock after the market price has gone up, he pays no tax on the paper profit until he later sells the stock, provided, of course, that the option qualifies as a restricted stock option under Section 421 of the Internal Revenue Code. If the price of the stock goes down after he gets the option he can wait for a later rise to complete his purchase.

The advantage of a qualified stock option program under Section 421 of the Code is that the employee pays no income tax at the time the option is granted or when the stock is purchased. The employee is given an opportunity to realize capital gains income if the profits of the company improve and the market price of the stock increases. When he sells the stock, he pays a capital gains tax on the difference between the price he paid for the stock originally and the selling price. Since the capital gains tax is limited to 25 per cent, restricted options of this type have become very popular in recent years. Many employees prefer stock options to cash salary increases.

### Handling a Decline in the Market

As long as the market on your company's stock is rising, your stock option program will be very appealing to your employees. On the other hand, some firms have found that a decline in the market will result in a loss of glamour that normally attaches to stock options. In the latter part of 1960, fewer firms appeared to be instituting stock option plans as compared with other years. The loss of appeal of stock options was due to the fact that they do not have the tax advantages where the market price of stock goes down. With a descending market, the option is worthless to the employee at least until such time as the market passes over and beyond the option price.

### When to Begin Option Plan

Many companies institute a stock option plan immediately prior to the time they go to the public with an initial stock offering. A review of some public stock offerings show the following:

> *Harcourt, Brace and Company, Inc.* On June 21, 1960 the Company adopted an Employee Stock Option Plan (the "Plan") which provides a means whereby certain key personnel of the Company will be granted an opportunity to purchase the Common Stock of the Company. The recipients of stock options thereunder are determined by the Board of Directors and there is no limit under the Plan as to the number of shares that may be optioned to any one employee. The options to be issued pursuant to such Plan are intended to be "restricted stock options" as said term is defined by Section 421 of the Internal Revenue Code of 1954, as amended. Under the Plan, 129,150 shares of the Company's Common Stock (including 4,500 shares held in the treasury) have been reserved for issuance and sale. The Plan provides that the option price must be at least 90% of the fair market value of the Common Stock on the day upon which the option is granted. Options to be granted under the Plan will be exercisable cumulatively in annual installments over a maximum period of eight years.

> The Registrant intends to grant on or about the effective date of this Prospectus options to 17 employees of the Company (including the three executive officers of the Company) to purchase an aggregate of 79,000 shares of the Company's Common Stock. The exercise price of these options will be the fair market value of the Common Stock of the Company on the day upon which the option is granted.

> *Del Electronics Corp.* As of the date of this Prospectus, no options to purchase stock pursuant to this Plan are outstanding. (The complete stock option is included in the Exhibits to the Registration Statement.) It is contem-

plated that options will be granted to approximately three present employees and to future employees as the occasion warrants. It is further contemplated that options will be granted to Officers and Directors to no more than an aggregate of 10,000 shares at a price equal to 110% of the fair market value or price prevailing at the time. The Plan does not provide any limit to the number of shares which may be optioned to any one person.

The aggregate number of shares of Common Stock which may be subject to stock options and warrants is 40,000, which is 13.1% of the Common Stock to be outstanding upon the completion of the financing.

# 33

## Selection of Board of Directors

Prior to a public stock offering, the Board of Directors of a typical family corporation, consists of the president, possibly his wife, a few executives of the company and the attorney or the banker for the company. The Board of Directors in these cases frequently meet on an informal basis.

Now, however, when you think of a public stock offering, you will have to give serious consideration to the membership of your Board of Directors, and the responsibilities which they will assume. Your underwriters may request of you that your company expand the size of your Board of Directors. They will want to be certain that the public will accept your board of directors and that it will have confidence in the directors selected.

Your underwriters may say to you, "We think you should expand your board of directors to eight or ten persons and we recommend that you select several persons from outside of your company to serve as directors." They will explain to you that the investing public will look with greater favor upon your company if there are outside directors who are highly respected in the business community. They might suggest to you the addition of several directors who have outstanding regional or national reputations and are skilled in corporate and business matters.

Upon first thought, you might not look favorably upon your underwriter's request to expand your board of directors. You might be opposed to bringing in outsiders, fearing the loss of control of your business. This will be a matter that you will want to discuss at great length with your own advisors as you try to arrive at a solution that will be satisfactory to you and your underwriters. In your thinking about this subject, you must keep in mind that the public will have an interest in your company as a result of the stock offering. The public has the right to know that your business will be directed by a competent and impartial Board of Directors, not by the president, alone.

## Duties and Responsibilities of the Board of Directors

It is well to have an understanding of the many subjects that must be brought to the attention of the board of directors for their consideration and decision. If you have been running a "one man" company it will be difficult to keep in mind that your directors must be consulted and given an opportunity to pass upon matters that rightfully should be decided by a board of directors. This is one of the difficult adjustments many owners must make as their companies become publicly owned.

It is the duty of a director to direct. A director cannot give up these responsibilities and duties to management. If he does not wish to exercise the authority and perform the duties imposed by law, he should not serve as a director. At the meetings of the board, the directors should consider every major question which affects the interests of the company. A director is presumed to have a certain knowledge of the corporation and its affairs. He is acting for the benefit of the stockholders and must exercise good faith along with good judgment in directing the affairs of the corporation. It is customary for the board of directors to delegate certain functions to an executive committee or to one or more officers of the company. Despite this delegation, the directors cannot abdicate their duties and responsibilities.

It is well to discuss with your attorney, the matters which must be brought before the board of directors of your company so that you will not find yourself in the position of having taken a course of action on your own which should have been the subject of a discussion and decision by the board of directors. It is advisable for you to develop a program of keeping your directors adequately informed about the corporation and its activities. Your directors can fulfill their responsibilities better if they are well informed. Directors may disagree with you but on balance, a good interchange of ideas will benefit the company. Consider the board of directors of your company as an important aid in managing the affairs of your company. Utilize the skills, background and judgment of your directors as you consider the many important problems that face the corporation executive today.

## Selection of Directors

The selection of your initial board of directors obviously is of great importance. In all likelihood, these directors will continue to serve for many years unless death or unavailability prevails. Once you have selected a director, and he has consented to serve, it is sometimes quite difficult to replace him merely because you are not pleased with the amount of work he does or the caliber of advice he is offering. Therefore, it is extremely important that you take every precaution when selecting your directors to find the very best people available.

Do not select people who will merely be "figure heads" on your board of directors. Rather choose men and women who can make a major contribution to your corporation. In casting about for suitable directors, you might wish to give some thought to placing a representative of your bank on your board. Some companies select a member of their investment banking firm, others their lawyer.

What are the qualifications to look for in selecting a member of the board of directors? You will want men and women of integrity, compatibility and honesty. Select people who have the ability to think "long range" and who can evaluate changing conditions. Naturally, you will want directors who will have a great interest in the welfare of your corporation—are conscientious and who will carry out their responsibilities faithfully.

### Representative of Underwriter on Board of Directors

The question quite often arises as to whether a representative of your investment banking firm should be placed on your board of directors. There are pros and cons on this subject which you should seriously consider. On the favorable side, of course, is the fact that a representative of your investment banking firm has a financial background that can be a great help to you in the operation of your business. Further, a representative of the underwriting firm, serving on your board of directors, can provide sound advice, particularly, as it affects your stockholder relations.

On the other hand, however, you should give consideration to the fact that by placing a member of your underwriter on your board of directors, you might well be committing your company for future underwriting services. There may be a time in the future when you may wish to have a further stock offering. At that time, you might not have freedom of action in selecting a new underwriter if one of the representatives of your present underwriting firm is serving on your board. Other conflicts of interest may arise from time to time.

Some of the larger underwriting firms have a policy against one of their representatives serving on the board of directors of a company for whom they have provided underwriting services. Other underwriting firms, as a condition to their handling of the public stock offering, might insist that one of their representatives serve on the board of directors for a period of time. If a representative of the underwriter is to serve on your Board, be certain that the one selected can make a valuable contribution to the operations of your company.

### Why Should Busy Men Serve on Your Board of Directors?

You might hesitate to ask your friend, Tom Peterman to serve on your board of directors because "Tom's a busy guy, he's running his own business, flying around the country and serves on six other boards." It may well be that Tom is not the man for you but somehow or other the busy men always seem to be the ones who make time to do the things they want. If Tom has the background, the ability and integrity, don't cross him off the list until you discuss with him whether he would like to serve on your board. It is not at all unusual for busy men to accept directorships in corporations even though they do not own any stock in the company.

Men serve on boards for a number of reasons, such as prestige, financial gain, experience and a desire to be of assistance. Many men feel that their own management skills can be sharpened by serving on other boards of directors. You will find that even the best executive likes to take on new challenges, particularly in companies that have a dramatic growth potential and may become one of the blue chip companies of the future. Very often the personal satisfaction which the directors receive from serving on a board far outweighs the compensation which they receive as directors.

If you have in mind the man that you would like to have on your board, don't pass him by merely because he is busy. He may be just the man that you are looking for and he may be very happy to accept the challenge which your directorship will offer to him.

## Conflicting Interests of Directors

In selecting directors for your company, make certain that there will not be a conflict of interest between the director and your company. If a director has a financial interest in a company that sells products or services to your organization, it is unwise to have him serve on your board. Try as he may to be impartial, there may be times when a conflicting interest might mitigate against your corporation. There have been in the past year several situations in some of America's large corporations where the directors were asked to resign because of conflicting interests. The corporation is placed in a position where it, as well as the director, might be subject to suit by stockholders. Periodically it is wise to check your directors to see whether they are adhering strictly to the principle of complete impartiality without any conflicting interest.

## Director's Compensation

In selecting directors, you will have to give consideration to the payment of fees for services which the directors will perform. There is a very wide range of fees paid to directors and every corporation sets its own policy. Many men serve as directors for nominal fees since the compensation is taxable and the net fee, after taxes, amounts to a token payment. Some Corporations do not pay directors fees when the directors are full time officers or executives of the company.

Some corporations pay a fixed fee per meeting, others pay an annual retainer.

In a survey conducted by the National Industrial Conference Board, Inc. in April 1960, it was determined that $100 per meeting attended is the most common fee paid to directors. The survey indicated that 45 per cent of the firms that pay regular meeting fees, pay $100 per meeting. 17 per cent pay $50 and 11 per cent pay $200. The balance of those queried paid various amounts. The survey indicated that in recent years an increasing number of companies are placing directors on a retainer or salary basis. Over one-half of the companies that reported, paying on this basis, indicated that they pay a retainer to outside directors of $2,000 a year or less. Directors normally receive reimbursement for expenses incurred in attending meetings, if held out of the city.

## Directors' Meetings

It will take a while for you to become reconciled to the need for calling directors' meetings, especially if you have been in the habit of calling merely token directors' meetings before becoming a public corporation. Since your directors have assumed certain responsibilities and must perform their duties as directors, you should pay particular attention to the requirements of your by-laws as they relate to the calling of meetings. Informal meetings will not suffice in meeting the requirements of your by-laws. The secretary of the company should send out the call for the meetings. Your attorney will advise you on the subjects to be discussed at the meetings, place of meeting, etc.

Your by-laws will provide for regular or special meetings. The regular meetings must be called at the time and place provided for in the by-laws. Be certain that the place where the meeting is to be held complies with the charter provisions or by-laws. Be certain at the meeting that you have a quorum which is necessary to enable the directors to transact business for the corporation. It is desirable for you to have your attorney present at the meeting since there are many technical requirements that must be met, in the calling and conducting of the meeting.

# 34

## Dividends

*What Commitments Will Your Company Be Required to Make
for Future Dividends?*

The stockholders of your company have the right to participate in the profits
of the Company and to receive their share of the dividends paid. The Board of
Directors has the discretion as to the amount of dividends to be paid. However,
from time to time stockholders attempt through court action to require the payment of dividends where the directors have decided not to pay out a portion of
the earnings to the stockholders. Courts hesitate to substitute for a Board of Directors in these cases, and will intervene only in cases where there is a flagrant
abuse of discretion by the Board.

Early in your discussions with your underwriters, the question will arise as to
the payment of a current as well as future dividends. The underwriters will want
some general commitments from the company, as obviously the dividend paying policy of your company will have an important bearing upon the initial sale
of your stock and subsequent sales in the future.

Many family owned corporations do not pay substantial dividends. However,
now that you consider a public stock offering for your company, you must keep
in mind that the public, in purchasing your stock, has a definite interest in the
dividends that you will pay in the years ahead. The amount of the dividends that
your directors will commit your company to may have a profound bearing upon
the price of the stock.

### Amount of Dividends

While the averages indicate that corporations pay out approximately 50 per
cent of their annual earnings, many companies pay out a very small percentage
of their earnings annually as dividends to stockholders. Some corporations
pay no dividends, since they need their total earnings to expand. Low dividends
do not necessarily make the stock less attractive since large investors are often

163

less interested in dividends and more interested in subsequent capital gains. The income tax laws help to create this situation, since capital gains carry a lower tax rate than dividends for the investor in the high income tax brackets.

It is important that due consideration be given by the Board of Directors to the needs of the business before paying out dividends. In many cases, it is advantageous for the corporation to plow back its earnings to provide additional working capital, reduce debt, expand, etc. Before voting a dividend, the directors should give serious consideration to the following:

(a) Current cash position
(b) Working capital position
(c) Future cash requirements
(d) Debt retirement and interest payments
(e) Needs for expansion of plant and equipment
(f) Amount of surplus
(g) Sinking fund requirements
(h) Projected earnings

In some cases the company will need to retain all of its earnings for the efficient operations of the company. For example, MCA, Inc., in its prospectus stated:

Although the company in the past has paid small cash dividends on its common stock, the management of the company believes that all funds available to the company will be required in the company's business. The company therefore, intends to retain all earnings for its corporate purposes during the foreseeable future.

The New York Stock Exchange reported on the dividend payment of some companies as follows:

The table presents stocks whose dividend payout in relation to recent earnings has tended to be lower than for most stocks. Dividend figures used are the totals for the past 12 months . . . the earnings shown are for the latest 12 months as computed from company reports. Obviously, the data may be used only when judged with other factors.

| Closing Price Apr. 29 1960 | Common Stocks with Small Dividend Payout in Relation to Latest Reported Earnings | Yield on Latest 12 Mos. Divs. | Cash Divs. Payable Latest 12 Mos. | Earnings Per Share 12 Mos. Ended Mar. 1960 | Cash Divs. Paid Ea. Yr. Begin'g |
|---|---|---|---|---|---|
| 64⅛ | Addressograph-Multigr. | 1.2% | $0.78 | $1.86 | 1935 |
| 45¼ | Aldens, Inc. | 2.6% | 1.17 | 3.74 | 1934 |
| 64½ | Amer. Mach. & Fdry. | 1.8% | 1.15 | 2.68 | 1927 |
| 14¼ | American Molasses Co. | 5.3% | 0.75 | 1.94 | 1927 |
| 16½ | Belding Heminway Co. | 5.2% | 0.85 | 2.02 | 1934 |
| 43⅝ | Bell & Howell Co. | 0.8% | 0.36 | 1.27 | 1915 |
| 73 | Brown Shoe Co. | 3.2% | 2.35 | 6.34 | 1923 |

| Closing Price Apr. 29 1960 | Common Stocks with Small Dividend Payout in Relation to Latest Reported Earnings | Yield on Latest 12 Mos. Divs. | Cash Divs. Payable Latest 12 Mos. | Earnings Per Share 12 Mos. Ended Mar. 1960 | Cash Divs. Paid Ea. Yr. Begin'g |
|---|---|---|---|---|---|
| 19⅝ | Burlington Industries | 6.1% | 1.20 | 2.70 | 1931 |
| 43 | Carborundum Co. | 3.7% | 1.60 | 4.46 | 1922 |
| 42¼ | Carpenter Steel Co. | 4.3% | 1.80 | 4.69 | 1907 |
| 69¼ | Carter Products, Inc. | 1.8% | 1.25 | 3.51 | 1883 |
| 39 | Chesapeake Corp. of Va. | 3.0% | 1.18 | 3.37 | 1933 |
| 52¾ | Clevite Corp. | 2.3% | 1.20 | 3.82 | 1922 |
| 39½ | Columbia Broadcasting | 3.2% | 1.27 | 3.01 | 1931 |
| 19½ | DWG Cigar Corp. | 3.9% | 0.76 | 2.05 | 1934 |
| 35 | Firestone Tire & Rubber | 2.6% | 0.92 | 2.42 | 1924 |
| 23 | Gamble-Skogmo, Inc. | 4.1% | 0.95 | 2.27 | 1929 |
| 24½ | General Cigar Co. | 3.3% | 0.80 | 2.02 | 1909 |
| 55⅜ | Georgia-Pacific Corp. | 1.8% | 0.98 | 2.70 | 1927 |
| 37⅜ | Gt. Atlantic & Pacific | 2.4% | 0.88 | 2.34 | 1905 |
| 87¾ | Heinz (H.J.) Co. | 2.5% | 2.20 | 6.79 | 1911 |
| 452½ | Int'l Bus. Machines | 0.6% | 2.60 | 8.31 | 1916 |
| 55¾ | Johnson & Johnson | 1.6% | 0.90 | 2.66 | 1905 |
| 38½ | Keystone Steel & Wire | 5.2% | 2.00 | 5.32 | 1934 |
| 32 | Masonite Corp. | 3.7% | 1.19 | 3.71 | 1935 |
| 29⅛ | McCall Corp. | 2.0% | 0.59 | 1.90 | 1926 |
| 17⅜ | McQuay-Norris Mfg. | 5.6% | 0.97 | 2.43 | 1927 |
| 30¼ | Midwest Oil Corp. | 3.5% | 1.05 | 2.94 | 1921 |
| 193 | Minn. Mng. & Mfg. | 0.8% | 1.55 | 3.74 | 1916 |
| 33¼ | Morrell (John) & Co. | 1.9% | 0.64 | 5.68 | 1916 |
| 32½ | National Standard Co. | 4.5% | 1.45 | 3.67 | 1916 |
| 70¼ | National Steel Corp. | 4.3% | 3.00 | 7.43 | 1907 |
| 45 | Olin Mathieson Chem. | 2.2% | 1.00 | 2.96 | 1926 |
| 39¾ | Otis Elevator Co. | 3.3% | 1.30 | 3.16 | 1903 |
| 50½ | Pet Milk Co. | 2.2% | 1.12 | 3.53 | 1922 |
| 47¾ | Plough, Inc. | 1.8% | 0.87½ | 2.17 | 1931 |
| 705 | Rohm & Haas Co. | 0.5% | 3.46 | 21.24 | 1927 |
| 20⅞ | "Shell" Transp. & Tr. | 3.2% | 0.66 | 2.04 | 1898 |
| 25 | Smith-Douglas Co. | 4.8% | 1.20 | 3.18 | 1922 |
| 39¼ | Standard Oil (Indiana) | 3.6% | 1.40 | 3.90 | 1894 |
| 25⅜ | Stevens (J.P.) & Co. | 5.9% | 1.50 | 4.79 | 1935 |
| 47 | Sun Oil Company | 2.1% | 0.98 | 3.28 | 1904 |
| 63¾ | Trane Company | 1.4% | 0.90 | 2.46 | 1934 |
| 40½ | Union Oil Co. of Calif. | 2.4% | 0.97 | 3.30 | 1916 |
| 64 | United Carbon Co. | 3.1% | 1.97 | 5.21 | 1933 |
| 34⅜ | Univ.-Cyclops Steel | 3.0% | 1.03 | 5.24 | 1934 |
| 56⅞ | Univ. Leaf Tobacco | 4.4% | 2.50 | 6.58 | 1927 |
| 47¼ | Upjohn Company | 1.4% | 0.66 | 1.71 | 1909 |
| 88 | Vick Chemical Co. | 1.0% | 0.90 | 3.20 | 1922 |
| 52 | Walgreen Co. | 3.0% | 1.58 | 4.55 | 1933 |

In determining the amount of dividends to be paid out, the following report of the New York Stock Exchange might prove helpful:

Almost nine out of ten common stocks on the New York Stock Exchange paid dividends in 1959. About half of these stocks paid dividends of 3.8% or more of their selling price on December 31, 1959, and half paid less.

During the past ten years, half the companies which paid dividends on their common stocks on the New York Stock Exchange paid more than the following rates, and half paid less (based on year-end prices):

| 1950—6.7% | 1955—4.6% |
|-----------|-----------|
| 1951—6.5% | 1956—5.2% |
| 1952—6%   | 1957—6.1% |
| 1953—6.3% | 1958—4.1% |
| 1954—4.7% | 1959—3.8% |
|           | 1960—4.2% |

Most companies attempt to maintain their customary dividend. The following report from the August, 1961 issue of "The Exchange" published by the New York Stock Exchange, indicates that 512 out of 1129 companies listed in the New York Stock Exchange paid the same dividend in the company the first six months of 1961 to the first six months of 1960.

CASH DIVIDENDS ON NEW YORK STOCK EXCHANGE LISTED COMMON STOCKS
1st 6 Months 1961 vs. 1st 6 Months 1960

| Industry | No. of Stocks Listed 6/30/61 | 1st 6 Mos. | More | Same | Less | Estimated Cash Payments 1st 6 Mos. 1961 | Per Cent Change |
|----------|------|------|------|------|------|------|------|
| 1. Aircraft | 38 | 30 | 12 | 15 | 4 | $   66,619,330 | —2.7 |
| 2. Amusement | 17 | 13 | 5 | 8 | | 21,313,950 | +5.0 |
| 3. Automotive | 53 | 41 | 9 | 24 | 12 | 400,893,980 | +2.0 |
| 4. Building | 44 | 35 | 6 | 23 | 9 | 76,585,050 | —6.9 |
| 5. Chemical | 101 | 94 | 36 | 53 | 6 | 556,217,240 | +2.3 |
| 6. Electrical | 63 | 40 | 12 | 22 | 9 | 213,697,220 | —2.5 |
| 7. Financial | 49 | 40 | 16 | 17 | 8 | 130,090,471 | +4.9 |
| 8. Foods Commodities | 78 | 69 | 29 | 37 | 6 | 188,901,380 | +3.5 |
| 9. Leather | 11 | 8 | 4 | 2 | 3 | 13,721,940 | —0.5 |
| 10. Machinery | 141 | 116 | 34 | 66 | 18 | 270,098,990 | +2.3 |
| 11. Mining | 39 | 27 | 7 | 17 | 4 | 120,763,580 | +0.8 |
| 12. Office Equip. | 12 | 6 | 4 | 1 | 2 | 13,841,050 | +4.4 |
| 13. Paper & Publng. | 42 | 38 | 14 | 22 | 3 | 106,960,950 | +4.7 |
| 14. Petrol & Nat. Gas | 44 | 37 | 13 | 23 | 2 | 734,637,460 | +1.3 |
| 15. Railroad & RR Equip. | 58 | 38 | 3 | 26 | 14 | 163,277,350 | —5.9 |
| 16. Real Estate | 9 | 8 | 3 | 3 | 2 | 11,916,860 | —0.4 |
| 17. Retail Trade | 65 | 60 | 21 | 34 | 6 | 218,657,950 | + * |
| 18. Rubber | 14 | 12 | 4 | 6 | 4 | 50,023,800 | —1.6 |
| 19. Services | 14 | 14 | 6 | 8 | | 21,930,210 | +4.2 |
| 20. Shipbuilding & Oper. | 11 | 7 | 2 | 4 | 2 | 7,454,400 | —18.9 |
| 21. Steel & Iron | 40 | 36 | 3 | 26 | 7 | 248,146,670 | —0.6 |
| 22. Textile | 37 | 31 | 11 | 15 | 6 | 37,775,410 | —1.5 |
| 23. Tobacco | 13 | 13 | 4 | 7 | 2 | 69,640,500 | +4.0 |
| 24. Utilities | 115 | 113 | 69 | 43 | 1 | 1,100,519,860 | +6.7 |
| 25. Foreign Stocks | 21 | 17 | 3 | 10 | 4 | 82,481,770 | —3.7 |
| | 1129 | 943 | 330 | 512 | 134 | $4,926,167,370 | +2.0 |

* Less than 1/20 of 1%

If the Directors contemplate paying a small dividend or passing a dividend completely, it is well to keep in mind the provisions of Sec. 531 of the Internal Revenue Code which imposes a tax on earnings which are retained beyond the "reasonable anticipated needs" of the business. While the Internal Revenue Service may question the amount of the dividend paid, the company has the right to point out its reasons for its dividend actions such as need of funds for expansion, additional plants, new equipment, inventory, etc.

### Types of Dividends

Corporations normally pay dividends to their stockholders in cash, stock, property or scrip. The directors will make this determination. In some instances a corporation will pay a combination of a cash and stock dividend.

### Cash Dividend

A cash dividend is customarily paid by most corporations on a quarterly basis although some payments are made on a semi-annual or annual basis. At the end of the year, many corporations declare an extra cash dividend or a stock dividend, along with the regular cash payment.

### Stock Dividend

Stock dividends ordinarily are paid to enable the company to retain its cash and at the same time provide the stockholders with a dividend. A stock dividend represents a pro-rata dividend among the stockholders, and they acquire no greater interest in the company than they had before the stock dividend. The stockholder will receive a greater amount of cash dividends after a stock dividend if the amount of dividend paid per share is continued.

It is important to distinguish between a stock dividend and a stock split. Basically, the differences are largely matters of accounting. The New York Stock Exchange distinguishes between the stock splits and stock dividends by considering any stock dividend of 25 per cent or more to be a stock split. Under accounting procedures, a corporation declaring a stock dividend, must transfer from retained earnings to permanent capitalization, an amount equal to the fair value of the additional shares issued. A stock split involves no change in the capital surplus accounts. The outstanding stated capital is divided into a larger number of shares with each share having a reduced par or stated value.

Under the current Internal Revenue Code, a stock dividend, unlike a cash dividend, is not taxable. This tax advantage makes the stock dividend very attractive to many stockholders. However, the stock dividend reduces the average cost of the investment.

The Goodyear Tire & Rubber Company, in explaining its 2 per cent stock dividend on the company's common stock, advised the shareholders of the company on November 1, 1960 as follows:

> This stock dividend is, in effect, a capitalization of earnings and permits the Company to conserve cash for working capital requirements. An amount

approximately equivalent to the fair market value of the additional shares issued in payment of such dividend will be transferred from the Company's earned surplus to stated capital and capital surplus.

Many firms pay a 2, 5 or 10 per cent stock dividend at the end of the year in addition to a cash dividend. Generally, these stock dividends are paid in place of an additional cash dividend so that the company can conserve its funds for working capital, expansion, retirement of its debt, etc. Some corporations at the end of the year find it necessary to eliminate a cash dividend and pay, in its place, a small stock dividend. The payment of a stock dividend in place of an increased cash dividend sometimes satisfies stockholders and eases the financial burdens on the corporation.

## Property Dividends

Some corporations pay dividends in property other than cash on their own stock to their stockholders. These dividends quite often consist of stock or securities of subsidiaries or other corporations. Some corporations pay dividends in bonds or merchandise.

## Scrip Dividends

Some few corporations prefer to issue scrip dividends which are a promise on the part of the corporation to pay cash, stock or other property at a future date. A dividend of this type is declared when the corporation determines that its cash position does not warrant a cash dividend at that time.

The disadvantage of this type of dividend is that it creates an obligation to pay a dividend at a future date. Before declaring a scrip dividend, the Board of Directors of the Company should seriously determine whether it is to the best interests of the company to make a commitment of this type. It might be advisable to pass the dividend completely rather than creating a future obligation through a scrip dividend.

## When Should Dividends Be Paid?

The question will be raised: "Should dividends be paid quarterly, semi-annually or annually?" Most companies declare and pay dividends quarterly; others pay semi-annually or annually. There are some companies that pay dividends on a monthly basis. This can prove to be a costly method as 12 checks must be written, 12 check reconciliations, 12 mailings to stockholders, etc. On the other hand, annual dividends are not generally recommended since many stockholders budget their income and depend on their dividends on at least a quarterly basis.

From time to time corporations are forced by business conditions or other circumstances to lower or eliminate dividends. This often has the effect of considerably reducing the price of the stock. When action of this type is taken, it is important that there be a full explanation to the stockholder.

*Report of Dividends*

As soon as a dividend is declared by the directors of a company, it is important that the public be advised immediately. It is customary to declare a dividend which will be payable on a specified future date to stockholders of record of a specified date.

For example, the Board of Directors might declare a dividend on October 1 to be paid on November 15 to stockholders of record on November 1. After the record date is past, the stock is quoted ex-dividend, and the subsequent purchasers will not receive the current dividend.

Press releases outlining the dividend action should be given immediately after the directors' meeting to your local newspapers and the financial newspapers.

Many metropolitan as well as financial newspapers publish a dividend digest daily. The regular dividend on your stock will be recorded showing the amount of the dividend, whether it is payable quarterly, monthly or annually, the record date for dividend purposes, and the date the dividend will be payable.

These dividend digests also report stock dividends—special, extra or irregular dividends.

*Dividend Notices*

When sending out dividend checks to stockholders, the company generally encloses a dividend notice. Many companies utilize the dividend notice as a vehicle to give their stockholders information about the company and its products.

For example, General Motors Corp. in its dividend notice of September 10, 1960 stated:

> As an owner of General Motors, you have a strong interest in your Corporation's products. We know you will inspect them at the showrooms of your neighborhood dealers at your earliest convenience. Should you or your friends be considering the purchase of a new car, we are sure you will find the value contained in any General Motors car outstanding in its class.

Sunray Mid-Continent Oil Company came up with a good suggestion to its stockholders in its dividend notice when it stated,

> IF YOU RECEIVED MORE THAN ONE CHECK IN PAYMENT OF THIS DIVIDEND, you have two or more accounts on Sunray's stock records because all your certificates have not been issued under an identical name

and address. Even slight variations in names (such as initials) or in addresses result in the creation of separate accounts, causing unnecessary handling by stockholders and extra expense for the Company.

Unless you have a special reason for not doing so, it will be helpful to you to have your name registered in the same way for all of your shares of the Company's stock. We will arrange for consolidation of accounts if you will complete the form printed on the reverse side of this notice and return it immediately to:

> Sunray Stock Bookkeeping Division
> The Corporation Trust Co.
> 120 Broadway
> New York 5, New York

Monsanto Chemical Company, in mailing out its 128th consecutive quarterly cash dividend, included the following advice to its stockholders:

In accordance with Internal Revenue Service requirements, Monsanto has reported cash dividends paid to shareowners in 1959 as follows:

| Payment Date | Record Date | Amount Per Share |
|---|---|---|
| March 16 | February 25 | $0.25 |
| June 15 | May 25 | .25 |
| September 15 | August 25 | .25 |
| December 15 | November 25 | .25 |
| | | —— |
| | | $1.00 |

The tax law provides that cash dividends received by a taxpayer are reportable on his individual tax return, subject to certain exclusions and credits; and you are referred to the instructions you will receive with your income tax forms. It is suggested that this notice be retained for use in preparing your 1959 tax return.

Many corporations publish a dividend notice in the Wall Street Journal, Barron's, Forbes, and other financial periodicals. These notices advise the stockholders as to the declaration of a dividend and the date the dividend will be paid.

# 35

## Stock Splits

Let us assume that the price of your company's stock has risen and is selling for $75 a share. You may want to give consideration to a stock split. Today an increasing number of corporations are splitting their Common Stock, to broaden the public interest in the stock. Also, splits are suggested since investors generally prefer low price shares. With a reduced per share price there is a wider distribution of a company's stock which helps to maintain a stable market for the issue.

Pressure to effect a stock split might well come from your underwriter who maintains a position in your stock. He may point out that the market is too thin and more stock is needed to prevent drastic price changes. The spread between the bid and asking price is also lower with more stock on the market.

The New York Stock Exchange has suggested that the most favorable price level for listed stock is in the range of $20 to $30 per share. The stock exchange takes the position that any issue selling above this range may be suitable for splitting. Stock splits generally are popular because they give the impression that the investor is getting something for nothing; however, a split does not actually increase your ownership; it just divides it into more pieces.

A split sometimes bears some promise of increased gain, for the split stock may subsequently rise in price above what the price was before the split. Many investors, particularly small investors, will be attracted because of the psychological stimulus of being able to buy more shares. Rumors of an impending split of a particular stock often cause the price of that stock to move up, sometimes substantially. At the time the split officially is announced, however, those investors who bought on the strength of the rumor may sell to realize their profits. This may cause the stock to move unevenly for a period, and even decline.

You may well find that your company should consider a stock split for the reasons mentioned and also to interest other dealers in taking a position in your company's stock. With limited shares outstanding, it is difficult to interest dealers

171

in your company. You might also want to keep in mind that broad stock ownership may help you in obtaining a listing on the various exchanges; see Chapter 39 for a discussion on the number of shares for listing. While the 2-for-1 split is the most usual, many companies split their stock on a 3-for-1, 3-for-2, or a 5-for-1 basis. A stock split requires no change in the capital or surplus account, while a stock dividend involves the transfer of earned surplus to the capital account. If the surplus of your company is relatively small, a split may be the answer rather than a stock dividend, which must be charged to surplus. In any event, whether it be a split or a stock dividend, both reduce the market value of the stock and place more shares within the reach of more investors.

The New York Stock Exchange in its August, 1961 issue of "The Exchange" analyzed the 33 listed stocks that were split in a ratio of 2 for 1 or better during the first half of 1961. The report showed

| *Company* | *Split Ratio* |
| --- | --- |
| ABC Vending Corp. | 2 for 1 |
| AMP Inc. | 3 for 1 |
| Amalgamated Sugar Co. | 3 for 1 |
| American Hospital Supply | 3 for 1 |
| American Machine & Fdry. | 2 for 1 |
| American Natural Gas Co. | 2½ for 1 |
| American Photocopy Equip. | 3 for 1 |
| Atlas Chemical Inds. (1) | 4 for 1 |
| City Products Corp. | 2 for 1 |
| Commercial Credit Co. | 2 for 1 |
| Corn Products Co. | 2 for 1 |
| Dayton Power & Light Co. | 3 for 1 |
| Field (Marshall) & Co. | 2 for 1 |
| Gerber Products Co. | 2 for 1 |
| Haveg Industries Inc. | 2½ for 1 |
| Heinz (H. J.) Co. | 3 for 1 |
| Idaho Power Co. | 2 for 1 |
| International Silver Co. | 3 for 1 |
| Interstate Dept. Stores | 3 for 1 |
| Kerr-McGee Oil Industries | 2 for 1 |
| Lehn & Fink Prod. Corp. | 3 for 1 |
| Lone Star Gas Co. | 2 for 1 |
| Martin Co. | 2 for 1 |
| McGraw-Hill Publ. Co. | 3 for 1 |
| Mergenthaler Linotype Co. | 4 for 1 |
| Pfaudler Permutit Inc. | 2 for 1 |
| Philadelphia Electric Co. | 2 for 1 |

| *Company* | *Split Ratio* |
| --- | --- |
| Procter & Gamble Co. | 2 for 1 |
| Ranco Inc. | 2 for 1 |
| Revlon, Inc. | 2 for 1 |
| Richfield Oil Corp. | 2 for 1 |
| Suburban Gas | 2 for 1 |
| Talcott (James), Inc. | 2 for 1 |

# 36

## Types of Buyers and Your Relations with Them

There will be many types of buyers who will be interested in acquiring the stock in your company at the initial offering and in subsequent years. These are as follows:

### Individuals

On the scale of your company's stock you will find that there are many individuals who will acquire your company's stock in varying amounts. These purchasers will reach the decision to acquire stock either upon their own study or upon the advice of a broker or an investment counselor. Many of these purchasers will buy your company's securities and continue to hold them for a long period of time. This type of purchaser has bought your company's securities because he or she is satisfied that the principal is safe and that there is a good likelihood of the price of the stock rising over a period of years.

On the other hand, there will be some purchasers called "free riders" who wish to come in for a quick profit. They will buy on the initial offering and will sell immediately after the initial market, if there is an increase of a few points. There are many individuals who purchase new issues with the thought in mind that there will be a heavy demand for the stock at the initial offering followed by a rise in the price. When the rise occurs, this type of purchaser sells his stock for a few points profit. With a quick rise, it is possible for the purchaser to pay for his stock within 4 days by using the proceeds of an immediate sale at a premium. Actually, in most public offerings the number who buy and sell on this basis are quite small in number because the underwriters attempt to restrict sales to such parties. Furthermore, the tax advantages provided for long term gains are not available on these transactions.

### Institutional Buyers

Many financial organizations and institutions will carefully analyze your company's "red herring" prospectus to determine whether they wish to acquire stock at the initial offering. These organizations normally purchase stock with the intention of holding the stock for a long period of time. Institutional investors play a key role in the stock market. The New York Stock Exchange in a five-day analysis of institutional transactions found that this group accounted for about 24 per cent of the volume. You can expect to find institutional investors among your list of stockholders since this group, while it is interested in blue chip companies, is becoming increasingly more interested in new issues with a "growth" potential. You can expect that the following classes of institutional buyers will show an interest in your stock:

1. Banks and Trust Companies
2. Insurance Companies
3. Charitable, Religious, and Educational Institutions
4. Pension and Profit-Sharing Funds
5. Investment Trusts and Mutual Funds

*Trust Departments of Commercial Banks.* The Trust Departments of Commercial Banks are faced with the problem of investing funds trusteed with them. Most investments are made in bonds, mortgages, and "blue chip" stocks. It is possible that in some instances, banks will have an interest in purchasing stock in a growth company.

There are large amounts of money invested by trust departments of banks throughout the country. While the trust departments are normally conservative in their investment policies, many today are finding that it is necessary to move into the area of common stocks, and limited purchases of growth companies are made.

*Insurance Companies.* Insurance companies receive millions of dollars annually in premium payments and these funds normally are invested in government securities, bonds, and in some common stocks. The insurance companies normally are conservative in their investments, considering safety of investment as a primary consideration.

Many of the insurance companies invest in common stocks and some insurance companies might be interested in your corporation if there is security in the investment.

*Charitable, Religious, and Educational Institutions.* Many colleges, religious groups and charitable organizations administer substantial trust funds. These groups quite often purchase common stocks with long-term growth potential.

*Pension and Profit-Sharing Funds.* There are today hundreds of pension funds jointly administered by a company, its union and a trust company. The pension funds do not speculate normally and their investments are generally in the "blue chip" stocks and bonds. It is possible, however, that the stock in your company may be acquired by a pension fund if it appears that there is a continuity of dividends and the investment is secure with a strong growth potential.

*Investment Trusts and Mutual Funds.* Many investment trusts have created growth funds which will buy new issues if the management of these funds can see long-term values. These funds will purchase a substantial amount of stock of growth companies and today are an important factor in the acquisition of new issues.

*Stock Held in Street Name.* A great portion of your company's stock will be purchased and held by stock dealers and brokers in "street name." Many buyers of stock in your company will prefer to leave their stock with their brokers, recorded in the name of their brokers. This stock is then held in what is known as "street name." This system enables the brokerage firm to deliver the stock easily upon sale.

Dividends on stock will be paid to the stock brokerage firm if the stock is held in "street name" and the firm will pay the dividend to the real owner of the stock. It is possible that 25 to 35 per cent of your company's stock will be held in "street name" and you will not know the name of the purchaser of the stock. All reports that you issue, as well as notices and letters to stockholders, will be mailed to the brokerage firm where the stock is held in "street name."

*Investment Clubs.* Throughout the country there are 20,000 investment clubs, some of which might well become stockholders in your company. The average investment club consists of 10 or 12 men or women who make monthly investments in the stock market. These groups study carefully the various market reports, analyze new issues, and are on the lookout for growth companies. They might well become interested in your company's stock as many of them have an interest in new issues with growth potentials.

Many investment clubs belong to the National Association of Investment Clubs, which claims 350,000 members. The association publishes a monthly bulletin which contains research material on various companies.

### Women Stockholders

Many women today own stock in America's corporations. In a recent survey by the New York Stock Exchange, it was reported that more women own stock than men. You will find many women listed among your company's group of stockholders.

### Stock Held by Parents as Custodian or Trustee for a Child

In recent years every state, as well as the District of Columbia, has simplified the steps to be taken for making gifts of securities to minors. It is now possible to give stock to children outright by registering the securities in the name of an adult as "custodian."

The custodian can be the parent, relative or friend, as well as the donor. The custodian will receive the dividends and has the power to sell the stock until the child reaches the age of 21. At that time, the stock is turned over to the child.

In some cases the parent is not desirous of making an outright gift of stock to a child, but prefers to place the gift in trust. The trustee may purchase stock in your company and will receive the dividends as trustee for a minor child.

You will find in the list of stockholders of your company many owners listed as "custodian" or "trustee."

### Who Will the Stockholders Be—What Is Your Preference?

Should the stock in your company be sold initially on a local, regional or a national basis? Your underwriter holds the key to this problem. By consulting with your underwriter, you can set up a pattern which will provide for distribution in accordance with your preference.

If you so desire, your underwriter can work with other underwriters from various parts of the country, and the distribution of the stock can be on a national basis. If you have customers located throughout the country, you might wish to have the stock sold on a national basis. While you may get national distribution at the original sale, the patterns of ownership change constantly due to sales and purchases of the stock.

How about selling to your friends? Many firms have no objection—some do. Very often this cannot be controlled. Eric Passmore, Executive Vice-President of Simplicity Manufacturing Company, advises,

> Make it difficult for personal friends to purchase. Obtain as wide a distribution outside of the state of domicile as possible. It appears to be a general experience that the public offering will be rapidly sold and will subsequently bring higher prices over-the-counter, perhaps higher than are warranted. The over pricing and economic conditions over which the company has no control, may result in lower prices. If the market then drops below the offering price, there will not only be discontented stockholders, but possibly a general belief that the company is not operating as well as expected. Personal friends may buy because of personal acquaintance with personnel and not with the business. If there are temporary setbacks, this is a fine way to lose friends.

### Stockholder Relations

After an initial public stock offering, it is extremely important to develop and maintain a strong public relations program with your company's stockholders and the financial fraternity. Consult with your public relations advisors and plan a program which will keep your stockholders informed as to the progress your company is making, new developments, appointments, etc. You will want to contact your stockholders by furnishing them with an interesting and readable annual report, interim reports, brochures and reports on stockholders' meetings. When you mail dividend checks to the stockholders, enclose a report or news letter. It costs no more to include this material.

Be sure that you answer promptly all letters from stockholders. You will receive many interesting suggestions—some good—others not so good. In all events, be sure you answer letters courteously and promptly.

Many companies invite stockholders to visit the plant. This can build important good will for the company.

### Initial Welcome Letter

Most public corporations send a letter of welcome to stockholders upon their acquisition of stock in the company. This is an important public relations gesture which every company should adopt as it creates a good relationship between the company and its stockholders.

Very often the company sells consumer products and by establishing good solid relationships with the stockholders, new customers can be developed. Many companies rely upon their stockholders to give preference to the purchase of the company's products.

In preparing a welcome letter to your company's stockholders, you may want to give consideration to making reference to the following subjects taken from letters of various companies:

### Company Brochure

*E. I. Du Pont De Nemours & Company.*   Under separate cover, I am sending you a booklet "This is Du Pont" which presents a pictorial summary of the Du Pont Company and its activities. I hope you will find the booklet interesting and informative.

### Credit Cards

*Texaco, Inc.*   If you do not already have a Texaco National Credit Card, our Sales Department would like to send you one. All you need to do is fill out the enclosed form and drop it in the mail.

### Customer Development

*P. H. Glatfelter Co.*   Your Company is widely known for its pulp and paper making achievements. Its products have earned a good reputation. Currently these include book, bond, mimeograph, envelope, tablet and offset papers, plus some specialties such as drinking cup, doily and box-lining. It would be of help if you would remind others, as the occasion arises, of the advantages of using Glatfelter papers.

## Dividends

*Republic Steel Corp.*   The Board of Directors considers the declaration of dividends on common stock four times a year and checks for dividends declared are mailed to stockholders about the 23rd of April, July, October and December.

## General

*American Hospital Supply Corp.*   Your Corporation plays an important role in the health of the nation. I feel that you as a shareholder will have reason to take pride in American's activities and achievements. Be assured that we will do our best to make your investment a happy and profitable experience.

## Protection of Stock Certificates

*E. I. Du Pont De Nemours & Company.*   Please give your stock certificates careful protection because it is difficult and costly to replace them. To secure a replacement you would be required to furnish an affidavit and an indemnity bond. You could expect the bond to cost at least 3% of your stock's market value.

## Quarterly Reports

*Simplicity Manufacturing Co.*   Your Company's business is seasonal and operations in any one quarter are not indicative of annual operations; therefore, quarterly statements are not sent shareholders, unless requested.

## Special Features

*United States Steel Corporation.*   We endeavor to keep our stockholders fully informed through the annual reports, issued about the end of March, through the U.S. Steel Quarterly and through releases to the press. You will also be interested in the messages on our program, "The United States Steel Hour," which is televised on alternate Wednesday evenings. However, we will be happy to answer any of your questions about the Corporation.

## Visits

*Shulton, Incorporated.*   If at sometime you are in the vicinity of our modern plant in Clifton, New Jersey, please feel free to stop in and visit with us. Your inquiries and suggestions concerning the company and its products are always welcome.

*Florida Power & Light Co.*   Florida is a grand place to live, work and play —but don't take our word for it. Come on down, visit some of our district offices, let members of our organization tell you more about their territory. You, too, may then decide to enjoy a longer and fuller life by making Florida your home.

## Words of Welcome

*General Electric Co.*   It is my hope that this letter will serve to express the very real sense of welcome that your management and Board of Directors desire to impart to you on becoming a share owner of General Electric.

Records should be checked before sending out a welcome letter to new stockholders to be certain that a letter isn't sent to a person who is already a stockholder.

Many corporations send a letter to a stockholder who sells his stock in the company. This builds future good will. The selling stockholder may some day become a stockholder again.

# 37

# Interim and Quarterly Reports

Periodically, after your corporation becomes publicly owned, you will issue reports to stockholders. While these reports are primarily intended to give stockholders information about sales, earnings and dividends, these reports offer an excellent opportunity for the corporation to acquaint its stockholders with new products, prospects for the future, executive changes, etc. A review of some recent reports show the following subjects discussed.

## Acquisitions

*Mead Johnson.* In August your Company announced the acquisition for $800,000 of Charles McDonald Pty., Ltd., of Sydney, Australia. The McDonald firm manufactures and markets a line of 25 products, including sedatives, analgesics, vitamins and hematinics. The company operates modern headquarters facilities, consisting of a manufacturing plant, quality control laboratory and administrative offices.

## Advertising Program

*The Siegler Corp.* During the past quarter, Siegler initiated a corporate advertising program. The schedule includes advertisements in Fortune, U. S. News & World Report, Aviation Week and Electronics magazines. For your information, we are enclosing a reprint of our first advertisement.

## Aims

*Coastal States Gas Production Co.* The entire management of Coastal States is fully aware of the responsibility which your support carries, and our earnest efforts are constantly being applied to advance the Company's success.

## Awards

*IBM.*   IBM's Federal Systems Division has won the largest non-military order for data processing machines ever awarded by the U. S. Government.

The Internal Revenue Service will install the machines in centers around the country during the next ten years. The IBM equipment will be used to automate the collection of tax revenues received by the Federal Government.

## Backlog

*Varian Associates.*   During the third quarter, order receipts of $16,327,217 brought the backlog for the Company's services and products to an all time high of $27,590,999. The Company's expansion program is proceeding on schedule to provide facilities required to meet the increased order volume.

## Citizenship Program

*The Ford Company.*   The Ford Effective Citizenship Program, aimed at encouraging greater political activity by Company employees, was launched in April. The purpose and nature of the program was described to supervisory personnel at all Company locations in the United States.

## Data Processing

*Texas Instruments Inc.*   The first IBM 7070 all-transistorized data processing system to be delivered to private industry was accepted by TI and installed in the company's new Data Processing Center in Dallas. The system incorporates more than 41,000 TI-manufactured transistors and significantly increases the company's data processing capabilities for accounting and research and engineering computations.

## Earnings

*Parke, Davis & Company.*   Company President Harry J. Loynd reported to the stockholders the sales and earnings figures which you will find elsewhere in this enclosure.

He cautioned the shareholders "not to project this first quarter earning rate for the full year by a simple multiplication of four.

*Thompson Ramo Wooldridge Inc.*   Earnings for both the third quarter and the first nine months reflect heavy non-recurring charges largely arising out of the reorientation of the role of Space Technology Laboratories, Inc., as reported in the last quarterly letter. The earnings also reflect a non-recurring gain of approximately $960,000 after taxes, resulting from a change in the method of pricing the inventory of a subsidiary in order to conform with practices elsewhere in the Company. In addition, expenditures for new product development and exploitation continued at a high level.

## Employment

*General Motors.* In the first six months of 1960 the number of people employed by General Motors throughout the world averaged 611,374 and payrolls totaled $1,795 million, compared with 580,488 employees and payrolls of $1,598 million in the first half of 1959. During the second quarter of 1960 average employment was 601,165 and payrolls totaled $861 million. In the corresponding period of 1959 average employment was 576,365 and payrolls totaled $803 million.

## Exhibits

*IBM.* The big trailer-truck pictured below is touring the United States with an exhibit of IBM's new check handling equipment for banks.

Bankers attending the exhibit are shown how this equipment can automatically process checks by reading numbers printed on them in magnetic ink. They are also invited to try the machines themselves, using magnetic ink checks from their own banks.

## Expansion

*Sears, Roebuck and Co.* Homart Development Co., a wholly-owned subsidiary, has been organized to own and develop shopping centers which will include a Sears store. Homart has under construction a shopping center at Fort Worth, Texas. In addition, land has been purchased for shopping centers in Austin, Texas, and Albany, New York.

## Foreign Operations

*Texaco, Inc.* Stockholders were informed by letter of July 5 of the Cuban Government's seizure on June 29 of Texaco's 20,000 barrel-a-day refinery and other properties in Cuba because of the Company's refusal to purchase and refine Russian crude oil.

## Growth

*American Hospital Supply Corp.* These gains were generated by three primary factors, probably with about equal weight: we are favored by operating in a growing market; we attracted a larger share of the health dollar to our companies in exchange for goods and services of the highest character; we acquired additional manufacturing and marketing components.

## Labor Relations

*Hamilton Cosco, Inc.* On September 13, a three-year contract including a no-strike clause was signed with the Teamsters and Carpenters Union, representing the company's production and maintenance employees at the Columbus plant. The company believes the terms of the contract are fair and workable.

## Litigation

*Alpha Cements.* Recently the Supreme Court of the United States rendered a unanimous decision against the taxpayer in a case involving percentage depletion on clay. It was in some respects similar but by no means identical to our own controversy with the Treasury Department. At present it is not possible to determine to what extent, if any, the principal factors involved in this case will apply to cement. Until this problem is resolved we will continue to report earnings on the more favorable basis as used in our recent reports.

## New Contracts

*Thompson Ramo Wooldridge Inc.* Among the new contracts recently awarded the company are two of particular importance on which work has already begun. One is a contract to develop new high-performance booster pumps for the North American B-70 "Valkyrie" 2,000 mph bomber, and the other is a contract to develop a miniature auxiliary power supply ("MIN-IAPS").

## Operations

*P. H. Glatfelter Co.* The demand for our papers during the second quarter enabled us to operate an average of 6½ days per week.

## Over-the-Counter Listing

*Hamilton Cosco, Inc.* The National Association of Securities Dealers, Inc. now quotes the bid and asked prices of Hamilton Cosco, Inc. stock. The Over-The-Counter National Listing is carried daily by leading financial newspapers.

## Products

*The Martin Company.* TITAN, with 24 firings, has the best performance record of any ICBM tested to date; and the PERSHING has, during this quarter, successfully completed the first stage of its test program, incidentally setting a new record at Cape Canaveral. BULLPUP deliveries now total several thousand and since the first practical production of the LACROSSE in 1957 sizable quantities have been delivered to the Army. In addition, foreign governments have displayed continuing interest in the MACE because it is the only guided missile which possesses unique low-level capability.

## Profits

*The Brunswick-Balke-Callender Co.* While the fourth quarter of the year normally yields lower sales and earnings than in the previous three months, and the steel strike may affect our shipments of some products, highly satisfactory results for the full year are assured. Equally important is the welding of a strong management structure that we believe will carry Brunswick to new successes in 1960 and future years.

*Kawneer.* The management of Kawneer is very disappointed with first quarter profits and is taking immediate actions necessary to improve profit margins. In spite of the poor first quarter we think that the final results for 1960 will compare favorably with 1959, providing the general level of business does not decline this year. Within the last few weeks we have noted a general increase in incoming orders.

## Research

*The Martin Company.* The Company's pure research organization known as RIAS stands as a prominent example of the ability of private industry to offer a means which eventually will permit basic research to become self-sustaining.

## Sales

*Shulton.* Domestic toiletry sales have shown excellent growth during the first six months and we expect this trend will continue for the remainder of the year. The new prestige line of men's toiletries under the brand name YORK TOWN has done well in test markets and will be available in better stores across the nation shortly.

## Sale of Stock

*Hamilton Cosco, Inc.* The sale of 300,000 shares of common stock of the corporation by major shareholders was registered with the Federal Securities and Exchange Commission on June 28th, 1960. The underwriting was managed jointly by Smith, Barney & Co., Inc., New York City, and City Securities Corporation, Indianapolis.

## Stock Dividend

*The Diners' Club, Inc.* The Company has been advised by counsel that shares of common stock received by a stockholder in payment of a stock dividend do not constitute taxable income for such purposes.

## Stockholders

*American Hospital Supply Corp.* The registry of owners of the corporation climbed to nearly 8,500, compared with about 4,500 at this time last year.

## Suggestion Program

*IBM.* The delighted lady is IBM employee Ruth D. Wilson who has just been awarded $4,100 for a suggestion that will result in significant savings for the Company.

Mrs. Wilson's idea, which received the highest employee suggestion award ever won by a woman in IBM, will reduce the time needed to produce components used in IBM accounting machines.

Some 17,000 IBM employees were awarded nearly $760,000 last year for suggestions that improved customer service, advanced product design, and reduced production costs.

Recommendations for improving our business are received every day from IBM employees throughout the world. Accepted suggestions are eligible for awards ranging from $25 to $25,000.

## Taxes

*Central and South West Corp.* All dividends paid by the Corporation in 1959 represent taxable income to stockholders for Federal income taxes. The dividends qualify under the Internal Revenue Code, however, for: (a) the $50 exclusion allowed individuals, and (b) the credit against one's tax of 4% of certain dividends received.

Some corporations are stressing the political responsibilty of shareholders. The president of the Glidden Company recently wrote to the shareholders of the company stressing the need for being vigilant in keeping our own economic system healthy and strong in the struggle between communism and the free world. The Glidden Company pointed out the ways that the stockholders of the company could be helpful in meeting the challenge of the sixties.

# 38

## Future Relationship with Dealers, Brokers, the SEC and Your Investment Banker

The professional investors and security analysts will adopt a close and continuing interest in your company after a public stock offering. It would be well for you to adopt a strong public relations program to keep this group advised of new developments, expansion plans, etc. Their opinions are valued by institutional buyers and potential stockholders.

Many dealers will be active in the sale of securities of your company and they will want to be kept current on the activities of your company. Provide them with information which will permit them to accurately appraise your company's stock. Give them the opportunity to make a judgment based on fact rather than hunch. Send to them your corporate reports—annual and interim, as well as company brochures, advertising pieces, copies of speeches before Societies of Security Analysts. They will appreciate your help in keeping their files on your company up to date. They will use this information to encourage investment in your company's stock if the facts and projections warrant this recommendation.

After a registration statement has become effective, it is necessary to file periodic reports with the SEC under the provisions of Section 13 and 15 (d) of the SEC Act of 1934. After the registration becomes effective, you will receive a letter from the SEC outlining the reporting requirements. The letter will be in the following form:

Gentlemen:

As you no doubt know, the registration statement of your Company which recently became effective under the Securities Act of 1933 contains an undertaking to file periodic reports with this Commission under Section 15 (d) of the Securities Exchange Act of 1934.

This is to advise you that the undertaking is now operative and that our records show that the periodic reports identified below will be due from

187

your Company. To avoid any misunderstanding, please let us know if you believe that our records are not correct in this matter.

*Report and due dates*                             *First such report and date due*

Annual reports on Form 10-K due within 120 days after the close of each fiscal year. (See Instruction F of Form 10-K for the requirement to furnish to the Commission copies of the Company's annual reports to stockholders.)

Semi-annual reports on Form 9-K for the first half of each fiscal year, due within 45 days after the close of such period.

Current reports on Form 8-K for each month in which any one or more of the events specified in Form 8-K takes place, due within 10 days after the close of the month in which event or events occur. Attention is directed particularly to Item 11 of Form 8-K regarding the requirement to file a report on this Form when matters are submitted to a vote of security holders.

One copy each of Forms 10-K, 9-K and 8-K is enclosed for your ready reference as to the type of information called for by these forms. If you need additional copies of these forms, you may request them directly from this Commission; blanks for filing purposes are not furnished.

A copy of the Commission's General Rules and Regulations under the Securities Exchange Act of 1934 is also enclosed for your information as to the formal filing requirements. Any additional copies of this publication that you may need must be purchased directly from the United States Government.

Form 10-K requires the filing with the SEC of four copies of the annual report to the stockholders of the company. The report must contain certified balance sheets, profit and loss statements, and information on registration on security exchanges, etc. If there has been a material change in the business, a disclosure must be made. The report must record the principal holders of voting securities, directors, remuneration of officers and directors, options to purchase securities, interest of management and others in certain transactions, etc.

The SEC requires that the registrant file semi-annual reports on Form 9K within 45 days after the end of the period. If the registrant makes available to its stockholders a report containing the information required, in Form 9K, the report may be incorporated by reference. Form 9K requires the reporting of six month's profit and loss and earned surplus information.

The SEC requires the registrant to file Form 8K with the Commission, in the 10 days after the close of the month where certain events have occurred. Current reports of this type must be filed to show changes in control of a registrant, acquisition or disposition if a significant amount of assets other than in the ordinary course of business, changes in securities, and defaults upon senior securities. The registrant must also report an increase or decrease in the amount of securities outstanding, granting of options to purchase securities, and re-evaluation of assets or a restatement of the capital share account. A disclosure must be made on Form 8K of any matters submitted to a vote of the security holders and other materially important events. Financial reports and exhibits covering certain transactions must be included with the filing of Form 8K with the Commission.

### Relationship with Your Investment Banker After Sale

In your talks with your investment banker you should talk about your relationship with them after the initial stock offering is completed. Your relationship with your investment banker will normally be a long and continuing one. If you are satisfied with the result of your initial stock offering, you will want to keep a close relationship with your investment banker. You can benefit from the financial advice that you will receive from your investment banker.

Mr. Frederick W. Straus, Partner in Straus, Blosser & McDowell, in stressing the importance of continuing relationships between investment, banker and the company, in a paper that he delivered before the American Management Association, stated:

> In any event, no underwriter will be particularly interested in handling your financing if he thinks this is the only business he is ever going to have with you. He goes into your deal with the hope that this will be the first of a succession of profitable pieces of business between the two of you. This can be done only if your stock enjoys a good market after the underwriting. It must have public acceptance and public confidence, and it can't have either unless you will help your banker by giving him your fullest cooperation. In this respect, the hiring of public relations counsel *can* be extremely helpful, but I do not recommend it in all cases.

> This brings me to a related and final point. Because of its importance in helping to maintain a good market after the underwriting, I consider it important enough to treat it by itself. I could call it "How *not* to win friends and influence shareholders," but I would rather call it "Don't withhold information—even if it is bad."

> In negotiating an underwriting you will have opened all the doors of your company to your banker. Make this open door policy a habit. Once your public offering is completed it is extremely important that you give your underwriter constant information regarding important events that are taking place in your company. It is essential that he know what is going on in your business so that he can in turn inform his customers, and other dealers who are interested in the stock of your company.

> I don't care whether the information you give is good or bad. Times can't

always be good. There must be some time in every company's life when its business is suffering a slight reversal. Don't hesitate to tell this to your banker. It is the fear of the unknown that is worse than any bad news that you can give out.

Mr. Straus also states, "Many people have compared the relationship between a company and its investment banker to that of a husband and wife in the early stages of their marriage. The marriage between the company and its investment banker can succeed only if there is mutual confidence. If there is suspicion and a lack of confidence or lack of understanding, this relationship, like that of husband and wife, is very likely to go on the rocks."

There will be many times where you will need to get the point of view of the investing public and your investment banker is in the best position to advise you.

It is also important to maintain a good relationship with your underwriter for future financing. There may well come a time when you wish to sell an additional amount of stock and your investment banker will be in a very good position to advise you on this. In some contracts between the company and the underwriter, it is provided that the company give to the underwriter the right of first refusal for future financing plans.

# 39

## Selling Stock on an Exchange or in the "Over-the-Counter" Market

In your total thinking about a public stock offering for your company, you will want to give consideration to the method of distribution of your company's stock in the future. Your company's stock will be sold initially on an "over-the-counter" basis, but at some point you will want to consider whether this stock should be listed on an exchange. You will ask your legal advisors and your underwriters "What are the advantages of listing our company's stock on an exchange—or should we continue to sell our securities over-the-counter?" Obviously, there are many advantages and disadvantages to both plans.

Actually, the "over-the-counter" market is the biggest securities market in the world. It has no one place of doing business. It is a method of doing business on a negotiated basis. It functions solely through securities dealers over a vast network of telephones and teletype equipment.

The term "over-the-counter" market itself is confusing. It is believed to have originated from the practice in the early 1800's before stock exchanges were established in this country, when securities were traded and settlements were made over the counters of private banking houses. On occasions, it is called the "unlisted" or "off board" market, indicating that it has no official roster of stocks and bonds it handles.

There are few exact statistics about the size of the over-the-counter market. National Quotation Bureau, Inc., a private firm which serves this segment of the stock market, publishes daily price quotations on around 5,000 over the counter stocks and 2,000 bonds. There are in excess of 4,000 broker-dealers who maintain markets in issues sold over-the-counter.

Many more securities are sold in the over-the-counter market than on the Exchanges. It is important to know that the over-the-counter market is referred to as "a negotiated" market, since prices are determined not through auction but through negotiation between representatives of buyers and sellers. There are

191

many top grade securities that are only traded in the over-the-counter market. There are also many issues that are traded in the over-the-counter market which do not qualify for the large Exchanges, because their earnings or number of stockholders have not reached the minimum provided by the Exchanges. There is no reflection upon a stock merely because it is sold over-the-counter and not on one of the Exchanges. If an issue is small, or there are few potential buyers, the security might well be sold in the over-the-counter market.

Some companies have not listed the securities on an exchange before, because they prefer the relative obscurity of "over-the-counter" trading, others are of the opinion that over-the-counter sales are less volatile. Some object to the additional SEC regulations which come into effect when stock is listed. Your underwriter will advise you against listing if your company stock is unseasoned. Often times dealers will place greater promotional efforts and conduct more activity in the sale of an unlisted security because of the larger commissions or earnings that occur in over-the-counter transactions.

### Functions

The over-the-counter market serves three major functions:

1. It provides a market for outstanding shares of unlisted companies.
2. It provides a distribution place for the sale of new security issues, operating as a selling arm in investment underwriting.
3. It is the market where many large blocks of securities are sold for individuals, estates and institutions.

Whereas the exchanges operate as auction markets, the OTC market generally conducts business by negotiation. Broker-dealers contact each other and negotiate the bid and asked (or offer) prices. The bid side represents the price at which a security can be sold; the ask side the price at which a security can be purchased.

When someone wants to buy or sell an over-the-counter security, they ask their broker to get the bid-asked prices. The broker then calls from one to four other broker-dealers for this information and reports back the best price he obtains.

In many transactions, the price for buying or selling that he quotes is the "net price"; that is, it is the price a buyer must pay; no commission is involved. The broker makes his profit on what he can buy or sell the security for in trading with another dealer.

To illustrate, let's assume that Mr. Jones wants to buy 100 shares of stock in your company. He goes to his broker who doesn't own any of your company stock. The broker will in turn call other dealers, including your principal underwriter, who may maintain an inventory of your company's stock. The lowest offering quote may be $25.00 a share. This is the "inside" price to Jones' broker, who will quote possibly $25.50 as a net price to Jones. No commission is paid. The broker makes his profit on the spread. Some firms will handle OTC transactions on an agency basis and charge a commission that approximates that charged on sales made on an exchange.

### Disadvantages

One of the disadvantages of purchasing stock in the over-the-counter market is the wide spread that often exists between the bid and asked quotations. There may be a difference of two to three points in the over-the-counter market, whereas on the New York Stock Exchange, for example, a stock is generally quoted on a much narrower spread, which is often one-eighth to one-half of a point.

The Board of Governors of the National Association of Security Dealers, Inc. has established a policy for its members with respect to mark-ups on the sale of securities traded in the over-the-counter market. Generally, the profit margin should not exceed 5 per cent. The Board has stated that under certain conditions, a mark-up in excess of 5 per cent may be justified, but on the other hand, 5 per cent is by no means always justified. The Board has stated that members of the Association should take into consideration in establishing the mark-up, such factors as type of security involved, availability of the security in the market, price of security, pattern of mark-ups, etc.

Over-the-counter dealers justify their higher charges on the grounds that they have to carry an inventory, that it often requires more time and effort to complete an OTC transaction than it does on an exchange, and that they often must take greater risks in their trading than is present on an exchange.

There are no fixed prices set for over-the-counter securities. They are not quoted on an Exchange. Newspapers carry quotations of the major stocks that are traded in the over-the-counter market. The dealers furnish information to the newspaper giving the bid and asked price. The price that appears in the newspaper is usually based upon an average of bid and asked prices from three different brokers.

*Over-the-Counter Securities Review,* a monthly magazine devoted to business and financial news of companies comprising the over-the-counter security markets, answered the question, "Why buy over-the-counter?" in this way:

> Our own belief is that the over-the-counter market should be inviting to the investor because it contains so many investment opportunities which have not been discovered or fully developed by the vast majority of the investment community. There are very few "undiscovered" stocks on the New York Stock Exchange or other exchanges, although occasionally an obscure issue

may take fire. By the very nature of the unlisted market and its lack of a definite perimeter within which all "unlisted" companies trade, there are many stocks which even in today's highly communicative society have not been discovered or are not widely known to most investors.

### National Quotation Bureau, Inc.

Each day an organization known as The National Quotation Bureau, Inc. publishes private reports showing the bid and asked price on the major companies selling stock in the over-the-counter market. Brokers and dealers report quotations daily to the Bureau. These reports are sold to a large number of investment brokers and stock brokers throughout the country, who use the quotations as a guide. The bid and offered prices shown are not for the general public but serve as a guide to brokers who are interested in getting information on the wholesale market. The spread between the bid and asked price in the wholesale market is generally narrower than the price quoted in the retail market—the market in which the general public trades in over-the-counter securities.

## THE EXCHANGE

### Advantages of Listing on an Exchange

There are many reasons why a company should consider listing its securities on an exchange. Some of the reasons are as follows:

### Corporations Viewpoint

1. Enhances Advertising Value—particularly where the products of the company are distributed to the general public.
2. Listing often enlarges the stockholder's list, both numerically and geographically.
3. Aids subsequent financing.
4. Increases prestige of company.
5. Facilitates acquisitions and mergers. Family owned corporations often prefer to exchange their stock for shares of a listed company.
6. Greater interest in stock by large stock brokerage firms.
7. Listing attracts institutional investors as well as individuals.

### Stockholders' and Investors' Viewpoint

1. Transactions are on an agency basis and sales are made at a lower commission cost.
2. Trading volume and prices are public.

3. Stockholders are kept abreast of price changes.
4. Ease of disposing of large blocks of stock.
5. Investors have a broader market.
6. Listed stock has greater collateral value for borrowing purposes.

While listed companies generally are of middle to large size, the majority of publicly held companies have not chosen to apply for a stock exchange listing because they cannot meet the listing requirements. Certain companies may refrain from listing because of the more detailed reporting requirements of the exchanges. Also some companies are of the opinion that the dealers will push unlisted stock because they earn more on over the counter sales.

Some companies are listed on more than one exchange. In such cases, their stock may trade at fractionally different prices.

The majority of the listed companies are on three exchanges—the New York Stock Exchange and the American Stock Exchange in New York City and the Midwest Stock Exchange in Chicago. There are more than 1,500 listed security issues on the New York Stock Exchange, more than 800 on the American and more than 500 on the Midwest. Several other larger cities across the country have exchanges but they do far less business.

There are many registered stock exchanges operating in America. The Securities Exchange Commission reports annually on the volume of sales effected on exchanges. The report for the year 1960 shows the following:

BREAKDOWN OF 1960 DATA BY REGISTERED EXCHANGES

| | Total Market Value (Dollars) | Stocks | |
|---|---|---|---|
| | | Market Value (Dollars) | Number of Shares |
| All Registered Exchanges | 46,900,630,211 | 45,218,847,358 | 1,388,609,692 |
| American Stock Exch. | 4,262,445,309 | 4,176,295,569 | 300,600,576 |
| Boston Stock Exch. | 272,155,515 | 272,155,515 | 5,606,360 |
| Chicago Board of Trade | 0 | 0 | 0 |
| Cincinnati Stock Exch. | 34,927,520 | 34,824,811 | 690,280 |
| Detroit Stock Exch. | 154,537,769 | 154,501,007 | 4,805,512 |
| Midwest Stock Exchange | 1,235,463,563 | 1,235,159,894 | 31,432,388 |
| New York Stock Exchange | 39,552,249,282 | 37,959,590,816 | 958,309,904 |
| Pacific Coast Stock Exch. | 883,358,081 | 881,155,042 | 43,414,811 |
| Phila.-Balt. Stock Exch. | 471,324,508 | 470,996,040 | 12,170,871 |
| Pittsburgh Stock Exch. | 28,271,079 | 28,271,079 | 792,714 |
| Salt Lake Stock Exch. | 2,396,023 | 2,396,023 | 16,727,002 |
| San Francisco Mining Exch. | 1,185,948 | 1,185,948 | 11,153,372 |
| Spokane Stock Exchange | 2,315,614 | 2,315,614 | 2,905,902 |

BREAKDOWN OF 1960 DATA BY EXEMPTED EXCHANGES

| | Total Market Value (Dollars) | Market Value (Dollars) | Number of Shares |
|---|---|---|---|
| All Exempted Exchanges | 12,990,862 | 12,712,064 | 1,086,420 |
| Colo. Springs Stock Exch. | 88,585 | 88,585 | 546,821 |
| Honolulu Stock Exch. | 11,654,025 | 11,375,227 | 509,728 |
| Richmond Stock Exch. | 807,663 | 807,663 | 17,598 |
| Wheeling Stock Exch. | 440,589 | 440,589 | 12,273 |

*New York Stock Exchange*

The largest stock exchange is, of course, the New York Stock Exchange located in New York City. This Exchange, also known as the "Big Board," while deciding each company application for listing on its own merits, generally requires the following:

1. Demonstrated earning power under competitive conditions of more than one million dollars annually after all charges and taxes.
2. Net tangible assets of more than ten million dollars.
3. At least 500,000 common shares outstanding (exclusive of concentrated or family holdings) among not less than 1,500 stockholders, after substantially discounting odd lot ownership.

The New York Stock Exchange, in a recent booklet entitled, *Understanding the New York Stock Exchange,* stated:

> At the time a company qualifies for listing on the Stock Exchange, it must be a going concern with substantial assets and demonstrated earning power. The Exchange places greater emphasis on such considerations as degree of national interest in the company, its standing in its particular field, the character of the market for its product, relative stability and position in its industry. The company's stock should have a sufficiently wide distribution to offer reasonable assurance that an adequate auction market in its securities will exist.

The listing agreement between a company and the New York Stock Exchange is designed to provide prompt disclosure to the public of earnings reports, dividend notices, and certain other information which may substantially affect security values or influence investment decisions. This exchange also expects companies to agree to solicit proxies for all meetings of stockholders. In applying for listing, a company also must furnish similar data to the Securities and Exchange Commission.

The initial fee for listing on the New York Stock Exchange is computed as follows: $100 per 10,000 shares, or fraction thereof, for the first 500,000 shares listed; $50 per 10,000 shares, or fraction thereof, for the next 1,500,000 shares and $25 per 10,000 shares, or fraction thereof, for shares in excess of 2,000,000. The minimum fee is $2,000.

The New York Stock Exchange charges a continuing annual fee for fifteen years. This fee is computed on the basis of $100 per 100,000 shares, or fraction thereof, for the first 2,000,000 shares and $50 per 100,000 shares or fraction thereof, in excess of 2,000,000. The minimum fee is $500 per year.

The minimum commission rates which may be charged by New York Stock

Exchange members on purchase or sale transactions of customers are figured on 100 share lots:

On a purchase or sale between $100 and $399.99, 2 per cent plus $3. The minimum commission is $6.

On a purchase or sale from $400 to $2,399.99, 1 per cent plus $7.

On a purchase or sale from $2,400 to $4,999.99, one-half of one per cent plus $19.

On a purchase or sale amounting to $5,000 or more, one-tenth of one per cent plus $39, provided that amount does not exceed $75 per 100-share transaction. On odd lots the commission is $2 lower per transaction.

The Federal Government collects a transfer tax of 4 cents per $100 of actual value of the shares sold or transferred. The minimum tax per transaction is 4 cents; the maximum tax per share is 8 cents on stocks selling at $200 or more.

New York State levies a transfer tax of from 1 to 4 cents a share, based on selling price of the stock.

Federal and State transfer taxes are paid by the seller.

Mr. T. G. Murdough, president of the American Hospital Supply Corporation, pointed out the responsibility of a company being listed on the New York Exchange by stating:

A company listing on the New York Stock Exchange must realize they have taken on a pretty direct partnership relationship with the Exchange in which full disclosure of even minor acts is generally necessary. Officers and directors of the company have additional responsibility for disclosures on any trading done in the company stock. Such disclosures on the part of the corporation, or its principals, are often costly in terms of legal and other professional opinions and counsel. Also, the company must realize the necessity of keeping stockholders more fully informed of corporate activity once they are listed on the Big Board, which is thus more costly.

The New York Exchange in its booklet entitled *Understanding the New York Stock Exchange* reported:

A primary objective of the Board is to maintain the kind of auction market the public expects for a listed security. The factors involved in continued listing on the Exchange are not measured mathematically; the Board may act to suspend or delist a security in any situation where it feels a security is not suitable for retention on the list. In considering a specific case, the Board will give weight to all factors affecting the security and the company.

For example, suspension of trading or delisting will normally be considered if a common stock is held by less than 250 stockholders after substantially discounting off lots; if common shares outstanding, exclusive of concentrated or family holdings, total less than 30,000 shares; or if total market value of the common shares, exclusive of concentrated or family holdings, is less than $500,000.

Other examples of circumstances under which suspension or delisting may be considered include situations where the size of the company has fallen below $2,000,000 in net tangible assets or aggregate market value of its common stock and average earnings after taxes have been below $200,000 for the last three years, or where liquidation of the company has begun, or substantially all of the company's assets have been sold. Delisting of a common stock will also be considered if the issuing company has violated its agreements with the Exchange.

## American Stock Exchange

The second largest exchange in the country is The American Stock Exchange, located in New York City. It was formerly known as the New York Curb Exchange. Its operations are very similar to the New York Stock Exchange. The requirements for listing on the American Stock Exchange are not as restrictive as the New York Stock Exchange. Under the rules of the American Stock Exchange, corporations applying for listing will be expected to show net worth of at least one million dollars; demonstrated earnings after all charges, including federal income tax, of at least $150,000 for the latest fiscal year preceding listing, and an average of at least $100,000 for the three years preceding listing; outstanding common shares must have a market value of at least two million dollars; publicly held common shares must have a market value of at least one million dollars; public distribution of at least 200,000 shares (exclusive of holdings of officers and directors and other concentrated or family holdings) among not less than 750 stockholders.

Of the 750 stockholders, not less than 500 must be holders of 100 shares or more.

## Midwest Stock Exchange

In 1949 the Chicago Stock Exchange consolidated its activities and organized the Midwest Stock Exchange. This exchange is the third largest in this country.

The listing requirements as expressed by the Midwest Stock Exchange are as follows:

### MIDWEST STOCK EXCHANGE LISTING POLICY

The prime requisite for listing on the Midwest Stock Exchange is the quality of the corporation. Its products and services must enjoy public acceptance and good reputation. Its management must operate the company in the public interest. Its securities must also meet the technical requirements of an auction market.

The Exchange is desirous of assisting new enterprises, as well as smaller businesses, but it is not interested in purely promotional ventures or a company whose products and services do not benefit the public. Therefore, the following requirements must be met in order for the Exchange to entertain an application for listing:

A. The Company must have at least $2,000,000, in net tangible assets.
B. It must be actively engaged in business and have been so operating for at least three consecutive years.
C. It shall have 250,000 or more shares outstanding of the common stock to be listed.
D. Such outstanding shares must be owned by 1,000 shareholders or more, a substantial majority of whom must own at least 100 shares.
E. It shall maintain stock transfer and registrar facilities independent of each other. The transfer agency may be the corporate office of the company, but the registrar must be a bank or trust company.
F. Its certificates of stock shall be fully engraved, prepared by an approved bank note company.
G. The Exchange must be satisfied (a) as to the adequacy of the company's working capital; (b) that the management enjoys a reputation of good character, competence and integrity; (c) as to its ability to show net earnings of at least $100,000 annually; and (d) that the company has agreed to publish periodic reports.

## National Stock Exchange

The Securities and Exchange Commission approved in August 1960 the registration statement of the National Stock Exchange, Inc. The new exchange was sponsored by the Mercantile Exchange of New York and operates in New York City. This exchange was the first new exchange organized in 30 years and will not list stocks traded on any other exchange. The majority of listings will come from over-the-counter securities. Minimum listing requirements for the National Stock Exchange are as follows: 500 stockholders, corporate net worth in excess of $1-million and 100,000 shares of stock outstanding. There is no requirement that an applicant's earning power exceed any minimum amount. The National Exchange will use tenths of dollars in trading instead of the customary fractions of eighths and sixteenths.

## Cincinnati Stock Exchange

The Cincinnati Stock Exchange does not have any specific rules on the number of shares or number of stockholders required as a condition to listing on its exchange. C. H. Steffens, president of the Cincinnati Stock Exchange, in discussing listing on the Cincinnati Stock Exchange stated: "A rule of thumb is that corporations should have outstanding at least 10,000 shares with 100 to 150 stockholders."

## Pacific Coast Stock Exchange

Under the requirements of the Pacific Coast Stock Exchange, a company attempting to qualify for listing must have:

- (a) a proven record of financial responsibility
- (b) ascertained and sound asset value and net worth
- (c) demonstrated earning power
- (d) at least 500 stockholders
- (e) at least 150,000 shares in public hands in relatively small lots exclusive of "control" stock and more than 250,000 shares issued and outstanding.

The applicant company must be an established concern or successor to a going concern. A history of successful business operations is also desirable. However, in the case of relatively new companies there must be adequate financing to attain successful production. Only in unusual cases will the Listing Committee give consideration to the application of a company in an exploratory or development stage. The Committee also is unwilling to consider applications of companies whose stock may be in the so-called "penny stock" class.

## Toronto Stock Exchange

In order to be listed on the Toronto Stock Exchange, the company must have a sufficient number of shareholders to insure an adequate public market and a substantial number of shareholders must be residents of Canada. The Governors of the Toronto Stock Exchange have not established a definite policy regarding the number of shares which they require to be outstanding and the dollar amount of the issue. This is left entirely to the discretion of the Board of Governors.

The Toronto exchange does not have any different requirements for American companies except that when less than 5 per cent of the company shareholders are residents of Canada, the initial maximum listing fee is $10,000 instead of $15,000.

## Montreal Stock Exchange

There are no set requirements as to the number of shares that must be outstanding for an issue to be listed on the Montreal Stock Exchange. The minimum number of shareholders required for listing an issue is 100 and 20 per cent of the outstanding shares must be in the hands of the public.

The determining factor for any company whether to become listed on a national stock exchange, assuming it qualifies for listing thereon, or to remain traded over-the-counter would be the amount of interest presently indicated in the stock of the company and the maintenance of this interest by the financial community. If there is assurance that this interest would be present when a company becomes listed, then it would be advisable to do so. To become listed without the proper amount of interest or without the broad distribution initially or a satisfactory number of shares in public hands, even though the minimum requirements of the exchanges may be met, would mean that the financial community may lose a great deal of interest. In the over-the-counter market interest is maintained by dealers—both members of the exchange and non-members—who maintain active trading in many securities and sponsor many securities in order to provide their own organizations with merchandise to sell or buy. Generally, over-the-counter trading is more profitable than acting as agent for listed stocks. Thus, there is a good business reason for a dealer to maintain his interest in over-the-counter securities. Listing on a local exchange does not appear, therefore, to have any distinct advantage. It obviously decreases the interest of the local dealers and in some respects makes it more difficult for the national dealers to participate in the trading. The only possible advantage may occur for a company that is truly local in nature with a product that is locally distributed and for some reason wants the distinction of being listed on a stock exchange. Statistics presented in the SEC Annual Report for the fiscal year ended June 30, 1960 indicate that the general trend for companies is to have their stock traded over-the-counter or to become listed on the N.Y.S.E. or A.S.E.

# 40

## Visits by Security Analysts

It is well that you become familiar with the operations of the investment research departments of the investment banking and brokerage firms. Most of them maintain a very active department which consists of a group of analysts who are continuously studying the progress of many companies.

They are aware of the latest developments and research. The analysts make field trips for the purpose of gathering on-the-scene information, and study all the statistical material that becomes available. Some will visit you.

Many of these investment research departments publish detailed reports which are circulated broadly throughout the country. In all likelihood your company will become the subject for analysis by the investment research department of various underwriting firms and reports on your company will be issued after field trips are made to your company.

### Who They Want to See and Talk With

The analysts want to talk to top management. Be prepared to spend time with them when they visit your company as it is their intention to obtain their own first-hand impressions of you and your management team. It will not be sufficient for the president of the company to exchange a few pleasantries when they arrive and then pass them off to someone else for a detailed discussion of your company. The analysts, through their discussions with the president, will formulate their opinions as to his qualities of leadership, creative ability, drive, and his personal plan as well as the company's. While they are interested in the financial aspects of your company, they can obtain this information from your reports and discussion with your financial officer. Their judgment of your company, however, will depend to a large degree upon their personal visit with your company's top executives.

### What They Want to Learn

On their visit, they will try to formulate their impressions of your management team as well as the depth of management. They want to know what would happen to the company if the principal executive officer of the company was to be removed through sickness, death, or any other reason. They are viewing your corporation from the long-term point of view and they will study carefully the role that each one of your executives plays in the management of your corporation. They will look for weaknesses as well as strengths.

On these visits you will quite frequently be asked to give your financial estimates of the future for your company. These questions quite often prove troublesome, particularly if your company is in the early stages of its development. There is no hard and fast rule for you to follow in making projections and estimates for the future. If you do not wish to make projections that might some day embarrass you, there is no objection to telling the visitors that you are not in a position to make any "guesstimates" at present.

It might be well for you to prepare your visitors before the meeting by sending to them financial information, literature about the company, its products, sales methods, customers, etc. If you have biographical material on your executives, send this to your visitor in advance of his coming to your office. Try to give him as much knowledge of your company as possible before the interview to save time for both of you.

Some companies employ a financial officer to meet with visitors. It is important, however, to keep in mind, as pointed out above, that the interview will not be complete without a substantial personal visit with the chief executive officer of the company.

Although these meetings are time-consuming, it is important that you give sufficient time and attention to them, as the results have an important impact upon the future marketability of your company's stock.

Lawrence K. Gessner, a senior security analyst for Smith, Barney and Company, a member of the New York Society of Security Analysts, suggests the following as a guide to busy executives to help plan the meetings with analysts in the company offices.

> There are no hard and fast rules here because of the variations in types of visitors, their desires and personality variations on both sides of the desk. There is certainly no necessity for a prepared "pitch" or for an "opening statement." These men have come to ask questions and your job is to answer fully, yet concisely. It will fast become apparent whether or not the visitor has done his homework and is really interested. The degree of his knowledge will allow you to tailor the detail of your answers. I believe that the visitor should direct these conversations (within reasonable limits) whereas you direct the large analyst meetings. I do not believe, therefore, that any prior preparation is necessary on your part.

> The question of time to be given and "whom to see" is difficult. It certainly

is helpful to have one officer designated as chief contact man. However, the choice rests not so much with the rank, but with who does the job best (including liking it or disliking it). As an aside, the public relations man is usually not as acceptable to the analyst as an officer. If the company is of moderate size I think the president should make himself available, for perhaps fifteen minutes or at lunch, aside from the visitor's main interview man. If he is an informed visitor he has the right to meet briefly with other top men.

Most interviews (the major portion) should not take more than an hour. An exception is the representative from your underwriter. He must get real depth because he is, in turn, a source of non-confidential information to the investment community.

*Some Specifics:*

1. It is your right, I think, to insist on reviewing material which is to be issued publicly, for accuracy of facts—not for editing the writer's opinions. (Some company attorneys disagree with this policy.)
2. Invite the analyst to visit your plant.
3. When arrangements are made, ask if you can be helpful on hotels and travel accommodations if you are located in a small town.
4. Try to get something out of these meetings yourself. Many questions can start a train of thought and no one has all the ideas.
5. Put visitors on the mailing list.
6. Whether you discuss budgets and other confidential information is optional. It is obviously necessary to know whom you can trust in this regard.

After the visit by the security analysts, they will normally write a report on your company. Such reports have wide circulation and it is important that they be accurate. Most analysts will send to you a copy of the proposed report based upon the results of their visit. These reports will contain in detail the background of your company, performance, an appraisal of management, financial data, projections and outlook for the future. It is important in analyzing these reports that you do not accept the projections if they are not in accordance with your own business estimates.

If you accept the proposed report without comment, the analyst will assume that you are agreeing with his projections. If it is not your intention to make statements as to the future earnings of your company, it will be well for you to point this out in your letter to the analysts, commenting on the proposed reports.

# 41

## Meeting of Societies of Security Analysts

"You are invited to meet with the Society of Security Analysts"—this invitation will be extended to you from time to time from various societies around the country. It would be well for you to attend whenever possible as this group plays an important role in the securities business. Appearances before these groups should be considered an integral part of your financial public relations program. Appendix D contains a list showing the cities in which there is a group known as the Society of Security Analysts.

The members of the Society are security analysts who work for investment bankers, brokers, trust companies, banks, investment trusts, insurance companies, etc. These people are in a position to recommend the purchase of your company's securities. It is important that you give the analysts complete financial and operating information about your company.

It is well to prepare your presentation carefully before the meeting. You will be asked many questions, some of which you can anticipate and include in your remarks.

What subjects should you cover in your presentation? The following is an outline prepared by the New Society of Security Analysts which might aid you.

A. *Background of Company*
1. Brief history.
2. Company organization and management.
3. Major products (description).
    (a) Breakdown by product group, type of consumer and geographical market.
    (b) Source and availability of raw materials.
    (c) Competitive position and advantages and patent position.
4. Plant Capacity (number, size, style, location and age).
5. Production Schedules (number of shifts, length of work day and week).

6. Method Distribution.
   (a) Organization, size and compensation of sales staff.
   (b) Pricing policy and history.
   (c) Advertising program.

B. *Recent Record* (Statistical data for past five years)
   1. Sales.
      (a) Explanation of percentage gain or loss.
      (b) Trend in relation to industry average and company's trade position.
      (c) Review of selling costs as related to sales.
      (d) Other expense factors (raw materials, labor, overhead, etc.).
      (e) Price changes and comparison with domestic, European and world levels.
   2. Earnings (Before and After Taxes).
      (a) Explanation of trend.
      (b) Direction of profit margins.
      (c) Description of any non-recurring items.
      (d) Nature and size of reserves.
      (e) Tax allowance and Government tax incentives.

C. *Results for Last Fiscal Year* (Sales and Earnings)
   1. Reason for increase or decrease over prior year.
   2. Effects of recession and extent of recovery.
   3. Unusual profits or losses.
   4. Special price or wage adjustments.
   5. Other local factors.
   6. Basis for consolidation from subsidiaries and overseas divisions.

D. *Research Policy and Program*
   1. Size and organization of staff.
   2. Amounts or per cent of sales (turnover) spent annually on research.
   3. Per cent of current sales from new products traceable to research over past five to ten years.
   4. New products under development and their prospects.

E. *Capital Program*
   1. Percent added to plant capacity annually in past five years and costs.
   2. Expansion program (size, location, cost and time).
   3. Method of financing capital improvements.
   4. Depreciation policy.
   5. Plans for financing new construction.

F. *Capitalization*
   1. Current capitalization.
   2. History of bond and stock offerings in past five to ten years.

    3. Plans for recapitalization.

    4. Dividend policy and prospects for increases, extras or stock dividends.

    5. Per cent of shares held by management and other large shareholders.

G. *Other Factors*

    1. Employee relations (degree of unionization, wage and social benefits).

    2. Possible mergers, acquisitions or reorganizations.

    3. Special company considerations.

H. *Outlook for the Current Year and Beyond*

Leave time for questions—there will be plenty—answer them fully and fairly. If you don't know the answer, it's better to say you don't have the information than to make a guess which may be inaccurate.

Your attendance at the analysts meetings should prove helpful to you as you will get an outsider's point of view on your company policies, dividends, reputation, etc. The reactions of the analysts might well be an indication of your stockholders' opinions and reactions to your company. Consider the analysts meetings as a two way street—an opportunity for you to give information and also to get reactions which will be helpful to you in your stockholder relationships.

Lawrence K. Gessner, a senior security analyst for Smith, Barney & Co. and a member of the New York Society of Security Analysts, suggests the following guide for an effective approach before a security analysts' meeting:

1. Have speech printed for distribution after presentation.

2. If possible, on the first "go around," top financial, sales and technical men should be present. A good way to bring them in is for answering questions.

3. First meeting presentation needs some history, but even then not too much.

4. Visual aids (chartbooks, perhaps) are important if they can be worked in.

5. A product display at the rear or at the entrance is good.

6. Speech should closely approximate one half hour with another half hour for questions.

7. Do not repeat that sales last year were $14,989,420, net income was $1,806,902 and earnings per share were $1.50 per share. Rather, say sales were $15 million and earnings $1.50 per share.

8. "Presents" or souvenirs are not necessary.

9. Aside from the short history at the first meeting and the necessity to tailor any discussions to your particular company, the following might be suggested topics for a typical manufacturer.

    (a) Review briefly what happened in period just past—last three, six or nine months.

    (b) Current industry situation.

(c) Current product mix or sales breakdown is as follows. . . .

(d) Company's current operations and near term projections if the speaker desires (not a necessity).

(e) What's new in products?
What's new in sales effort?
What's new in research effort?
What's new in plant?
What expansion is going on?

(f) How have all the above affected sales and earnings?

10. Invite analysts to visit you and designate a person as primary contact man. (Usually the president or treasurer.)

11. Put your faith in and work with the chairman of the meeting—he has been through this many times.

12. Make sure someone in your organization is there to handle speeches, displays, slides, etc.

13. Give thought to distributing the speech to analysts throughout the country immediately after the presentation.

14. If possible, show how you compare and contrast with competitors and name them.

15. For the first meeting, do you have a company philosophy on such items as integration, national vs. regional character, mergers, diversification, long range planning, financing vehicles, dividends, etc.

16. What is the inter-relationship between your sales and earnings and general business indices or broad economic factors?

17. Above all, tell the bad along with the good. These are experienced men who will respect you for it. Speaking before analysts' groups is excellent public and financial relations—so make the most of it!

## Informal Meetings with Dealers

Your investment banker can be very helpful to you in arranging for informal meetings in various parts of the country with dealers, trust company analysts, representatives of investment banking firms, etc. It is important that you keep the financial community informed as to the progress that your company is making. These informal meetings are sometimes much more effective than an appearance before the Analysts' Societies.

If you are planning a business trip and can devote a few hours to attend an informal meeting of the type described, your underwriter can make the necessary arrangements for you. These meetings can be held in the office of the underwriter or at a club or hotel. You will be expected to present the facts and figures concerning your company's operations and the material that you should discuss will follow the outline contained in this chapter relating to appearances before the Security Analysts' Societies.

Leave plenty of time for questions. By all means, even if the meetings are informal, be prepared. You will be talking to a sophisticated group of people and they will expect you to come well armed with facts and figures. Don't overlook this opportunity to build good will for your company.

# 42

## Types of Financing Available If You Cannot Have a Public Stock Offering

If your company is not ready for a public stock offering, it might well have to continue its prior loan arrangements or develop new plans for obtaining credit or increased capital. It is impossible to discuss in detail the various methods of raising additional funds. A book could well be written on this subject. The following will serve merely as a check list and not a detailed analysis of methods used to provide additional funds:

1. *Short Term Bank Loans.* These loans are normally made by commercial banks on a short-term basis for up to one year. A bank in many cases will establish a line of credit which is available to the borrower from time to time to finance inventories and accounts receivable. Occasionally the bank asks the borrower to pay up the full amount owing and be out of the banks for a short period of time before it will make a new loan.

2. *Term Loans.* Many commercial banks, insurance companies and pension funds will make loans for a period of more than one year. These are called "term loans" and are normally payable in two to five years or longer. Loans of this type are important to many firms seeking long term financing. Generally, installment payments of principal are made during the term of the loan. There is, however, a fixed interest commitment and a fixed maturity date when each installment must be paid.

3. *Loans Secured by Equipment.* Many companies obtain additional financing through borrowing from banks and other lending institutions which accept loans against equipment as security. Chattel mortgages are often given to the lending institution representing the security for loans of this type.

4. *Pledging Accounts Receivable.* Many organizations obtain financing through pledging the accounts receivable of the company as security for the loan. The borrowing company is responsible for any collection losses.

The commercial financing company does not handle the collections. This is the responsibility of the borrower. Many banks have commercial finance departments to make loans against the accounts receivable. This type of financing is used most often by smaller business firms.

There are some financial organizations that look with disfavor upon firms that borrow against accounts receivable. It is not necessarily a stigma against a company if it borrows on this basis. It is important whether a loan will be made on a basis of notification to the debtor. It is desirable, from the borrower's standpoint, that his account not be notified of the assignment.

5. *Factoring Accounts Receivable.* Many companies sell their Accounts Receivable outright to a finance company. This procedure is known as "factoring" and the purchaser of the receivables usually buys them without recourse. If there are any losses, the factor agrees to take the loss. In this type of financing arrangement, the factor usually notifies the customer who pays directly to the factor.

6. *Loans Secured by Warehouse Receipts.* Banks and finance companies make loans when they can receive as security a receipt from a public warehouse certifying that it holds goods or property belonging to the borrower. Arrangements can also be made for a similar loan when the goods are in the plant or warehouse under a fixed warehouse arrangement. Under this plan, a public warehouse separates and takes possession of the property even though it is in the company warehouse. The warehouse company issues a receipt which is used as security for the loans.

7. *Mortgage Loans.* Companies borrowing funds on a long-term basis, provide a mortgage for security. It is customary that these mortgage bonds are paid off over a period of years ranging from 15 to 30 years. Many bonds contain sinking fund provisions and restrict the dividend payments on the common stock. The interest paid on these loans is deductible under the Federal Income Tax laws.

8. *Debentures.* Many companies borrow money on a long-term basis and issue debentures in preference to mortgage bonds. Large institutions are often willing to loan money and receive in return long-term debentures. Debentures may be subordinated to bank loans or they may be convertible into common stock.

Again it must be kept in mind that a debenture calls for a fixed interest rate and a maturity date. There is an advantage to the issuing company in comparing debentures to preferred stock since interest on the debentures is deductible for income tax purposes whereas the dividends on preferred stock are not.

9. *Sale and Leaseback.* Many companies, particularly those in the merchandising field, have found it advantageous to enter into a sale and lease back arrangement. Under this plan, the company sells its store, factory or warehouse to a financial institution which leases back the property to the company under a long

term lease. This plan frees working capital and permits the selling company to use the proceeds of the sale for additional inventory and accounts receivable. Many companies with limited capital, wishing to expand, use the sale-lease back arrangement in constructing new facilities which are sold to a lending institution with a lease back to the seller.

10. *Sale of Preferred Stock.* In order to obtain long term financing in the nature of equity capital, consideration should be given to the sale of preferred stock. This will require the payment of a specific dividend each year before dividends are paid to the common stockholders. Consideration should be given to issuing participating or convertible preferred stock. Keep in mind that the dividends paid on preferred stock are not deductible for Federal Income Tax purposes whereas interest on debentures can be deducted.

11. *Loans from Officers of the Company.* In many family-owned corporations, it is customary for the officers of the company to loan money on either a short term or long term basis.

12. *Offering of Stock Rights.* Many corporations raise additional capital by offering "rights" to their present common stockholders on a pro-rata basis. Normally the rights are offered to the stockholders at a price which is lower than the current market quotations. Certain states require that stockholders be given this opportunity to purchase a pro rata portion of the common stock under statutes relating to "pre-emptive rights." Normally the rights provide that they can be exercised during a certain period.

The rights generally are transferable and are represented by warrants. Rights are purchased and sold and are obviously more attractive as the market price for the stock increases beyond the subscription price. When the rights are exercised, the corporation receives a cash payment in the amount of the subscription price.

13. *Loans Against Cash Value of a Life Insurance Policy.* Many corporations own insurance on the lives of the corporate executives. Banks as well as the insurance company itself will make loans with the insurance policy as security for the loan.

14. *Loans by Small Business Administration.* The United States Government, through the Small Business Administration, is authorized to make loans to small businesses needing funds to finance plant construction and expansion or to finance the purchase of equipment, machinery and supplies. The Small Business Administration can also make loans to provide working capital for companies that qualify under the regulations of the Small Business Administration. These loans, however, cannot be made by the Small Business Administration unless no other lending organizations are available to make the loan.

15. *Small Business Investment Companies.* Over 300 companies have been licensed under the Small Business Investment Act of 1958. These companies,

known as SBIC's, make long term loans and receive convertible debentures or warrants to purchase stock. Most SBIC's loan and invest in companies with assets of less than 5 million dollars and a net worth of less than 2½ million dollars. The net income of these companies, after taxes, is under $250,000. Many banks have invested in the SBIC's and a large number are publicly owned.

16. *Mergers.* It is possible that your company might be interested in a merger with a public corporation. Under this plan you could exchange your stock for stock in a company that is publicly owned. There are tax advantages in this type of transfer and, of course, it is less costly than a public issue. Under a merger with a larger company you must keep in mind that you would lose your control of your corporation.

17. *Financial Help for American Firms Expanding Abroad.* If a company is expanding abroad and needs additional funds to finance new facilities, there are many ways of obtaining money for this purpose. Some firms are selling subsidiary bonds guaranteed by the parent company in the Swiss market. Foreign insurance companies also purchase bonds. Foreign banks are available for loans.

# 43

## Diversification Through Transfer of Stock to a Mutual Fund

Numerous swap type funds also known as Centennial-type funds, have been organized recently to help holders of common stock diversify their holdings without incurring immediate capital gains. This new type of fund was created to aid the investor who is locked in to a capital gain.

The Centennial Fund was the first fund of this type organized. It received a ruling from the Federal Internal Revenue Service to the effect that an exchange of stock of the type indicated above would be a tax free exchange under Section 351 of the Internal Revenue Code. Other funds have been organized along similar lines by investment company groups. Under these plans, initially, the stockholder deposits his shares with the fund under an escrow arrangement. The fund, during a 30 to 60 day period, determines whether it wishes to accept the securities offered. If the fund accepts the shares, the stockholder has a period of 10 days to 20 days in which to accept or reject the plan.

All stockholders in the fund in effect pool their unrealized capital gains and share the burden of any taxes payable if and when the fund sells stock and realizes any gains.

In exchange for their shares the investors receive shares in the Fund.

The advantages of a transfer of this type appear to be that the payment of a capital gains tax is deferred and there is an opportunity to diversify, provided the Internal Revenue Service has issued a favorable ruling to the Fund.

By exchanging their securities for shares of the fund, investors become participants in a securities portfolio which has the benefit of diversification and investment management. Some funds will accept a minimum of $15,000 worth of securities from an investor; others require $25,000 to $50,000. Most funds are interested in securities having long range growth and income.

Commissions on the exchange of the stock vary, but a typical fee arrangement is as follows:

| *Exchange Value* | | | | *Total Fee* |
|---|---|---|---|---|
| $50,000 but less than $ 100,000 | | | | 4.0% |
| 100,000 but less than 250,000 | | | | 3.5% |
| 250,000 but less than 500,000 | | | | 3.0% |
| 500,000 but less than 750,000 | | | | 2.5% |
| 750,000 but less than 1,000,000 | | | | 2.0% |
| 1,000,000 or more | | | | 1.5% |

## Future Sales of Stock by Stockholders and the Company

In many offerings, the selling stockholders agree that they will not sell any additional stock within a stated period without the approval of the Underwriter. For example:

*Kingsport Press, Inc.* The Selling Stockholders have agreed not to sell any other shares of the Common Stock owned by them during 90 days after commencement of this offering without the consent of the Underwriters.

*Liberty Records, Inc.* The owners of 4,500 shares of Class B Common Stock have agreed not to sell their holdings for one year following this offering without the consent of Crowell, Weedon & Co.

The company may enter into an agreement with its Underwriter to give it first refusal rights on future public offerings. For example:

*American Properties, Inc.* The Company and the Organizers, upon the condition that all the shares offered hereby are sold, have agreed for a period of five years from the completion of the offering (1) to use their best efforts to elect a designee of the Underwriter as a director of the Company and (2) have granted the Underwriter a right of first refusal as to any future public financing engaged in by the Company, its subsidiaries and its controlling stockholders at terms equal or better than those which might be obtained elsewhere. The Underwriter has informed the Company that it will designate Franklyn I. Steinberg, the Underwriter's President, as a director.

*Victor Paint Company.* The Underwriting Contract provides that, subject to certain conditions, Charles Plohn & Co. shall have the right to handle any public distributions of securities of the Company requiring the services of an Underwriter, whether by the Company or by the Selling Stockholder, which may be made within three years after the date of this offering under the most favorable terms and conditions available to the Company or the Selling Stockholder from any other Underwriter.

# Your First Annual Meeting of Stockholders

## General

"How many stockholders will be present at the first annual meeting of stockholders? What will the stockholders want to know? Will there be disgruntled stockholders present?" These are some of the questions that will run through your mind prior to the date of your first stockholders' meeting. You have no experience to draw upon as to the number of stockholders that will be present at your meeting. How can you adequately plan for the meeting if you have no idea as to the number of people that will be present?

Basically you can use as a guide, the relative success of your company. If your company is doing well and you are meeting your dividend commitments, the odds are that there will be very few stockholders at your meeting. If on the other hand the profits of your company are down and there is a group that is unhappy with your management, the odds are that there will be a greater number of people present at your meeting. Certainly if there is an attempt on the part of any one group to seize control of the company, there will be a large number of stockholders present at the meeting.

Your attorney can be very helpful to you in estimating the number of people to expect at your meeting. Assuming that your first years' operations since you have gone public are satisfactory to the stockholders, you may well end up with under ten stockholders at your first annual meeting.

Enlightened management today does not look upon the annual meeting as a formality. It should be a vital and important part of a corporation's affairs.

## Proxies

A proxy notice will be sent to your stockholders inviting them to be present at the meeting or to send in their proxy on the form that will be enclosed with the notice. Since in most cases there will not be a large turnout of stockholders at the meeting, most of the stockholders will send in their proxies.

If the business of the company is being well run with adequate profits and an acceptable policy, most stockholders will sign the proxies and send them in. This will authorize the persons named in the proxy to vote at their own discretion unless there are specific questions raised in the ballot.

Meetings are held in the city designated in the bylaws of the company. The requirements for notice of meetings must be carefully followed.

Many corporations are organized under the laws of the State of Delaware and maintain an office in that state. Wilmington, Delaware, particularly, has become the corporate capital of the world, serving as the corporate office of more blue chip American corporations than any other American city. A large number of these corporations hold their annual meetings at Wilmington, Delaware.

### Proceedings at Meeting

General Electric has departed from the customary business type annual meeting. The company makes the best part of the meeting the center of a larger sphere of activity which includes production exhibits, tour of company facilities, and special programs and events. In 1959 the company held its first meeting outside of New York State and encouraged its stockholders through special bulletins to attend the annual meeting.

A recent meeting of General Electric attracted 3,722 shareholders. Ralph J. Cordiner, Chairman of the Board of Directors of General Electric, in pointing up the company's policy for increased participation on the part of stockholders at the annual meeting stated:

> If this economy is to be preserved and developed, it needs the participation of an active and informed investor group, the larger the better. General Electric's development of the Annual Meeting fits into the context of our long-term efforts to broaden share ownership and to win better public understanding of the share owner's role. The efforts devoted to adding depth and meaning to the Annual Meeting comprise what we believe to be a positive contribution to the continuing healthy development of our economic system based on private capital and individual initiative.

While the annual meeting is intended solely as a business affair, it can be given social overtones that do not detract from its seriousness and simultaneously build the corporate image.

Your new stockholders largely are strangers to you and your fellow officers and directors. The annual meeting is one opportunity for cultivating good relations with your stockholders. Unfortunately, you'll only be able to reach a small percentage of them, for not many stockholders find it possible to attend such meetings. Nevertheless, you can demonstrate your managerial capacity, your integrity and intelligence to the shareowners present. Word of mouth will help to spread whatever impression you make.

Stockholders will come to listen and welcome the opportunity to ask questions. Conduct the meeting in a democratic manner and answer the questions fairly. You may have some critics at the meeting. There may be the perennial nuisance stockholder, but he is serious in his attitude, and his questions also deserve answers. Allow time for complaints and suggestions. Remember, the meeting affords the stockholders an opportunity to meet the management of the company. This can be an important advantage for the company. On the other hand, the company can be hurt if the attitude toward stockholders at the meeting is unfair and unfriendly.

Chock Full o'Nuts Corporation had 500 stockholders at their annual meeting at the Biltmore Hotel in New York. Many suggestions were made by stockholders at the meeting, including the opening of offices in the major cities of Europe and the placing of ropes in the restaurants to keep customers in line. It was also suggested that sugarless doughnuts be served and customers should be asked whether they want cream in their coffee before being served.

### Questions at Meetings

A review of some questions asked at the 1960 stockholders' meeting of United States Steel Company are of interest. The management was asked such questions as:
1. "How much was spent for the solicitation of proxies?"
2. "Have you considered building a steel mill abroad?"
3. "Do we have any investments of any amount in Cuba?"
4. "Are you spending enough money on automation and on research to meet foreign competition?"
5. "Wouldn't a stock split increase the market price of the stock and benefit the economy?"

### Report of Stockholders' Meeting

Many corporations send to their stockholders a report of the annual meeting. Reports are sent either in letter, booklet or newspaper form and describe the important features of the meeting. Very often there are pictures taken at the meeting showing stockholders with executives of the company.

The New York Stock Exchange, in its recent booklet entitled *Telling Your Corporate Story* reported:

> Post-Meeting Reports. Shareowners are attending annual meetings in growing numbers, but the problem of geography will always limit attendance.

Therefore, a post-meeting report is a valuable addition to corporate literature—helpful in permitting shareowners to weigh matters which were discussed, and to better understand decisions and policies voted on.

A wide variety of post-meeting reports include a "big picture" treatment by International Business Machines; a tabloid newspaper by the Chesapeake & Ohio; pictures-and-text by American Telephone & Telegraph, Sinclair Oil and Texaco; sketches-and-text by Charles Pfizer; and an attractive report, without illustration, by Macy's.

General Motors Corporation issued a report of their 52nd Annual Meeting which was attended by 3,000 individuals from 25 states and elsewhere. The report contained the following information:

1. Remarks by Frederic G. Donner, Chairman of the Board of Directors, on the following subjects:
   (a) Number of shareholders in attendance.
   (b) Resignation of certain directors.
   (c) Comments as to value of meeting being held in a General Motors plant.
   (d) Introduction of 21 directors and officers who were present.
2. Remarks by President John F. Gordon, who commented on the following subjects:
   (a) Business conditions at General Motors.
   (b) Customer acceptance of company's new products.
   (c) Discussion of change in transportation needs.
   (d) Defense production.
   (e) Recent plant improvements.
   (f) Australian visit.
3. Remarks by Frederic G. Donner, Chairman of the Board of Directors, on the following subjects:
   (a) Motors by GM.
   (b) Opportunities ahead.
   (c) Overseas program.
   (d) Description of 3 new cars.
   (e) The outlook.
   (f) Company's position in the future.
4. Election of directors.
5. Ratification of independent public accountants.
6. Other comments and discussions.
7. Questions and answers.

Ampex Corporation publishes reports of its Annual Meeting of shareholders. Its report of August 23, 1960 contained the report of George I. Long, Jr., President, who commented on the prior year's activities, current fiscal year, and the future. The questions that were raised at the meeting and the answers that were given were set out in detail. The questions covered such subjects as what is the projected growth rate for the year, pressure of competition on profit margins, new products, proposed mergers, merchandising new products, dividends, and foreign sales.

If a report of the meeting is prepared, consider sending copies to analysts and the financial press as well as the stockholders.

# 45

## Annual Reports

Once you admit the public to joint ownership in your corporation by means of a public offering, you have committed your company to keeping your share-owners informed. You will attempt through the annual report to make your new stockholders true partners in the business.

With the continually increasing participation of the public in ownership of corporate stock, more and more attention is being given to building a "corporate image." When corporations were largely owned by families, or by only a small group of stockholders, the image the public was likely to see was that of the principal owner. John D. Rockefeller was the image of the early day Standard Oil Company; J. P. Morgan of New York banking; Andrew Carnegie of the steel industry; W. C. Durant, Henry Ford and a few others of the automobile industry.

There still are business leaders of stature, but with the widespread owner-ship of common stock today, these men have become professional managers rather than principal owners of the companies they direct. Consequently, the image—the picture in the public mind—of a corporation has tended to become obscured. Recognizing this, many corporations now work hard to create an image for the hitherto impersonal and intangible corporation. This can be materially accomplished through effective Annual Reports.

The New York Stock Exchange, in describing the importance of annual reports, has stated:

> Most companies recognize the annual report as the single most effective means of reaching shareowners. The techniques of presentation, as well as over-all content, differ markedly: some are illustrated extensively; others use no pictures at all. Some emphasize products and services in the main body of the report; others carry special sections for this material. Yet each in its own way accomplishes its task of building the "corporate image."
>
> Representative examples include: Litton Industries, which devotes a spe-cial section to its products; Olin Mathieson, which relies on typography,

rather than illustration, for impressive effect; General Electric, which discusses economic topics of interest to shareowners; Lone Star Gas, which reports in detail on the characteristics of its shareowners; Hilton Hotels, which features a ten-year growth record in the main section of the report.

What should be included in the Annual Report? The best advice would be to try to anticipate the questions your stockholders would like to have answered. Your stockholders not only will want to know the sales and earnings but related figures as well—per share earnings, for example, and how much of net income was paid to stockholders in dividends. If the company took on additional debt in the form of bank loans, the shareowners would like to know, as that could affect what they anticipate in dividends.

They also are interested in what the company is doing to improve the business: Are new products being developed? Are plants and facilities being expanded or properly maintained? Is the sales organization adequate to obtain full market coverage?

And they may want to know what the company does in granting stock options to employees and whether large bonuses are paid to executives. Furthermore, they are interested in what the company's outlook is for the next year. Is their investment in your company going to be worth retaining?

To answer these questions, you may want to call upon additional executives of your company in preparing the annual report. Larger companies often call upon their public relations departments, or outside public relations counsel, to assist in preparing this segment of the corporate image. You may not have a public relations department, but you can bring your advertising, sales, manufacturing, personnel and other departments into consultation with your purely financial assistants.

If you're going to do it right, it no longer can be a one-man job.

What about the cost of an annual report? Some companies try to make their reports simple—without a great deal of art work to show the stockholders that the company is cost conscious. Other companies prepare lavish reports, not only to impress their stockholders, but sell their products as well. The cost can range from 10¢ a copy for a simple report to $2.50–$3.00. The average report for smaller companies would appear to run around $1.00 a copy.

Many companies use their four color national magazine ads for their annual reports. This can reflect savings in art work. Most reports are mailed First Class, although some send reports by Third Class mail.

"Where will the reports be distributed?" The New York Stock Exchange reports:

Today the 1,000 leading corporations distribute an estimated 40,000,000 copies of these reports every year. They go not only to stockholders, but also to the press, company employees, schools of business administration, investment firms and other financial organizations. And anyone—whether he owns securities or not—can usually obtain an annual report merely by mailing a written request to the company.

In the last decade, a number of companies have supplemented issuance of the annual report in new ways, their objective being to get additional readership out of the assembled material.

One way is to publish the report in a financial or daily newspaper, either taking a full page to reproduce the report in a somewhat condensed form, or having the report reproduced in full as a supplement to the newspaper. While this method is not inexpensive, it can reach millions of readers—potential customers or stockholders.

American Telephone & Telegraph Company, the giant of the communications industry, sent blind shareholders reports printed in braille and on phonograph records. An estimated 3,600 shareholders received such reports.

Allis-Chalmers Manufacturing Company, a major producer of, primarily, capital goods, had a color film strip produced of its 1959 report. This strip reviewed Allis-Chalmers products, employee benefit programs and the company's financial picture, particularly as it affected employees. It was shown in noontime periods at various locations in the company's factories about the country.

Some companies reproduce the highlights of the annual report on a card of playing card size and distribute these to employees. Carried in the wallet, such a card can be useful to an employee in settling an argument with a friend over a glass of beer.

These innovations are not ones you must consider and adopt immediately, of course. But they suggest means not only of keeping your stockholders informed, but of selling more of your products or service, of building good will, and of establishing your company in the minds of investors. It is certainly possible that you may want to sell additional stock at a later date.

The New York Stock Exchange in its booklet, *Telling Your Corporate Story,* stated:

> Every employee wants to know how his company is doing—and many companies include employees on their annual report distribution list. But the special report to employees—frequently in company publications—is a widely accepted technique. Individual approaches vary: illustrated charts, cartoons, pictures and interviews are some of the ways in which financial data are made more readable and informative for employees.

Some excellent examples of reporting to employees include Babcock & Wilcox's question-and-answer session with its president; Hercules Powder Company's *The Story of Tom Jones' Sawmill*; Toledo Edison's "wallet-sized edition" of the annual report; C.I.T.'s *If I Had $27,539.59*; a complete issue of *The Standard Oiler* (Calif.) featuring pictures of employees in all departments; W. T. Grant's comic-strip technique; J. C. Penney's cartoons; and others.

In preparing your annual report for your company, it might be well to review portions of reports from other companies. The following excerpts from various reports serve as a guide of items to be included in an annual report for your company.

### Acquisition

*Shulton.* The Acquisition program moved ahead with the purchase of Technique, Inc., a progressive manufacturer of hair coloring products. This gave us an opportunity to enter a rapidly growing field, and we are fortunate to have obtained an excellent product of proven worth. Meanwhile, other companies are continually being investigated to see if their acquisition would aid our long-range growth.

### Advertising

*Texaco, Inc.* Advertising and sales promotion campaigns were accelerated to direct consumers' attention to the high quality of Texaco's products and services. In mid-year, the Company assumed sponsorship of the Texaco Huntley-Brinkley News Report, a 15-minute nation-wide network program telecast five evenings a week. This award-winning program continues the Company's traditional association with public service presentations. Outstanding among these are the Saturday afternoon radio broadcasts of the Metropolitan Opera, which were Texaco-sponsored for the 20th consecutive year.

### Aim of Company

*The Chemstrand Corporation.* Our aim is to be prepared to meet all competition with consistently high quality products, through continued efforts in market and applications research, production efficiency, effective marketing programs, fiber development, and intensive long-range research.

### Back Orders

*Leeds & Northrup Company.* Because shipments exceeded new orders, the backlog was reduced from about $11,000,000 to about $9,000,000. We have been aiming to achieve such a reduction in order to give better service to our customers by shortening the average time for deliveries.

## Capital Expansion Program

*Parke-Davis.* We are projecting for the next five years, a capital expansion program involving some $60,000,000, all of which we plan to finance out of present and future retained earnings. Approximately $18,000,000 will be spent during the next twelve months.

*The Chemstrand Corp.* Our aim is to be prepared to meet all competition with consistently high quality products, through continued efforts in market and applications research, production efficiency, effective marketing programs, fiber development, and intensive long-range research.

*General Electric.* The next decade is one in which United States business enterprises must take into account not only the prospect of more vigorous competition among themselves but also from competitors abroad. Foreign producers, with lower wage, salary and tax costs, and in many instances with automated equipment the equal of that in use in this country, are cutting into sales of United States products both abroad and at home.

## Contributions

*Weyerhaeuser Timber Company.* During 1958 the Company donated $392,000 to Weyerhaeuser Timber Foundation. Contributions by the Foundation in 1958 continued to be mainly in the field of education, including undergraduate scholarships, graduate fellowships and unrestricted grants-in-aid to nontax supported colleges and universities.

## Cooperation with Educational Institutions

*Consolidated Edison Company of New York, Inc.* Cooperation is extended to educational institutions of all levels, from grade school to university. A prime example was an atomic energy seminar staged with Company help for New York City's junior high school science teachers.

## Cost Control

*Standard Oil Company.* At the same time, efficiency has been raised to new levels and utilization of manpower improved. Expenses have been substantially reduced and are under careful control in line with your management's determination to keep the company a low-cost operator in the oil business.

## Decentralization

*General Electric. Depth in Management* at General Electric is provided by the decentralized organizational structure. The decentralization program, which has undergone steady evolution since 1950, has resulted in the establishment of 21 major operating Divisions and 105 business Departments, each with management assigned responsibility and accountability for the successful conduct of its business on a profitable and successful basis within the framework of over-all objectives, policies, plans and programs.

## Diversification

*The Norwich Pharmacal Co.*   The Norwich Pharmacal Company is today a strong, diversified corporation making a specialty line of consumer drug products in the proprietary field, a growing number of professional medications for human and veterinary use, and a group of chemical specialties, limited in number, but important in volume. This diversification affords us balance and opportunities for growth in this country and abroad.

## Dividends

*Rexall Drug and Chemical Co.*   We continued our policy of regular quarterly cash dividends and an annual three per cent stock dividend. Because of the Company's rapid rate of growth, and the desirability of retaining a large proportion of earnings, it would be reasonable to expect your Directors to continue the present dividend policy for the year 1960.

*Texas Instruments Inc.*   Your Board of Directors determined that the interests of the shareholders could be served best by reinvestment of all earnings to sustain company growth and competitive position, thereby deferring dividend payments.

*Nalley's Inc.*   Your Board of Directors, at a recent meeting voted to adopt a policy of paying dividends quarterly instead of annually. In fact, at the time you are reading this report, you will have already received the first quarterly payment under this newly adopted plan. In addition to the obvious benefit of receiving dividend payments earlier, this newly adopted plan will enable us to keep you currently informed about the progress of your company.

## Employee Relations

*Chesapeake and Ohio Railway.*   Our chairman and president have stated repeatedly that C&O's men and women are the railroad's greatest asset. No truer statement was ever made.

Chesapeake and Ohio maintains 57 different labor agreements with 30 brotherhoods and other labor groups. In 1958, not a single day was lost as a result of labor disputes.

This enviable record is a testament to the philosophy of labor relations which C&O has followed over the years.

We are fortunate also that maturity prevails when we deal with railroad brotherhoods. They are among the oldest labor organizations in this country, and their leaders possess a degree of statesmanship which I believe to be unrivalled.

*Texaco Inc.* For the fourth consecutive year there was no dispute resulting in a work stoppage. As part of a continuing program for stable operations and effective dealing with legitimate needs of employees, training workshops were conducted for the labor relations staffs of all departments.

## Employee Suggestion Plan

*United States Steel Corporation.* During 1958 U.S. Steel's Suggestion Plan produced many ideas. Approximately 11,500 ideas were accepted and installed in the year. For these suggestions, employees were awarded over $375,000 in 1958.

## Expansion

*Rexall Drug and Chemical Company.* In 1959 the Company continued its program of intensifying its franchise campaign with special emphasis in fast growing key market areas. The numerical growth in franchise holders in no way signifies the Company's over-all growth. While there has been a decrease in the number of drug stores per se, the number of Rexall stores has continued to increase each year. Emphasis continues to be on quality and not quantity. Marginal and sub-marginal franchise holders are being replaced by efficient stores which are a credit to the Rexall name.

## Expression of Appreciation to Employees

*Motorola Inc.* A record year such as 1959 does not occur without an imaginative, responsible, and responsive group of people making it occur. I am particularly grateful this year, when the loss of my father weighs heavily, to the management and all the employees of the company for their devotion to Motorola. No memorial would have pleased him more.

*MCA Inc.* To all of our employees we take this opportunity to acknowledge, with appreciation, their loyalty and efforts beyond normal duty, thereby helping make possible our success in the past, and upon whom we rely for the future progress of the Company.

## Expression of Appreciation to Suppliers

*Sears, Roebuck & Co.* We also wish to thank our many fine sources of supply for their splendid cooperation in producing quality goods necessary to meet the demands of Sears customers.

## Extension of Services

*A. C. Nielsen Company.* After two years of careful investigation, a Retail Audit Service is now being established in France under the direction of Mr. Justin Power, with Mr. Henry Burk as resident manager. This undertaking was encouraged by the increasingly important role of France in the European Common Market, and the substantial expansion of the French economy which is currently under way. The new service is scheduled to cover all of metropolitan France, and to measure the purchasing habits of her 44 million citizens.

## Freedom

*American Hospital Supply Corp.* Our economic system has demonstrated since the day the Mayflower sailed out of England its vitality and infinite capacity for meeting the needs and goals of our people. In the 240 years since that day, no other economic system anywhere has achieved such dramatic success in providing a framework for human progress.

Some of our freedoms are being diminshed by people who are willing to let government take over more and more responsibilities historically reserved for individuals and private institutions. This erosion attacks the very rootholds of America's strength. To guard our heritage, we must repulse every unnecessary government encroachment into our free institutions and processes as resolutely as we defend against threats from abroad.

## Future Predictions

*Alpha Portland Cement Company.* Most predictions for the next decade forecast a surging economy in which construction bolstered by the demands of an exploding population will play an important part. With the development of the urban areas of the immediate future, the use of concrete and concrete products must necessarily increase even though the per capita consumption of 1.85 barrels remains constant. Our industry must necessarily benefit from the increasing need for public works and from both residential and non-residential building.

## Government Controls

*Scott Paper Co.* As Americans we can look back on the year just ended with real pride and with renewed confidence. Our institutions and our ways of life were put to the test and came through with flying colors. We should be grateful that, despite the pressure for precipitous government action, President Eisenhower determined to let natural economic forces operate as the primary means of bringing about recovery. He had the necessary faith in our economic strength and the courage to believe that a sound and orderly adjustment would be accomplished.

## Income Tax Audits

*Lone Star Gas Co. and Subsidiary Co.* The officers are pleased to advise you that Federal income tax returns through 1957 have been audited by the United States Treasury Department and no liability exists for any prior year.

## Industrial and Public Relations

*P. H. Glatfelter Company.* Opinion Research Corporation of Princeton, New Jersey, was engaged to conduct an attitude survey among our personnel. It was encouraging to note the genuine interest of the 96% of our employees who participated. The objective of this survey was: (1) to determine how employees feel about their jobs and the Company, (2) to provide information for formulating an effective program of improvement if weaknesses were revealed.

## International Operations

*Schering Corp.* The continued growth of international operations during 1959 has been most impressive. The International Division now accounts for approximately 22% of corporate sales. Important expansion of subsidiary operations in Argentina and Australia was accomplished during the year. Our Mexican pharmaceutical subsidiary, Scheramex, demonstrated significant progress during 1959, as did our Mexican chemical manufacturing subsidiary, BEISA.

## Labor Turnover

*Western Union.* The average monthly voluntary separation rate among non-messenger employees during 1959 was .8 for each 100 employees. This is substantially lower than the average of 1.2 for the communications field generally and assures the Company of continuity of employee experience in the diverse skills essential to its service.

*Texaco Inc.* Percentage depletion is again under attack, as you have no doubt seen in press reports. If anything, the allowance of 27½% should be increased to assure the availability of low cost energy which is so paramount to the continued prosperity of our country.

## Litigation

*General Electric.* On February 16 and 17, 1960, Grand Jury indictments were returned and companion civil suits filed against your Company and a number of other firms alleging price fixing conspiracies involving a number of electrical apparatus products. It has been the long standing policy of the Company to insist on conduct even beyond the requirements of the antitrust laws. This Company policy has been forcibly and repeatedly emphasized to all management employees. We condemn all restrictive practices and shall continue to insist on pursuing a policy of creative and aggressive competition.

## Loans

*Ling-Altec Electronics, Inc.*   One of the most substantial developments during the past year, and certainly significant recognition of your Company's position in financial circles, was the private placement of $5 million in long term Senior Notes with prominent insurance companies and other investors. These funds, in addition to lines of credit established with leading banks, provide adequate working capital to insure the successful completion of the Company's expansion program.

## Modernization Program

*Republic Steel Corporation.*   The most significant occurrence of the year, apart from the lengthy labor dispute, was the decision by Republic's directors to proceed with a major program of capital expenditures directed at further improving the efficiency, profitability and competitive strength of the company.

## New Orders

*United Electrodynamics Inc.*   New orders booked totaled $5,739,246, also a new high, representing a 56 per cent increase over the equivalent new orders of $3,776,749 for 1958. New business for United Geophysical Corporation equipment of $137,000 represents only 25 per cent of the equivalent 1958 volume of $555,000.

## New Products

*Kawneer Company.*   We recently held a general sales meeting attended by our sales organization from the United States, Canada and Mexico. At this meeting the new building product line for 1960 was introduced and the sales program for the year reviewed. The reception was outstanding and enthusiasm is running at a new high.

## New Stockholders

*Sears, Roebuck & Co.*   Finally, we should make special reference to those individuals, institutions, and trusts who last year became shareowners. During the year there was a net increase of 6,292.

## Organization Changes

*General Electric.*   General Electric's 1959 organization change, establishing the International Group as one of five major Company Groups, brings fresh emphasis to a long-established business.

## Prices

*United States Steel Corp.*   Except for a few minor changes both upward and downward in the prices of certain of its individual products, U.S. Steel maintained the general level of its steel prices throughout the year.

## Product Design

*The Mead Corporation.*   In our container and packaging plants, Mead engineers and designers are at work creating the packages that will brighten the looks and guard the condition of the things you're going to want, day after tomorrow.

## Profits and Freedom

*United States Steel Corporation.*   There is a big difference between the American economy and the Russian economy. In the American economy productive effort, through the voluntary and competitive decisions of free men, is automatically and continuously devoted to meeting with maximum satisfaction the wants of all the people; in Russia production is by governmental compulsion directed toward satisfying the aspirations of its ruling class with mere subsistence for the people. But the American economy cannot function if there is interference with the voluntary and competitive markets by which the community bestows its rewards. These rewards are in terms of income or profits to those who most ably produce what the community wants at prices it is willing to pay, while those who serve to its lesser satisfaction receive lesser incomes or experience losses.

Our system rests on its provision of opportunity for free men to benefit themselves by saving and investing, but only if in so doing they serve the public's economic interest. If the benefits from so doing are removed, then progress must stop, unemployment arise and government compulsion replace the voluntary decisions of free men.

A profit and loss system can be practiced only by free men. They cannot sacrifice that system without sacrificing their freedom.

## Public Relations

*Hilton Hotels Corporation.*   It is our creed that every Hilton hotel in a foreign setting should serve as a showcase for the best of what is termed the

American Way of Life. Fortunately, a hotel is not remote words on paper, or impersonal sounds heard over a loudspeaker, but a physical edifice manned by fellow human beings with whom one comes into contact on a face-to-face basis. Our overseas hotels provide United States citizens and our foreign friends and acquaintances with an unprecedented opportunity to meet on a truly cosmopolitan basis.

## Purchase of Company Products

*The Goodyear Tire & Rubber Company.* More than 23,000 employees throughout the domestic organization joined enthusiastically in the "Buy Goodyear—Sell Goodyear" program conducted during the summer months. This resulted in sales of more than one and one-quarter million dollars.

## Research

*Itek.* After two years of rapid growth, the company has become an effective research-oriented organization. Our scientific and technological talents are at work in areas that have significant promise. Our decentralized operating managements are consolidating gains made to date and building the business in their respective markets in accordance with approved objectives. The top executive group is integrating these divisional operations and planning for growth in new fields.

## Retained Earnings

*Western Union.* Continued growth of your Company is dependent upon large capital expenditures. In recognition of this need, 52 percent of the year's earnings were retained for reinvestment in the business, in addition to funds made available by the provision for depreciation and amortization. Further, a standby bank credit up to $60,000,000 was negotiated on favorable terms to accommodate major expansion projects scheduled for 1960–1961.

## Safety Record

*General Motors.* The safety performance in GM plants during 1959 was outstanding, and merited the National Safety Council's annual Award of Honor for the 14th time. This record was achieved by the continued cooperative efforts of supervisory and plant personnel throughout the company.

## Sales Force

*The Mead Corporation.* Some of the busiest people in the world of Mead are those who tell the "outer" world about the service and value we have to offer. We expect our salesmen to be able to find imaginative answers to the questions they encounter day after day: What paper is best suited to a job?

## Standards of Conduct

*Schering Corp.* Your management has been, and will continue to be, guided by the highest ethical standards in the conduct of its business with the basic interests of stockholders, employees, professional public and patients in mind.

## Stock Certificates

*E. I. Du Pont De Nemours & Company.* Suggested safeguards for your certificates are:
1. Leave them unendorsed until actual delivery for sale or transfer;
2. Store them in a safe fireproof place, preferably a bank safekeeping department or safe deposit box;
3. Keep a separate record of their numbers and amounts;
4. Use registered mail if you send them by mail.

## Stock Split

*Western Union.* One anticipated result of the 4-for-1 stock split in May 1955 has been an increase in investor interest, as evidenced by the steadily growing number of share owners. There were 38,274 stockholders as of December 31, 1959, an all-time high and an increase of 97 percent since the end of 1954. At year end approximately 3,800 Company employees and pensioners owned shares.

## Stockholders

*Hilton Hotels Corporation.* Common stocks of major hotel companies are currently being accepted by private and institutional investors as attractive vehicles for income and capital growth. Over 500,000 shares, or 13 percent, of Hilton common stock are presently held by investment trusts, banks, and pension funds.

## Stockholders as Salesmen

*Nalley's Inc.* I would like to take this opportunity to remind each of you that you can help your company to grow by being a salesman and goodwill ambassador for Nalley's products. You can do this by always buying the Nalley's brand when you shop for goods we make, and by reminding your friends and acquaintances of the wide variety of quality Nalley products available and suggesting that they try both new and old products in our lines which you have found to be exceptionally pleasing. No advertising message, no matter how well conceived and presented can ever take the place of a personal recommendation from a friend. Won't you start to be a Nalley sales ambassador today and help us make your company grow.

## Television

*United States Steel Corporation.* Televised also on "The United States Steel Hour" in the last year were several economic messages seeking to explain the profit story and other facts about U.S. Steel. The vital part played by profits in the effective functioning of the American economy is described in the Financial Summary of this Report. Plans have been completed for televising further messages of this type in 1959.

## Training

*United States Steel Corporation.* During 1958 U.S. Steel's Advanced Technical Study program had an enrollment of over 2,000 employees. Approximately 740 employees participated in the Trade Apprentice Training Program and 30,000 in other formalized training programs. In addition, 55 management employees participated in advanced management programs at 21 colleges and universities.

*Schering Corp.* This past summer, carefully selected college students with medical, scientific and business school backgrounds were given vacation employment in a summer training program developed after consultation with several educational institutions. Students were given opportunities to become acquainted with Schering's products and methods of operations and management was afforded the opportunity of evaluating prospects for future employment.

*P. H. Glatfelter Company.* Employees are encouraged to improve themselves through Company-sponsored or outside educational courses. In the supervisory group, quite a few took advantage of the courses offered by the American Management Association, National Industrial Conference Board and others.

# Appendix A

DEFINITIONS

The New York Stock Exchange has prepared the following definitions for investors:

*At the Market:* An order to buy or sell a security "at the market" calls for its execution at the best possible price when the order reaches the trading floor.

*Balance Sheet:* A condensed statement showing the nature and amount of a company's assets, liabilities and capital on a given date. In dollar amounts the balance sheet shows what the company owned, what it owed, and the ownership interest in the company of its stockholders.

*Bear:* Someone who believes the market will decline.

*Bear Market:* A declining market.

*Bid and Asked:* Often referred to as a quotation or quote. The bid is the highest price anyone has declared that he wants to pay for a security at a given time; the asked is the lowest price anyone will take at the same time.

*Big Board:* A popular term for the N. Y. Stock Exchange.

*Blue Chip:* Common stock in a company known nationally for the quality and wide acceptance of its products or services, and for its ability to make money and pay dividends in good times and bad. Usually such stocks are relatively high priced and offer relatively low yields.

*Blue Sky Laws:* A popular name for laws various states have enacted to protect the public against securities frauds. The term is believed to have originated when a judge ruled that a particular stock had about the same value as a patch of blue sky.

*Boiler Room:* High pressure peddling over the telephone of stocks of dubious value. A typical boiler room is simply a room lined with desks or cubicles, each with a salesman and telephone. The salesmen call what is known in the trade as sucker lists.

*Book Value:* An accounting term. Book value of a stock is determined from a company's records, by adding all assets (generally excluding such intangibles as good will), then deducting all debts and other liabilities, plus the liquidation price of any preferred issues. The sum arrived at is divided by the number of common shares outstanding and the result is book value per common share. Book value of the assets of a company or a security may have little or no significant relationship to market value.

*Broker:* An agent, often a member of a Stock Exchange firm or an Exchange member himself, who handles the public's orders to buy and sell securities or commodities. For this service a commission is charged.

*Bull:* One who believes the market will rise.

*Bull Market:* An advancing market.

*Capital Stock:* All shares representing ownership of a business, including preferred and common.

*Capital Gain or Capital Loss:* Profit or loss from the sale of a capital asset. A capital gain may be either short-term (6 months or less) or long-term (more than 6 months). A short-term capital gain is taxed at the reporting individual's full income tax rate. A long-term capital gain is taxed at a maximum of 25 per cent, depending on the reporting individual's tax bracket. Up to $1,000 of net capital loss—that is, when you sell securities at a lower price than you paid for them—is deductible from the individual's taxable income during the year reported. If the capital loss is more than $1,000, as much as $1,000 annually is deductible in each of the next five years. The amount of capital loss which may be deducted is reduced by the amount of any capital gain.

*Capitalization:* Total amount of the various securities issued by a corporation. Capitalization may include bonds, debentures, preferred and common stock. Bonds and debentures are usually carried on the books of the issuing company in terms of their par or face value. Preferred and common shares may be carried in terms of par or stated value. Stated value may be an arbitrary figure decided upon by the directors or may represent the amount received by the company from the sale of the securities at the time of issuance.

*Cash Flow:* Reported net income of a corporation *plus* amounts charged off for depreciation, depletion, amortization, extraordinary charges to reserves, which are bookkeeping deductions and not paid out in actual dollars and cents. A yardstick used in recent years because of the larger non-cash deductions appearing to offer a better indication of the ability of a company to pay dividends and finance expansion from self-generated cash than the conventional reported net income figure.

*Certificate:* The actual piece of paper which is evidence of ownership of stock in a corporation. Watermarked paper is finely engraved with delicate etchings to discourage forgery. Loss of a certificate may at the least cause a great deal of inconvenience—at the worst, financial loss.

*Commission:* The broker's fee for purchasing or selling securities or property for a client. On the N. Y. Stock Exchange commissions average about one per cent of the market value of the stocks involved in the transaction and approximately one-quarter of one per cent on bonds.

*Common Stock:*   Securities which represent an ownership interest in a corporation. If the company has also issued preferred stock, both common and preferred have ownership rights, but the preferred normally has prior claim on dividends and, in the event of liquidation, assets. Claims of both common and preferred stockholders are junior to claims of bondholders or other creditors of the company. Common stockholders assume the greater risk, but generally exercise the greater control and may gain the greater reward in the form of dividends and capital appreciation. The terms common stock and capital stock are often used interchangeably when the company has no preferred stock.

*Consolidated Balance Sheet:*   A balance sheet showing the financial condition of a corporation and its subsidiaries.

*Cumulative Preferred:*   A stock having a provision that if one or more dividends are omitted, the omitted dividends must be paid before dividends may be paid on the company's common stock.

*Cumulative Voting:*   A method of voting for corporate directors which enables the shareholder to multiply the number of his shares by the number of directorships being voted on and cast the total for one director or a selected group of directors. A 10-shareholder normally casts 10 votes for each of, say, 12 nominees to the board of directors. He thus has 120 votes. Under the cumulative voting principle he may do that or he may cast 120 (10 × 12) votes for only one nominee, 60 for two, 40 for three, or any other distribution he chooses. Cumulative voting is required under the corporate laws of some states, is permissive in most others.

*Current Assets:*   Those assets of a company which are reasonably expected to be realized in cash, or sold, or consumed during the normal operating cycle of the business. These include cash, U. S. Government bonds, receivables and money due usually within one year, and inventories.

*Current Liabilities:*   Money owed and payable by a company, usually within one year.

*Dealer:*   An individual or firm in the securities business acting as a principal rather than as an agent. Typically, a dealer buys for his own account and sells to a customer from his own inventory. The dealer's profit or loss is the difference between the price he pays and the price he receives for the same security. The dealer's confirmation must disclose to his customer that he has acted as principal. The same individual or firm may function, at different times, either as broker or dealer. For example, the specialist on the floor of the N. Y. Stock Exchange acts as a dealer when he buys or sells stock for his own account to maintain a market. He acts as a broker when he executes the orders commission brokers have left with him.

*Debenture:*   A promissory note backed solely by the general credit of a company and not secured by a morgage or lien on any specific property.

*Director:*   Person elected by shareholders at the annual meeting to direct company policies. The directors appoint the president, vice presidents, and all other operating officers. Directors decide, among other matters, if and when dividends shall be paid.

*Discretionary Account:*   An account in which the customer gives the broker or someone else discretion, which may be complete or within specific limits, as to the purchase and sale of securities or commodities including selection, timing and price to be paid or received.

*Dividend:*   The payment designated by the Board of Directors to be distributed pro rata among the shares outstanding. On preferred shares, it is generally a fixed amount. On common shares, the dividend varies with the fortunes of the company and the amount of cash on hand, and may be omitted if business is poor or the directors determine to withhold earnings to invest in plant and equipment. Sometimes a company will pay a dividend out of past earnings even if it is not currently operating at a profit.

*Earnings Report:*   A statement—also called an income statement—issued by a company showing its earnings or losses over a given period. The earnings report lists the income earned, expenses and the net result.

*Equity:*   The ownership interest of common and preferred stockholders in a company. Also refers to excess of value of securities over the debit balance in a margin account.

*Ex-dividend:*   A synonym for "without dividend." The buyer of a stock selling ex-dividend does not receive the recently declared dividend. Open buy and sell stop orders in a stock on the ex-dividend date are ordinarily reduced by the value of that dividend. Every dividend is payable on a fixed date to all shareholders recorded on the books of the company as a previous date of record. For example, a dividend may be declared as payable to holders of record on the books of the company on a given Friday. Since four business days are allowed for delivery of stock in a "regular way" transaction of the N. Y. Stock Exchange, the Exchange would declare the stock "ex-dividend" as of the opening of the market on the preceding Tuesday. That means anyone who bought it on and after Tuesday would not be entitled to that dividend.

*Ex-Rights:*   Without the rights, Corporations raising additional money may do so by offering their stockholders the right to subscribe to new or additional stock, usually at a discount from the prevailing market price. The buyer of a stock selling ex-rights is not entitled to the rights.

*Extra:*   The short form of "extra dividend." A dividend in the form of stock or cash in addition to the regular or usual dividend the company has been paying.

*Fiscal Year:*   A corporation's accounting year. Due to the nature of their particular business, some companies do not use the calendar year for their bookkeeping. A typical example is the department store which finds December 31 too early a date to close its books after the Christmas rush. For that reason many stores wind up their accounting year January 31. Their fiscal year, therefore, runs from February 1 of one year through January 31 of the next. The fiscal year of other companies may run from July 1 through the following June 30. Most companies, though, operate on a calendar year basis.

*Growth Stock:* Stock of a company with prospects for future growth—a company which over a period of time seems destined to expand materially.

*Investment Banker:* Also known as an underwriter. He is the middleman between the corporation issuing new securities and the public. The usual practice is for one or more investment bankers to buy outright from a corporation a new issue of stocks or bonds. The group forms a syndicate to sell the securities to individuals and institutions. Investment bankers also distribute very large blocks of stocks or bonds—perhaps held by an estate. Thereafter the market in the security may be over-the-counter, on a regional stock exchange, the American Exchange or the N. Y. Stock Exchange.

*Investment Counselor:* One who is professionally engaged in rendering investment advisory and supervisory services.

*Investment Trust:* A company which uses its capital to invest in other companies. There are two principal types: the close-end and the open-end, or mutual fund. Shares in close-end investment trusts, some of which are listed on the N. Y. Stock Exchange, are readily transferable in the open market and are bought and sold like other shares. Capitalization of these companies is fixed. Open-end funds sell their own new shares to investors, stand ready to buy back their old shares, and are not listed. Open-end funds are so-called because their capitalization is not fixed; they issue more shares as people want them.

*Investor:* An individual whose principal concerns in the purchase of a security are regular dividend income, safety of the original investment, and, if possible, capital appreciation.

*Liabilities:* All the claims against a corporation. Liabilities include accounts and wages and salaries payable, dividends declared payable, accrued taxes payable, fixed or long-term liabilities such as mortgage bonds, debentures and bank loans.

*Listed Stock:* The stock of a company which is traded on a national securities exchange, and for which a listing application and a registration statement, giving detailed information about the company and its operations, have been filed with the Securities & Exchange Commission and the exchange itself. The various stock exchanges have different standards for listing. Some of the guides used by the N. Y. Stock Exchange for an original listing are national interest in the company and its stock, at least 1,500 share owners, 400,000 shares outstanding in the hands of the public, an earning power at the time of listing of at least $1,000,000 annually.

*Margin:* The amount paid by the customer when he uses credit to buy a security, the balance being advanced by the broker. Under Federal Reserve regulations, the initial margin required in the past 20 years has ranged from 40 per cent of the purchase price all the way to 100 per cent.

*Market Price:*   In the case of a security, market price is usually considered the last reported price at which the stock or bond sold.

*Member Corporation:*   A securities brokerage firm, organized as a corporation, with at least one member of the N. Y. Stock Exchange who is a director and a holder of voting stock in the corporation.

*Member Firm:*   A securities brokerage firm organized as a partnership and having at least one general partner who is a member of the N. Y. Stock Exchange.

*NASD:*   The National Association of Securities Dealers, Inc. An association of brokers and dealers in the over-the-counter securities business. The Association has the power to expel members who have been determined guilty of unethical practices. NASD is dedicated to—among other objectives—"adopt, administer and enforce rules of fair practice and rules to prevent fraudulent and manipulative acts and practices, and in general to promote just and equitable principles of trade for the protection of investors."

*Off-Board:*   This term may refer to transactions over-the-counter in unlisted securities, or, in a special situation, to a transaction involving a block of listed shares which was not executed on a national securities exchange.

*Over-the-Counter:*   A market for securities made up of securities dealers who may or may not be members of a securities exchange. Over-the-counter is mainly a market made over the telephone. Thousands of companies have insufficient shares outstanding, stockholders, or earnings to warrant application for listing on a stock exchange. Others may prefer not to make public all the information which listing requires. Securities of these companies are traded in the over-the-counter market between dealers who act either as principals or as brokers for customers. The over-the-counter market is the principal market for U. S. Government bonds, municipals, bank and insurance stocks.

*Par:*   In the case of a common share, par means a dollar amount assigned to the share by the company's charter. Par value may also be used to compute the dollar amount of the common shares on the balance sheet. Par value has little significance so far as market value of common stock is concerned. Many companies today issue no-par stock but give a stated per share value on the balance sheet. Par at one time was supposed to represent the value of the original investment behind each share in cash, goods or services. In the case of preferred shares and bonds, however, par is important. It often signifies the dollar value upon which dividends on preferred stocks, and interest on bonds, are figured. The issuer of a 3 per cent bond promises to pay that percentage of the bond's par value annually.

*Passed Dividend:*   Omission of a regular or scheduled dividend.

*Preferred Stock:*    A class of stock with a claim on the company's earnings before payment may be made on the common stock and usually entitled to priority over common stock if company liquidates. Usually entitled to dividends at a specified rate—when declared by the Board of Directors and before payment of a dividend on the common stock—depending upon the terms of the issue.

*Principal:*    The person for whom a broker executes an order, or a dealer buying or selling for his own account. The term "principal" may also refer to a person's capital or to the face amount of a bond.

*Proxy Statement:*    Information required by SEC to be given stockholders as a prerequisite to solicitation of proxies for a listed security.

*Quotation:*    Often shortened to "quote." The highest bid to buy and the lowest offer to sell a security in a given market at a given time. If you ask your broker for a "quote" on a stock, he may come back with something like "45¼ to 45½." This means that $45.25 is the highest price any buyer wanted to pay at the time the quote was given on the floor of the Exchange and that $45.50 was the lowest price which any seller would take at the same time.

*Record Date:*    The date on which you must be registered on the books of a company as a shareholder in order to receive a declared dividend or, among other things, to vote on company affairs.

*Registration:*    Before a public offering may be made of new securities by a company, or of outstanding securities by controlling stockholders—through the mails or in interstate commerce—the securities must be registered under the Securities Act of 1933. The application must be filed with the SEC by the issuer. It must disclose pertinent information relating to the company's operations, securities, management and purpose of the public offering. Securities of railroads under jurisdiction of the Interstate Commerce Commission, and certain other types of securities, are exempted. On security offerings involving less than $300,000, only limited information is required.

Before a security may be admitted to dealings on a national securities exchange, it must be registered under the Securities Exchange Act of 1934. The application for registration must be filed with the Exchange and the SEC by the company issuing the securities. The application must disclose pertinent information relating to the company's operations, securities and management. Registration may become effective 30 days after receipt by the SEC of the certification by the Exchange of approval of listing and registration, or sooner by special order of the Commission.

*Rights:*    When a company wants to raise more funds by issuing additional securities, it may give its stockholders the opportunity, ahead of others, to buy the new securities in proportion to the number of shares each owns. The piece of paper evidencing this privilege is called a right. Because the additional stock is usually offered to stockholders below the current market price, rights ordinarily have a market value of their own and are actively traded. In most cases they must be exercised within a relatively short period. Failure to exercise or sell rights may result in actual loss to the holder.

*SEC:*   The Securities and Exchange Commission, established by Congress to help protect investors. The SEC administers the Securities Act of 1933, the Securities Exchange Act of 1934, the Trust Indenture Act, the Investment Company Act, the Investment Advisers Act, and the Public Utility Holding Company Act.

*Secondary Distribution:*   Also known as a secondary offering. The redistribution of a block of stock sometime after it has been sold by the issuing company. The sale is handled off the Exchange by a securities firm or group of firms and the shares are usually offered at a fixed price which is related to the current market price of the stock. Usually the block is a large one, such as might be involved in the settlement of an estate. The security may be listed or unlisted. Exchange approval is required for member firms to participate in a secondary distribution of a listed stock.

*Short Sale:*   A person who believes a stock will decline and sells it though he does not own any has made a short sale. For instance: You instruct your broker to sell short 100 shares of ABC. Your broker borrows the stock so he can deliver the 100 shares to the buyer. The money value of the shares borrowed is deposited by your broker with the lender. Sooner or later you must cover your short sale by buying the same amount of stock you borrowed for return to the lender. If you are able to buy ABC at a lower price than you sold it, your profit is the difference between the two prices—not counting commissions and taxes. But if you have to pay more for the stock than the price you received, that is the amount of your loss. Stock Exchange and Federal regulations govern and limit the conditions under which a short sale may be made on a national securities exchange.

*Split:*   The division of the outstanding shares of a corporation into a larger number of shares. A 3-for-1 split by a company with 1 million shares outstanding would result in 3 million shares outstanding. Each holder of 100 shares before the 3-for-1 split would have 300 shares, although his proportionate equity in the company would remain the same, since 100 parts of 1 million are the equivalent of 300 parts of 3 million. Ordinarily splits must be voted by directors and approved by shareholders.

*Stock Dividend:*   A dividend paid in securities rather than cash. The dividend may be additional shares of the issuing company, or in shares of another company (usually a subsidiary) held by the company.

*Stockholder of Record:*   A stockholder whose name is registered on the books of the issuing corporation.

*Syndicate:*   A group of investment bankers who together underwrite and distribute a new issue of securities or a large block of an outstanding issue.

*Thin Market:*   A market in which there are comparatively few bids to buy or offers to sell or both. The phrase may apply to a single security or to the entire stock market. In a thin market, price fluctuations between transactions are usually larger than when the market is liquid. A thin market in a particular stock may reflect lack of interest in that issue or a limited supply of or demand for stock in the market.

*Transfer Agent:*   A transfer agent keeps a record of the name of each registered share-owner, his or her address, the number of shares owned, and sees that certificates presented to his office for transfer are properly cancelled and new certificates issued in the name of the transferee.

*Transfer Tax:*   A tax imposed by New York State, a few other states, and the Federal Government when a security is sold or transferred from one person to another. Paid by the seller. The Federal Government collects a transfer tax of 4 cents per $100 of actual value of the shares sold or transferred. The minimum tax per transaction is 4 cents; the maximum tax per share is 8 cents on stocks selling at $200 or more. New York State levies a transfer tax of from 1 to 4 cents a share, based on selling price of the stock.

*Treasury Stock:*   Stock issued by a company but later re-acquired. It may be held in the company's treasury indefinitely, reissued to the public or retired. Treasury stock receives no dividends and has no vote while held by the company.

*Voting Right:*   The stockholder's right to vote his stock in the affairs of his company. Most common shares have one vote each. Preferred stock usually has the right to vote when preferred dividends are in default. The right to vote may be delegated by the stockholder to another person.

*Yield:*   Also known as return. The dividends or interest paid by a company expressed as a percentage of the current price—or, if you own the security, of the price you originally paid. The return on a stock is figured by dividing the total of dividends paid in the preceding 12 months by the current market price—or, if you are the owner, the price you originally paid. A stock with a current market value of $40 a share which has paid $2 in dividends in the preceding 12 months is said to return 5 per cent ($2.00 ÷ $40.00). If you paid $20 for the stock five years earlier, the stock would be returning you 10 per cent on your original investment. The current return on a bond is figured the same way. A 3 per cent $1,000 bond selling at $600 offers a return of 5 per cent ($30 ÷ $600). Figuring the yield of a bond to maturity calls for a bond yield table.

# Appendix B

PURCHASE AGREEMENT BETWEEN UNDERWRITER, COMPANY AND SELLING
STOCKHOLDER

150,000 Shares
Common Stock
(Par Value $1 Per Share)

*Purchase or Underwriting Agreement*

To The Managing Underwriter:

Dear Sirs:

Certain holders (the "Sellers") of issued and outstanding shares of Common Stock, par value $1 per share, of ................, a Delaware Corporation (the "Company"), propose to sell, severally, to the Underwriters named in Schedule I hereto, an aggregate of 150,000 of such shares (the "shares"), which Shares are more fully described in the registration statement and prospectus hereinafter mentioned. Such sale of the Shares will benefit the Company by creating a public market for its Common Stock. We wish to confirm as follows our agreement with you and the other Underwriters, on whose behalf you are acting as representative, for the several purchases of the Shares.

1. *Registration Statement and Prospectus:* The Company has prepared and filed with the Securities and Exchange Commission (the "Commission") in accordance with the provisions of the Securities Act of 1933 and the rules and regulations of the Commission thereunder (collectively called the "Act"), a registration statement including a preliminary prospectus relating to the Shares, and has filed one or more amendments thereto. The Company expects to file on or prior to the effective date of the registration statement a further amendment thereto. As used in this Agreement the term "Registration Statement" means such registration statement in the form in which it becomes effective, and the term "Prospectus" means the prospectus in the form included in the Registration statement.

2. *Agreement to Sell and Purchase:* Upon the basis of the representations and warranties and subject to all the terms and conditions set forth herein, each seller severally agrees to sell and each Underwriter severally agrees to purchase at $13.80 a share that proportion of the number of Shares set

opposite the name of such Seller below which the number of Shares set opposite the name of each Underwriter in Schedule I bears to 150,000.

The Sellers hereby agree not to sell or otherwise dispose of any Common Stock of the Company owned by them on the date of this Agreement, other than the Shares to be sold by them under this Agreement for a period of 90 days after the date of the initial public offering of the Shares by the Underwriters without the consent of the managing underwriters as representative of the several Underwriters.

3. *Terms of Public Offering:* The Sellers and the Company are advised by you that the terms of the initial public offering of the Shares will be as set forth in the Prospectus.

4. *Representations and Warranties of Sellers:* Each Seller, severally and not jointly represents and warrants to each Underwriter that such Seller now is, and at the time of delivery will be, the lawful owner of the number of Shares set forth in Section 2 hereof opposite the name of such Seller, and at the time of delivery thereof will have valid marketable title to such Shares, free and clear of any claims, liens or encumbrances; that such shares are, and at the time of delivery thereof will be, legally issued, fully paid and nonassessable; and that such Seller has, and at the time of the delivery of such Shares will have, full legal right and power and authorization and any approval required by law to sell, assign and transfer such Shares in the manner provided in this Agreement. The Sellers represent and warrant to the Company and to each Underwriter that when the Registration Statement becomes effective, such parts thereof as relate to the Sellers and are based on information furnished to the Company by or on behalf of the Sellers expressly for use in the Registration Statement or Prospectus will not contain any untrue statement of a material fact or omit to state any material fact required to be stated therein or necessary to make the statements therein not misleading. Each Seller has duly authorized the Representative of the Sellers, as defined in Section 7 hereof, to act for it in all matters in respect of which action is to be taken by such Representative as provided in this Agreement.

The foregoing representations and warranties, the representations and warranties set forth in Section 5 hereof, and the indemnity agreements set forth in Section 6 hereof shall remain operative and in full force and effect, regardless of (a) any investigation made by or on behalf of any person indemnified, (b) acceptance of any Shares and payment therefor hereunder, and (c) any termination of this Agreement.

5. *Representations and Warranties of the Company:* The Company represents and warrants to each Underwriter and Seller that:

(a) the Registration Statement and Prospectus in the form in which they are when the Registration Statement becomes effective and also in such form as they may be when any post-effective amendment thereto shall become effective, will fully comply with the provisions of the Act: and the Registration Statement and Prospectus will not at any such times contain an untrue statement of a material fact or omit to state a material fact required to be stated therein or necessary to make the statements therein not misleading; except that this representation and warranty does not apply to statements or omissions in the Registration Statement and Prospectus made in reliance upon information furnished to the Company in writing by or on behalf of any Underwriter, or upon information furnished to the Company by or on behalf of the Sellers, expressly for use in connection therewith;

(b) the Shares have been validly authorized and are validly issued and outstanding and are fully paid and nonassessable;

(c) the Common Stock of the Company conforms to the description thereof in the Prospectus under the caption "Description of Common Stock"; and

(d) the accountants who have certified or shall certify the financial statements and schedules filed or to be filed with the Commission as parts of the Registration Statement and Prospectus are independent public accountants, as required by the Act.

6. *Indemnification of the Underwriters and the Sellers:* The Company agrees to indemnify and hold harmless each Underwriter and each person who controls any Underwriter within the meaning of Section 15 of the Act against any and all losses, claims, damages, liabilities and expenses (including reasonable costs of investigation) caused by any untrue statement or alleged untrue statement of a material fact contained in any preliminary prospectus or in the Registration Statement or Prospectus, or in any amendment or supplement thereto, or caused by any omission or alleged omission to state therein a material fact required to be stated therein or necessary to make the statements therein not misleading, except insofar as such losses, claims, damages or liabilities are caused by any such untrue statement or omission or allegation thereof based upon information furnished in writing to the Company by or on behalf of any Underwriter expressly for use in connection therewith, provided that the foregoing agreement, insofar as it relates to any preliminary prospectus, shall not inure to the benefit of any Underwriter from whom the person asserting any losses, claims, damages or liabilities purchased the Shares which are the subject thereof (or to the benefit of any person controlling such Underwriter), if a copy of the Prospectus has not been sent or given by or on behalf of such Underwriter to such person prior to or together with the written confirmation of the sale of such Shares to such person.

The Company agrees to indemnify and hold harmless each Seller to the same extent, against the same liabilities, and on the same conditions (except to the extent loss to any Seller is caused by an untrue statement or omission or allegation thereof based on information furnished to the Company by or on behalf of the Sellers) as it agrees to indemnify each of the Underwriters and each person who controls any Underwriter, provided that such indemnification shall be subordinate in all respects to the indemnification provided in the preceding paragraph and the Sellers shall not be entitled to collect or retain any amounts in respect of such indemnity unless all amounts required to be paid or claimed under the preceding paragraph shall have been finally settled.

If any action shall be brought against any Underwriter or any Seller or any person controlling an Underwriter, in respect of which indemnity may be sought from the Company pursuant to the provisions of the preceding paragraphs, such Underwriter, Seller or controlling person shall promptly notify the Company in writing, and the Company shall assume the defense thereof, including the employment of counsel and the payment of all expenses. Any Underwriter or any Seller or any person controlling an Underwriter or a Seller shall have the right to employ separate counsel in any such action and participate in the defense thereof, but the fees and expenses of such counsel shall be at the expense of such Underwriter, Seller or controlling person unless (a) the employment thereof has been specifically authorized by the Company in writing, or (b) the Company has failed to assume the defense and employ counsel.

The foregoing indemnity insofar as it may permit or require indemnification of a director or controlling person of the Company is subject to the undertaking of the Company contained in Item 29 of the Registration Statement but only to the extent stated in said Item 29.

Each Underwriter agrees to indemnify and hold harmless the Company, its directors and officers, the Sellers, and each person, if any, who controls the Company within the meaning of Section 15 of the Act, against any and all losses, claims, damages, liabilities and expenses (including reasonable costs of investigation) caused by any untrue statement or alleged untrue statement of a material fact contained in any preliminary prospectus or in the Registration Statement or Prospectus, or in any amendment or supplement thereto, or caused by any omission or alleged omission to state therein a material fact required to be stated therein or necessary to make the statements therein not misleading, but only with respect to any untrue statement or alleged untrue statement, omission or alleged omission, which is based on information relating to such Underwriter furnished in writing by it, or on its behalf expressly for use in connection therewith.

If any action shall be brought against the Company or its directors or officers, or any such controlling person, based on any preliminary prospectus or the Registration Statement or Prospectus and in respect of which indemnity may be sought from any Underwriter pursuant to the provisions of the preceding paragraph, such Underwriter shall have the rights and duties given to the Company, and the Company, its directors or officers and any such controlling person shall have the rights and duties given to the Underwriters by the third paragraph of this Section.

7. *Representative of Sellers:* The undersigned shall act as Representative of the Sellers pursuant to powers of attorney, satisfactory to counsel for the Underwriters, granted by each of the Sellers, copies of which powers of attorney have been furnished you. Such Representative is authorized on behalf of the Sellers to execute this Agreement and any other documents necessary or convenient in connection with the sale of the Shares, take any action on behalf of the Sellers as fully as they or any of them might do personally, receive the proceeds of the sale of the Shares, to receipt for such proceeds, to pay therefrom the expenses to be borne by the Sellers in connection with the sale and public offering of the Shares and to distribute the balance to the Sellers in proportion to the number of Shares sold by each Seller.

8. *Delivery of Shares and Payment Therefor:* Delivery to the Underwriters of and payment for the Shares shall be made at 10:00 A.M., Central Daylight Saving Time, on ———— day of ———— (the "Closing Date"), at the office of the principal underwriters. The Closing Date may be varied by agreement between you and the Representative of the Sellers.

The Stock certificates for the Shares shall be registered in such names and in such denominations as you shall request by at least two business days notice in writing to the Representative of the Sellers. Such certificates shall be delivered to you on the Closing Date for the respective accounts of the several Underwriters against payment of the purchase price by certified or bank cashier's check or checks payable in Chicago Clearing House funds to the order of the Sellers. For the purpose of expediting the checking and packaging of the certificates by you, it is agreed that the certificates shall be made available to you a reasonable time in advance of the Closing Date.

9. *Conditions of Obligations of Underwriters:* The obligations of each Underwriter hereunder are subject to the accuracy of and compliance, as at the Closing Date, with the representations and warranties of the Sellers and the Company contained in this Agreement and to the following further conditions:

(a) The Registration Statement shall have become effective not later than 6:30 P.M., Central Daylight Saving Time, on ............... or at such later date and time as shall be consented to in writing by you.

(b) No stop order suspending the effectiveness of the Registration Statement shall be in effect and no proceedings for such purpose shall have been taken or to the knowledge of the Company shall be contemplated by the Commission and you shall have received on and as of the the Closing Date a certificate signed by the Chairman of the Board or the President of the Company to the foregoing effect.

(c) You shall have received on and as of the Closing Date, an opinion, or opinions, satisfactory to counsel for the Underwriters, . . . . . . . . . . . . . . . . ., as counsel for the Company and from the Sellers, to the effect that:

(i) The Company is a corporation duly organized and validily existing in good standing under the laws of the State of Delaware and has adequate corporate power to carry on the business in which it is now engaged and is duly authorized to carry on and conduct such business in all states wherein the Company now operates, subject at all times to the applicable laws of such states;

(ii) Each of the domestic subsidiaries of the Company listed in Item 27 of the Registration Statement is a corporation duly organized and validly existing under the laws of its state of incorporation and has adequate corporate power to carry on the business in which it is now engaged and is duly authorized to carry on and conduct such business in all states wherein each such subsidiary now operates, subject at all times to the applicable laws of such states;

(iii) That all of the issued and outstanding shares of stock of each of the subsidiaries of the Company listed in Item 27 of the Registration Statement are validly issued fully paid and non-assessable, and that all of such shares are owned by the Company as of the date of closing;

(iv) The Shares have been validly authorized and are validly issued and outstanding, fully paid and non-assessable, the certificates therefor are in proper legal form and the Common Stock of the Company conforms as to legal matters to the description thereof contained in the Prospectus.

(v) The Registration Statement and the Prospectus (except as to the financial statements and schedules included therein as to which counsel need not express an opinion) comply as to form in all material respects to the Act and such counsel has no reason to believe that the Registration Statement or the Prospectus (except as aforesaid) contains any untrue statement of a material fact or omits to state a material fact required to be stated therein or necessary in order to make the statements therein not misleading; and

(vi) This Agreement has been duly authorized, executed and delivered by the Company and is a valid and binding agreement of the Company in accordance with its terms.

(vii) This Agreement has been duly executed and delivered by or on behalf of each of the Sellers and is binding upon each of the Sellers in accordance with its terms; and

(viii) Delivery of the certificates for the Shares pursuant hereto will pass good and marketable title thereto free and clear of any claim, lien or encumbrance.

(e) You shall have received on and as of the Closing Date a favorable opinion of ...............,  counsel for the Underwriters, to the effect that the Company is a corporation duly organized and validly existing in good standing under the laws of the State of Delaware and in addition, covering the matters in subdivisions (iv) through (viii), of paragraph c of this Section 9, provided, however, that with respect to all matters referred to in subdivisions (ii) and (iii) of paragraph c, counsel for the underwriter may rely upon the opinion of counsel for the Company to the extent such matters are pertinent to said opinion.

(f) That at the Closing Date the accountants for the Company shall have furnished you a letter in form and substance satisfactory to you stating that they are independent public accountants as required by the Act and stating further that the financial statements and schedules of the Company certified by them and included in the Registration Statement or the Prospectus comply as to form in all material respects with the requirements of the Act, and stating further that (a) nothing has come to their attention which would indicate that during the period from ...... .......... to a specified date not more than five days prior to the Closing Date there was any change in the financial position or results of operations of the Company or any of its subsidiaries except as set forth in, or contemplated by, the Registration Statement and the Prospectus and (b) on the basis of a limited review (as distingiushed from an examination or audit made in accordance with generally accepted auditing standards), of the financial statements of the Company for the two years ended .... ............. and ................., consultations with officers of the Company responsible for financial and accounting matters and other specified procedures and inquiries, nothing has come to their attention which in their judgment would lead them to believe that the statements of unaudited consolidated earnings of the Company and the companies which became subsidiaries thereof in ................ for the two years ended ............... and ................, set forth under "Earnings Summary" in the Prospectus do not comply as to form in all material respects with the applicable requirements of the Act, or that any material adjustments thereto are required, or that the accounting principles and practices followed in their preparation are not substantially in accordance with generally accepted accounting principles applied on a basis consistent with those followed in the preparation of the audited financial statements in the Prospectus:

(g) That (i) there shall not have been since the date of this Agreement any material adverse change in the condition of the Company, financial or otherwise from that set forth in the Registration Statement nor shall the Company have incurred any material liabilities or obligations, direct or contingent, other than those arising from transactions in the ordinary course of business; and (ii) you shall have received at the Closing Date a certificate dated the Closing Date signed by the Chairman of the Board or the President of the Company to that effect; and

(h) That neither the Company nor the Sellers shall have failed at or prior to the Closing Date to have performed any of the agreements herein contained and required to be performed by it or them, as the case may be, at or prior to the Closing Date.

10. *Effective Date of Agreement:* This Agreement shall become effective at 10:00 A.M., Central Daylight Saving Time, on the next full business day following the effective date of the Registration Statement, or at such earlier time after the Registration Statement becomes effective as you may fix either by notice to the Sellers, or by release for publication of any advertisement of a public offering of the Shares, or by release by you of the offering to dealers, whichever shall first occur. Until this Agreement so becomes effective, either the Sellers, or the Representatives of the Sellers, by notice to you, or you, as representative of the several Underwriters, by notice to the Sellers, may terminate this Agreement and prevent its becoming effective without assigning any cause whatsoever for such action, without obligation by any party to any other party except as otherwise specifically provided in this Agreement. Any notice under this Section may be made by telephone or telegraph, but shall be subsequently confirmed in writing.

11. *Certain Agreements of Sellers:* If this Agreement shall be terminated pursuant to any of the provisions hereof (otherwise than by notice given by you pursuant to Section 10 hereof and otherwise than on account of the default by any Underwriter hereunder), or if the Sellers fail to perform any of the agreements herein contained and required to be performed by them, the Company will reimburse the several Underwriters for all out-of-pocket expenses (including the fees and expenses of counsel), reasonably incurred by them and upon such reimbursement the Company and the Sellers shall be absolved from any liability for loss of anticipated profits hereunder. Failure of any of the Sellers to fulfill any obligation hereunder shall not increase the obligations of any of the other Sellers or release any of them from their obligations hereunder.

The Sellers will pay, or will reimburse the Company for, all costs and expenses incident to the performance of their obligations under this Agreement, including, without limitation, all stamp taxes payable with respect to the initial transfer of the Shares to the Underwriters but excluding other costs and expenses listed in Item 23 to the Registration Statement.

12. *Agreements of the Company:* The Company agrees as follows:

(a) The Company will advise you promptly and, if requested by you, will confirm such advice in writing (i) when the Registration Statement has become effective, (ii) of any request by the Commission for amendments or supplements to the Registration Statement or the Prospectus or for additional information, (iii) of the issuance by the Commission of any stop order suspending the effectiveness of the Registration Statement or the initiation of any proceedings for that purpose, and (iv) of the happening of any event which in the judgment of the Company makes any material statement made in the Registration Statement or the Prospectus untrue or which requires the making of any changes in the Registration Statement or the Prospectus in order to make the statements therein not misleading. If at any time the Commission shall issue any stop order suspending the effectiveness of the Registration Statement, the Company will make every reasonable effort to obtain the withdrawal of such order at the earliest possible moment.

(b) The Company will furnish to you, without charge, two signed copies of the Registration Statement as originally filed and of all amendments thereto, in each case including financial statements and all exhibits filed therewith, and will also furnish to you for transmittal to each of the other Underwriters, without charge, a copy of the Registration Statement as originally filed and all amendments thereto without exhibits.

(c) The Company will not file any amendment to the Registration Statement or make any amendment or supplement to the Prospectus of which you shall not previously have been advised, or to which you shall reasonably object in writing.

(d) Prior to the effective date of the Registration Statement, the Company has delivered or will deliver to you, without charge, in such quantities as you have requested or may hereafter reasonably request, copies of each form of preliminary prospectus. The Company consents to the use of such documents, in accordance with the provisions of the Act, by the Underwriters and by dealers.

(e) On the effective date of the Registration Statement and thereafter from time to time, for a period of 40 days after that date (or for such longer period as you may request if the Prospectus is required by law to be delivered in connection with sales by an Underwriter or dealer after the expiration of such period of 40 days) the Company will deliver to you, without charge, as many copies of the Prospectus (and of any amendments or supplements thereto) as you may reasonably request. If during such period of time any event shall occur which in the judgment of the Company or in the opinion of counsel for the Underwriters should be set forth in the Prospectus in order to make the Prospectus not misleading, or if it is necessary to supplement or amend the Prospectus to comply with law, the Company will forthwith prepare appropriate supplements thereto or an amended Prospectus and will furnish to you, without charge, a reasonable number of copies thereof, which the Underwriters shall use thereafter. Provided that if the Underwriters or any of them are required to deliver a Prospectus more than a year after the effective date of the Registration Statement, the Company at the expense of such Underwriters will revise such Prospectus in such manner as to conform with the requirements of the Act.

(f) Prior to any public offering of the Shares the Company will cooperate with you and your counsel in conection with the registration or qualification of the Shares for offering by the several Underwriters under the securities or Blue Sky laws of such states as you or your counsel may request and will file such consents to service of process or other documents as may be necessary in order to effect such registration or qualification; provided that in no event shall the Company be obligated to qualify to do business in any state where it is not now so qualified or to take any action which would subject it to taxation or the service of unlimited process in any state where it is not now so subject.

(g) The Company will make generally available to its security holders a consolidated earnings statement covering the twelve-month period commencing on the first day of the month next succeeding the month in which the Registration Statement becomes effective, soon as is reasonably practicable after the end of such period, which earnings statement shall satisfy the provisions of Section 11(a) of the Securities Act of 1933. The Company will annually mail to the holders of its Common Stock a consolidated balance sheet and consolidated statements of profit and loss and earned surplus of the Company and its subsidiaries, certified by independent public accountants and will mail to such holders quarterly consolidated statements of profit and loss, which may be uncertified.

(h) During the period of ten years hereafter, the Company will furnish to you, and upon request, to each of the other Underwriters, as soon as practicable after the end of each fiscal year, a consolidated balance sheet and statements of income and surplus of the Company and its subsidiaries as at the end of and for such year, all in reasonable detail and certified by independent public accountants; and the Company will furnish to you (i) as soon as practicable after the end of each quarterly fiscal period (except for the last quarterly fiscal period of each fiscal year), a consolidated balance sheet and statements of income and surplus of the Company and its subsidiaries as of the end of and for such period, all in reasonable detail and certified by a principal financial or accounting officer of the Company, (ii) as soon as available, a copy of each report of the Company mailed to stockholders or filed with the Commission, and (iii) from time to time such other information concerning the Company as you may reasonably request.

(i) The Company will pay all expenses in connection with (1) the preparation, printing and filing of the Registration Statement, each preliminary prospectus, the Prospectus and the Purchase Agreement and all amendments to any thereof, (2) furnishing to the several Underwriters copies of each preliminary prospectus, the Prospectus, the Registration

Statement and all supplements to the Prospectus, (3) the preparation, countersignature by a transfer agent and registration by a registrar of certificates representing the Shares to be delivered by the Sellers pursuant hereto, and (4) the registration or qualification of the Shares for offer and sale under the securities or Blue Sky laws of the various states (the expenses of the Underwriters, including fees and disbursements of counsel, so payable in connection with such registration or qualification of Shares not to exceed $5,000).

Except as otherwise expressly provided, this Agreement has been and is made solely for the benefit of and shall be binding upon the Sellers, the Underwriters, and controlling person referred to herein and the Company, and their respective legal representatives, successors and assigns, all as and to the extent provided herein, and no other person shall acquire or have any right under or by virtue of this Agreement. The term "legal representatives, successors and assigns" shall not include any purchaser of any of the Shares from any of the several Underwriters merely because of such purchase.

Please confirm that the foregoing correctly sets forth the agreement between the Sellers, the Company and the several Underwriters.

Very truly yours,

. . . . . . . . . . . . . . . . . . . . . . . . . . . . . . .

. . . . . . . . . . . . . . . . . . . . . . . . . . . . . . .

Acting, pursuant to Powers of Attorney, on behalf of the Sellers named in Section 2 hereof

COMPANY

By . . . . . . . . . . . . . . . . . . . . . . . . . . . .

President

Confirmed on the date first above mentioned, on behalf of themselves and the other several Underwriters named herein.

. . . . . . . . . . . . . . . . . . . . . . . . . . . . . . .

Managing Underwriter

# Appendix C

AGREEMENT AMONG UNDERWRITERS

To The Managing Underwriter:

Dear Sirs:

We wish to confirm as follows our agreement with you with respect to the several purchases by you and the other Underwriters listed in Schedule I to the Purchase Agreement, including ourselves, severally, and the offering of an aggregate of 150,000 shares of Common Stock, $1 par value (the "Shares") of, ............... (the "Company").

1. Purchase Agreement: Attached hereto as Exhibit A is a proposed Purchase Agreement with the Company and the Selling Stockholders named in the Purchase Agreement (the "Sellers") providing for the several purchases from the Sellers by each Underwriter, severally, of the number of Shares set opposite each Underwriter's name in Schedule I thereto. We authorize you to execute the Purchase Agreement, substantially in the form attached hereto, on our behalf.

2. Method of Offering: We authorize you, as representative of the several Underwriters, to manage the underwriting and the public offering of the Shares and to take such action as may seem advisable to you in respect of all matters pertaining thereto, including the determination of the time of the initial public offering of the Shares pursuant to the Prospectus, the initial public offering price thereof, and the making of any change in the public offering price. We understand that you will advise us when the Shares are released for public offering.

We authorize you to reserve for sale and sell for our account such number of Shares as you may elect (a) to institutions and other retail purchasers in the proportion that our number of Shares bears to the total Shares, and (b) to dealers in the proportion that the number of our Shares reserved for sale to dealers bears to the total Shares reserved therefor. Such dealers (the "Dealers") are to be members of the National Association of Securities Dealers, Inc., or foreign dealers agreeing to conform to the Rules of Fair Practice of such Association and may include any of the Underwriters. We authorize you to fix the concessions and reallowance in connection with any sales to Dealers.

You shall advise us of the number of Shares sold or reserved for sale for our account. We shall retain for direct sale any Shares purchased by us and not sold or reserved. With your consent, we may obtain release from you for direct sale of Shares so reserved for sale to Dealers but not sold and paid for, in which event the number of Shares reserved for our account for sale to Dealers shall be correspondingly reduced.

If, prior to the termination of this Agreement, you shall purchase any Shares sold directly by us but not effectively placed for investment, you may charge our account with an amount equal to the concession to Dealers with respect thereto and credit such amount against the cost thereof, or you may require us to purchase such Shares at a price equal to the total cost thereof, including commissions, if any, and transfer taxes on redelivery.

We will advise you from time to time, at your request, of the number of Shares retained by us. You may at any time (a) reserve any of such Shares for sale by you for our account or (b) purchase any of such Shares which, in your opinion, are needed to enable you to make deliveries for the accounts of the several Underwriters pursuant to this Agreement. Such purchases will be made at the public offering price or, at your option, at such price less any part of the Dealers' concession.

3. Delivery and Payment: At 8:45 A.M., Central Daylight Saving Time, on the Closing Date, determined as provided in the Purchase Agreement, we will deliver to you a certified or bank cashier's check or checks payable in Chicago Clearing House funds to your order or otherwise, as you may direct, for the full purchase price of the Shares which we are obligated to purchase from the Sellers, such check or the proceeds thereof to be delivered by you against delivery to you for our account of certificates for such Shares. Prior to the Closing Date we will furnish any papers and specimen signatures required for valid transfer of such Shares.

You will promptly deliver to us certificates for Shares purchased by us and not sold or reserved for sale. Certificates for all other Shares which you then hold for our account shall be delivered to us upon termination of this Agreement, or prior thereto in your discretion, and may at any time be delivered to us for carrying purposes only, subject to redelivery upon demand. If, upon termination of this Agreement, an aggregate of not more than 15,000 Shares reserved by you pursuant to Section 2 hereof remain unsold, you may, in your discretion, sell such Shares at such prices as you may determine.

We authorize you, in connection with the purchase, distribution and resale of the Shares to advance your own funds or to arrange loans for our account, and to hold or pledge as security therefor all or any part of the Shares purchased by us. Any lending bank is hereby authorized to accept your instructions with respect thereto.

You shall promptly remit to us or credit to our account (a) the proceeds of any loan made on our behalf, and (b) upon payment to you for any Shares sold for our account, an amount equal to either the purchase price paid by us, or the price received by you therefor, as you may determine.

4. Trading in the Shares: We authorize you during the term of this Agreement in your discretion (a) to make purchases and sales of the Company's outstanding Common Stock in the over-the-counter market or otherwise (in addition to purchases and sales of Shares made under the authority of Section 2 hereof), either for long or short account, on such terms and at such prices as you may determine, and (b) in arranging for sales of Shares pursuant to Section 2 hereof to over-allot and to make purchases for the purpose of covering any over-allotment so made. All such purchases, sales and over-allotments shall be made for the respective accounts of the several Underwriters as nearly as practicable in proportion to their respective commitments to purchase Shares as set forth in Section 2 of the Purchase Agreement; provided, however, that at no time shall the aggregate of our net commitments resulting from such purchases and sales and over-allotments, for either long or short account, exceed 10% of the aggregate number of Shares which we are obligated to purchase from the Sellers. We agree to take up at cost on demand any Shares so purchased for our account and to deliver on demand any Shares so sold or so over-allotted for our account. Without limiting the generality of the foregoing, you may buy or take over for the respective accounts of the several Underwriters all in the proportion and within the limits set forth, at the price at which reserved, any Shares of any Underwriter reserved for sale by you but not purchased and paid for.

You will notify us promptly if you engage in any transaction hereunder which in your judgment may be deemed to be a "stabilizing transaction" within the meaning of the applicable rules of the Securities and Exchange Commission. We authorize you to file with the Commission, on our behalf, any and all reports required by such rules.

Except as permitted by you, we will not bid for, purchase, sell, or attempt to induce others to purchase, directly or indirectly, any shares of the Company's outstanding Common Stock, otherwise than by (a) purchases and sales of Shares as provided in the Purchase Agreement and in this Agreement, and (b) purchases from or sales to other Underwriters or Dealers of Shares at the public offering price, or at such price less any part of the Dealers' concession; provided, however, that the foregoing shall not prohibit the purchase or sale by us of the Common Stock of the Company as agent on unsolicited orders for the account of others.

5. Termination and Settlement: This Agreement shall terminate either (a) on the 15th business day after the Closing Date, or (b) on such earlier or later date, not more than 30 business days after the Closing Date, as you may determine, or (c) if the Purchase Agreement shall be terminated as permitted by its terms. You may at your discretion on notice to us prior to the termination of this Agreement terminate or suspend the effectiveness of Sections 2 and 4 hereof or any part thereof, or alter any of the terms or conditions of offering determined pursuant to Section 2 hereof.

Upon termination of this Agreement, all authorizations, rights and obligations hereunder shall cease, except (a) the mutual obligations to settle accounts hereunder, (b) our obligation to pay any claims referred to in the last paragraph of this Section 5, (c) our obligation with respect to purchases which may be made by you from time to time thereafter to cover any short position incurred hereunder, and (d) the indemnity set forth in Section 6, all of which shall continue until fully discharged.

The accounts arising pursuant to this Agreement shall be settled and paid as soon as practicable after termination. The determination by you of the amounts to be paid to or by us shall be final and conclusive.

As compensation for your services in connection herewith, we authorize you to charge our account and pay to yourselves, when final accounting is made, an amount equal to —— cents for each of the Shares which we have agreed to purchase from the Sellers.

We authorize you to charge our account with (a) all transfer taxes on sales made for our account and (b) our proportionate share of all expenses (other than transfer taxes) incurred by you, as representative of the several Underwriters, in connection with the negotiations for, purchase of, and distribution of the Shares. You shall be under no duty to account for any interest on our funds at any time in your hands. Notwithstanding any settlement upon the termination of this Agreement, we will pay our proportionate share of any amount asserted against and discharged by the Underwriters, or any of them, based on the claim that the Underwriters constitute an association, unincorporated business or other separate entity, or based upon or arising out of a claim that this Agreement or the Purchase Agreement is invalid or illegal for any reason, including any expense incurred in defending against such claim, and will pay any transfer taxes which may be assessed thereafter on account of any sale or transfer of Shares or of the Company's outstanding Common Stock for our account.

6. Indemnity: Each Underwriter, including yourselves, agrees to indemnify, hold harmless and reimburse each other Underwriter, each person who controls any other Underwriter within the meaning of Section 15 of the Securities Act of 1933, and any successor of any other Underwriter, all to the extent that each Underwriter will be obligated in the Purchase Agreement to idemnify, hold harmless and reimburse the Company, and regardless of any investigation made by or on behalf of any Underwriter.

7. Authorizations under Purchase Agreement: The Purchase Agreement provides that the obligations of the Underwriters thereunder are subject, among other things, to the condition that the Registration Statement shall have become effective not later than 6:30 P.M., Central Daylight Saving Time on ............ You are hereby authorized, in your discretion, to extend such date to not later than 6:30 P.M., Central Daylight Saving Time, on the day following such date and, with the consent of Underwriters, in-

cluding yourselves, who have agreed to purchase in the aggregate at least a majority of the Shares, to extend one or more times such date to any subsequent date, and to take on our behalf any action that may be necessary for such purpose.

With respect to the Purchase Agreement, you are also authorized in your discretion (a) to postpone the Closing Date or any other date specified therein, (b) to exercise any right of cancellation or termination, (c) to arrange for the purchase by other persons (including yourselves or any other Underwriters) of any Shares not taken up by any defaulting Underwriter and (d) to consent to such other changes in the Purchase Agreement as in your judgment do not materially and adversely affect the substance of our rights and obligations thereunder.

8. Blue Sky Qualification: Upon request, you will inform us as to the states in which you have been advised by counsel that the Shares have been qualified for sale under the respective securities or Blue Sky laws, but you do not assume any responsibility or obligation as to our right to sell the Shares in any state.

We authorize you to cause to be filed with the State of New York a Further State Notice with respect to the Shares to be offered to the public in New York and to send by registered mail to the Pennsylvania Securities Commission a copy of the Prospectus and a list of dealers to whom you expect initially to offer Shares on behalf of the several Underwriters in Pennsylvania.

We will not advertise over our name until after the first public advertisement made by you on behalf of the Underwriters and then only at our own expense and risk.

9. Registration Statement: We hereby confirm (a) that we have examined the registration statement as amended to date and are familiar with the proposed amendment thereto, (b) that the information therein is correct and is not misleading in so far as it relates to us, (c) that we are willing to accept the responsibilities under the Securities Act of 1933 of an Underwriter named in the registration statement, and (d) that we are willing to proceed with the underwriting of the Shares in the manner contemplated. You are authorized, in your discretion, on our behalf, with approval of counsel for the Underwriters, ...................., to approve of or to object to any further amendments to the Registration Statement or supplements to the Prospectus.

10. Miscellaneous: In taking any action under this Agreement you shall act only as agent of the Underwriters, and you shall be under no liability to us, except for lack of good faith, for obligations expressly assumed by you in this Agreement and for any liability imposed by the Securities Act of 1933.

Nothing herein contained shall constitute us partners with you or with the other Underwriters and the obligations of ourselves and of each of the other

Underwriters are several and not joint. Default by any of the other Underwriters with respect to the Purchase Agreement shall not release us from any of our obligations thereunder or hereunder.

Any notice from you to us shall be deemed to have been duly given if mailed or telegraphed, or if telephoned and subsequently confirmed in writing, to us at the address stated in Schedule I of the Purchase Agreement.

We confirm that we are a member of the National Association of Securities Dealers, Inc.

This Agreement is being executed by us and delivered to you in duplicate. Please indicate your receipt of identical agreements from each of the other Underwriters by confirming this Agreement, whereupon it shall constitute a binding contract between us.

Very truly yours,

. . . . . . . . . . . . . . . . . . . . . . . . . . . . . . . . .

By . . . . . . . . . . . . . . . . . . . . . . . . . . . . . .

Confirmed . . . . . . . . day of . . . . . . . .

. . . . . . . . . . . . . . . . . . . . . . . . . . . . . . .

Managing Underwriter

# Appendix D

SOCIETIES OF SECURITY ANALYSTS

The following is a roster of the various Societies of Security Analysts, showing the local meeting dates:

The Baltimore Security Analysts Society
   Meets Monthly (Sept.–June)
The Boston Security Analysts Society
   Meets every Monday (Sept.–May)
The Investment Analysts Society of Chicago
   Meets most Thursdays (Sept.–May)
The Cincinnati Society of Financial Analysts
   Meets monthly (Sept.–June)
The Cleveland Society of Security Analysts
   Meets each week, usually Wednesday
The Dallas Association of Investment Analysts
   Meets periodically
The Financial Analysts Society of Detroit
   Meets once a month in June, July, Aug., Jan.—1st and 3rd Wed. of other months
The Houston Society of Financial Analysts
   Meets monthly except in summer months
The Indianapolis Society of Financial Analysts
   Meets monthly
Kansas City Society of Financial Analysts
   Meets 3rd Tuesday of each month
The Los Angeles Society of Security Analysts
   Meets usually every Thursday and sometimes on Tuesday
The Montreal Institute of Investment Analysts
   Meets every 3rd week
The New York Society of Security Analysts
   Meets every day
The Omaha-Lincoln Society of Financial Analysts
   Meets 3rd Tuesday of each month
Financial Analysts of Philadelphia
   Meets every Thursday
Phoenix Society of Financial Analysts

The Providence Society of Financial Analysts
    Meets monthly (Sept.–June)

The Richmond Society of Financial Analysts
    Meets once each month

The Rochester Society of Investment Analysts
    Meets 3rd Wed. of each month (Sept.–May)

The St. Louis Society of Financial Analysts
    Meets 3 or 4 times a month

The Security Analysts of San Francisco
    Meets Thursdays

The Security Analysts Association of Toronto
    Meets every 2nd Wednesday (October–April)

The Twin Cities Society of Security Analysts, Inc.
    Meets on call of President

The Washington Society of Investment Analysts
    Meets Bi-monthly

# Index